MORETON HALL
WESTON RHYN
OSWESTRY
SHROPSHIRE SY11 3HW

Teach the Latin, I Pray You

by Paul Distler

Published by
WPC Classics

Teach the Latin, I Pray You

by Paul Distler

General editor: Professor John Traupman

Published by Wimbledon Publishing Company Ltd.

WPC Classics USA
4117 Hillsboro Pike, Suite 103-106
Nashville, TN 37215 USA

Fax: 801 749 2983

E-mail: sales@wpcpress.com

ISBN: 1898855 40 4

Produced in UK
Printed in Hungary

WPC Classics is an imprint of the Wimbledon Publishing Company
P.O. Box 9779, London SW19 7QA Fax: (+44) 20 8944 0825

Preface

Teaching is an art and possibly the greatest. It deals not with inanimate things such as clay or marble, color or sound, but is bent upon molding and shaping that which is alive and pulsating in the realm of the spirit. Hence its excellence as a vocation and its responsibilities.

The exercise of any art is not achieved without a mastery of skills — skills that are generally acquired by hard work and study coupled with abundant practice. The art of teaching is no exception. Teachers too must work hard to acquire the skills that are consonant with their high calling.

Besides a mastery of the subject matter and a thorough knowledge of psychology, the teacher must possess the ability to impart to those entrusted to him his own knowledge, and this imparting of knowledge is largely dependent upon skills that so many seem to possess quite naturally but which most people must acquire.

The acquisition of the skills proper to teaching can be observed in action in the classroom of the experienced teacher and this is possibly the best way of acquiring a knowledge of teaching skills. However, most aspiring teachers will not have an abundance of opportunities for such observation. It is for these that this book is written.

It is the hope of the author that this volume may help teachers secure greater efficiency in the exercise of the art of teaching. If it does this in but a small way, the author will feel that he has contributed something to the teaching profession. And he would like this contribution to be a concrete way of expressing his thanks to the many teachers who inspired him and who have guided him along the paths of learning.

The techniques outlined in this book are not restricted to any one modern or traditional way of teaching Latin. Rather, it is hoped that all teachers of Latin may find some help toward a more effective teaching of the reading of Latin.

Bibliographical lists of helpful books have been omitted as such listings are outmoded by the time they are printed. Current periodicals do keep teachers abreast of new and timely publications.

Listings of classroom helps such as slides, movies, projects, and so forth are purposely omitted as such listings become obsolete by the time they are completed. This is evident when one notes the wealth of materials that are offered the teachers in each succeeding issue of current periodicals. It is to these periodicals, then, that the teacher is referred as well as to the listings of the American Classical League.

Techniques involving the use of teaching machines have been omitted as undoubtedly books in that field will appear shortly since much time, effort, and money is being currently expended in their development.

Contents

Speak the speech, I pray you,
as I pronounced it to you,
trippingly on the tongue....
Be not too tame neither,
but let your own discretion be your tutor.
Suit the action to the word,
the word to the action....

(Hamlet, Act III, Scene 2)

Chapter 1

Objectives

Any presentation or discussion of the objectives in the teaching of Latin is likely to be somewhat controversial because it necessarily involves and reflects the personal attitudes of the participants. However, there are certain fundamentals about which most teachers agree. It is these fundamental objectives of language teaching, and in particular of the teaching of Latin, that will be discussed in this chapter. What, then, are some of the basic objectives in Latin teaching?

Since language is a means of communication, the ultimate objective in the teaching of Latin is comprehension. By study and hard work the student is to be brought to the level of knowledge that permits him to secure what the Latin wishes to communicate to him. There can be no true communication if English is involved as the interpreter. So long as English is the intermediary there is no direct communication. Hence our goal must be the ability to receive a direct communication from the Latin. In other words, the ultimate goal is the understanding of Latin — getting the thought directly from the Latin either spoken or written. Some may refer to this goal as the reading of Latin as Latin.

Translation then is not our goal in the teaching of Latin. Rather this process is considered as skill over and above that of comprehending directly what the Latin wishes to communicate. Once we have taught the student to comprehend what the Latin says, then it will be proper to proceed to the next step, that of translation. This teaching of translation might will be deferred to the third and fourth years of the study of a non-native language.

Teaching the student to comprehend directly from the Latin what the Latin communicates involves us in the attainment of other goals. Quite obviously there will be no communication if the student does not know the inflection of nouns and verbs. A knowledge of these forms is one of the necessary steps that will put the student on the path toward direct comprehension.

How this first step is taught will greatly aid or hinder the student's ultimate comprehension. If the forms are memorized as disparate items, just as one memorizes the component parts of sulphuric acid, then there will be no eventual comprehension because we have not taught the student how to use the form. The true chemist must not only know the components of sulphuric acid but he must also know how to use it. Just so, the Latin student must not only know the component parts of «amābat», but he must also know how to use it. Hence, Latin forms should be mastered functionally — the student must be taught from the first to react to «amābat» as telling him that the action of loving took place in the past.

Necessary as it may be, the knowledge of the inflection of nouns and verbs as well as a thorough acquaintance with other parts of speech is only the beginning. There can be no true comprehension of the Latin without the next step — that of understanding how these forms are combined into a meaningful expression. This involves us in the study of grammar.

Grammar is not to be taught as a science. Rather just as forms must be learned largely through observation of what they do, so also grammar must be presented functionally. Students can easily memorize the conditions for the use of «cum» but this will forever remain just theoretical knowledge unless it is reduced to practice. Hence, students should meet «cum» in their reading and learn to react to what the author wishes to communicate when he uses that word. If the student correctly understands that «cum» followed by a verb in the indicative mood wishes to tell him something about the time only when a certain event transpired, there is no added comprehension if he can classify this usage as a «cum-temporal» clause. Comprehension does involve grammar but it need not involve the science of grammar. The learning of the science of grammar can be deferred until the third and fourth years if it is felt that such learning is helpful or necessary.

Some terminology is serviceable even in first year. Once a student has understood what «cum» and the indicative wish to say, then the term «cum-temporal» is a handy way of summing up the grammatical function.

A knowledge of forms (morphology) and how these function in a language (grammar) are the two basic steps needed for comprehension. If students remain at this level they will comprehend much of what the Latin expresses but by no means will they understand perhaps the most important part of the communication.

In order to more fully understand what the author wishes to say we must study his choice of words and their arrangement. Individual words may need some elucidation by the teacher if the student is fully to understand what is said. For example, «īra» when used in the plural by Vergil expresses an idea that is quite similar to our English word "passions". Then there are the apt phrases to express exactly what the author wishes to convey. «Invidēre alicuī» contains the idea of looking at (against) someone to his disadvantage. This expresses in a more concrete way what we express by the word "envy".

The author's use of words, phrases, and clauses and how he arranges them can be considered elements of his style. In Roman oratory and poetry, more so than in English, many stylistic devices were used to heighten the expression of the idea. These the student must understand to fully appreciate an author.

What the author says and how he says it does not constitute the final fullness of understanding for the student because he must be taught to project the author and his work against a larger background — the environment and culture of the people for whom the author is the spokesman. Knowing something about housing conditions in Rome will help the student understand the bitterness in Juvenal's description of the poor person who lived in the attic and was the last to perish in the fire. Similarly, knowing that the orator was for a long time the ideal of Roman education will help us understand more fully the devotion of men like Cicero to this form of writing. A knowledge, therefore, of Roman customs, social conditions, and religious attitudes will enable the student to undersand more completely what the author wishes to say.

The goal then in the study of Latin should be a full comprehension of the Latin author's communication. This goal can be achieved at least partially in the student's first comprehension of the literal meaning and this is perhaps a sufficient goal for the first year of the study of Latin. As the student progresses in his acquaintance with the language and through it with the people who spoke and wrote it, he can ever more thoroughly comprehend what the author wishes to convey. The final stages will have been reached when the student can read the author with a keen appreciation of all that constitutes the culture which the author represents. The language itself is the key to that culture.

The study of Latin that ever progresses toward a full comprehension as we envisaged it here will result in a language experience that is truly educative, especially for students who are monolinguals. The student's vision will be broadened and he will come to a more sympathetic view of cultures other

3

than his own. He will come to a realization that his way of expressing a thought is not the only way; his view of life is not always fully the same for all peoples. His interests are broadened, his sensibilities refined through contact with great personalities. Thus his own personal development is enriched.

It is not to be assumed that students will have achieved these goals at the end of one year's study of Latin, but they should have taken the first steps that will lead eventually to a full comprehension of the Latin as they read — a comprehension that bypasses the English and does not make use of instantaneous translation.

Chapter 2

General norms

In order to bring students to a direct comprehension of the Latin there are some general norms or principles that will govern the teaching procedures.

1 If students are to be taught to comprehend the Latin directly, then quite obviously it follows that English is to be used just as little as possible. This general norm affects all the areas of learning: vocabulary, syntax, and reading.

At the beginning students should learn their Latin vocabulary mostly from pictures and from the spoken word of the teacher. When they have acquired some vocabulary, new words are explained insofar as possible in Latin without reference to English.

Syntax should also be taught without reference to the English. If students know that «quod» and the indicative can express the cause or reason, then this knowledge can be used to teach them that «cum» and the subjunctive can also express this same idea.

Using English as little as possible also affects the teaching of reading. Instead of translating a story, the teacher reads it in the original, gives a synopsis of it in simpler Latin, and then proceeds to a further reading of the story as originally told.

2 The use of induction in the teaching of Latin is admittedly slow but it does help toward establishing the habits that will help to a direct comprehension of the Latin. Ideally the student will meet the particular construction or usage in his reading. Observation, reflection, organization, and the formulation of the rule governing the usage will follow in order. This principle affects all the areas of learning: vocabulary, syntax, and reading.

After meeting repeated occurrences of words ending in «-tor» the student can readily enough infer that such an ending will indicate the doer of the action. Similarly the «-tās» ending will indicate the abstract quality. Soon the student realizes that it is important to know the meaning of base forms. The actual meaning of a new word can be largely determined from context. Proper training of the student in vocabulary will eliminate the fear that most students have of comprehending passages that they have not seen before.

Meeting new forms in context and determining what they do is a slow way of learning them but it is an effective way of establishing direct comprehension. If the student knows that the story he is about to hear has already occurred, then it is natural for him to associate forms like «amābat» with the continued past action. Of course he will want to know what element signals such an action and this can be readily answered when he sees many such verbs in the past and finally notes the element that is common to all of them.

If a teacher retells a story with which the students are familiar and uses new grammatical constructions, the same inductive procedure can be followed to bring the students to a knowledge of what the new construction indicates. If they are familiar with «postquam» and the perfect indicative, they need but meet situations in which a definite time element is expressed and note that the pluperfect tense is used. The student was not given the rule in advance, he learned it from his own observation.

Reading levels can be increased by the use of induction. If a story is told a second time and if new words and constructions are slowly introduced, the student can through his own observation come to a knowledge of what the words mean and what the constructions indicate.

3   After a child has frequently put together a jigsaw puzzle, he can do it with ease and rapidity and with a minimum of attention. We say that such a child has overlearned how to put the puzzle together. Overlearning is important in the mastering of a language. When a student can automatically manipulate the elements of communication in a language, he knows the language.

In view of this principle the student must have an abundance of opportunities to practice the various combinations that are part of a language. This practice is not had in writing as that is too slow a process. Situations must be created then that will enable the student to orally produce the combinations. Because the student is no longer a child, the situations for the manipulation of the elements of language can be created in what are called "Drill masters" by some and "Pattern practices" by others.

We might term this principle the "stimulus–response" type of learning. In the oral drills the stimulus is given and the response is made. When the response can be made automatically then the student may be said to have overlearned. Such overlearning is a help in directly comprehending the Latin when reading.

4 Overlearning as was indicated above can best be accomplished by what is known as the oral-aural approach to the teaching of Latin. And that for several reasons.

The ear has been trained from our earliest days to catching the sound of language. We also learned to speak when still quite small. Both skills were acquired before we were taught to read. Both the hearing and the speaking were acquired through abundant practice that had little to do with the eye. Hence, it would seem quite profitable to use these highly developed skills in the learning of a second language.

Psychologically, too, the oral-aural approach has advantages over the "eye" approach. Our senses are the avenues to the soul in accord with the philosopher's dictum, «Nīl in intellectū nisi prius in sēnsū.» If, therefore, we use three senses to learn a language instead of one, the learning should be faster and should also be more permanent.

The typed page is wholly inarticulate and consequently many helps to understanding are wanting. On the other hand, when a story is read interpretatively and even with a certain amount of mimicry, or better still if the story is told, the teller can by his very intonation, phrasing and gesturing make it easier for the listener to comprehend. Then there is true communication. For the teacher, I might add, there is no greater thrill than to see on the faces of his listeners the pleasure they experience when they understand what he wishes to communicate to them. The situation is quite akin to the wrapt attention that youngsters in grade school give their teacher when he tells them a story.

The oral-aural approach also permits a more effective use of time. Writing is always slow and time consuming. Writing the transformation of ten Latin sentences consumes at least three times as much times as making those same transformations orally.

Because so much more can be accomplished in a short time by the oral-aural methods the student is enabled to concentrate more thoroughly. He will not be distracted by erasures that must be made on the page, by the changing of pens since the first went dry, and by other such nuisances. Because of this concentration we secure what might be termed "mass learning". The correct form or usage is constantly bombarding his consciousness through a relatively short period of time, thus paving the way for automatic response.

5 For the person who is totally color blind, this world presents itself as a series of small contrasts between the shades of grey. What a wealth of contrast on the other hand there is in it for the person whose color perception is good. And this contrast of color is a help in easily distinguishing items. The contrasts that occur between languages are a source of sound learning if presented properly. Contrast teaching then should be exploited by the language teacher. Students will enjoy the search for the differences between Latin and English.

If at the outset the teacher presents clearly the contrast between English and Latin, the student will readily see it and adjust to the new way of thinking. In English, for example, meaning is conveyed by the positions in which the words appear in the sentence. Latin on the other hand signals the meaning by changing the endings of words.

When strong contrasts are had between the native language and the language the student wishes to learn, the teacher knows in advance that there will be difficulty. Hence he is careful to explain the contrast and then to drill the students until such time as the contrast no longer affords difficulty. On the other hand where the contrast is small the teacher knows that he can proceed rather rapidly.

Contrast teaching has a place within the new language itself. A student has a definite degree of knowledge when he knows the meaning of «audit», but this knowledge is deepened if it is seen in contrast with «audiet» and «audiat». Similarly his knowledge of grammar is deepened when he sees the contrast between purpose and result clauses that are introduced by «ut», especially when he sees that the negative conjunctions are «nē» and «ut nōn».

6 Observing the points of contrast between the student's native language and the Latin is good for determining where the student will find difficulty and in what elements he must be more thoroughly drilled. At first glance this principle may seem to conflict with that of stressing similarities rather than focusing upon dissimilarities. The conflict though is only an apparent one.

In accord with contrast the teacher will present the first and second declensions together in order to take advantage of the contrasts in gender and in endings. At the same time, in accord with the principle of focusing attention on similarities, the teacher will help the student see that the final "m" is an indication of the accusative singular, that "s" preceded by the characteristic vowel of the declension indicates the accusative plural, and that "īs" indicates the ablative and dative plurals.

Similarly in the teaching of syntax the teacher will present conditions and wishes, if not simultaneously, then at least in rapid succession; when presenting the wishes he will stress the similarities with conditions.

7 The teacher that trains his students to focus upon similarities will quite naturally observe the principle of unity in his teaching. He will be intent upon presenting the things that are closely allied whether in vocabulary or syntax.

When the student meets the verb «capiō» he will be given the compounds that are formed from this verb together with allied words such as «captor» and «captivitās». This might be characterized as "unit building" in the study of vocabulary. Soon the similarities such as the «tās» ending will further build the student's vocabulary.

Other forms of "unit building" can be developed. For example, a picture of a human face can be presented and the vocabulary given for all the features; or if the student is to study Vergil, he can learn as a unit the various words that are used when describing a ship, together with the words for the sea, the weather, and other related items.

The principle of unity will also bear upon the teaching of syntax. After the student has met several uses of «cum» the teacher should present all the uses of «cum» and by examples show what usage can be expected in a given situation. For example, in a narrative it is likely that «cum» will mean "when" rather than "because" or "although".

8 Once the student has learned the various meanings of «cum» as a conjunction, the teacher can further the student's reading and comprehension by training him to observe the principle of expectancy. In any partial communication there are indications of what is to follow. For example, «Mīlitēs bonī herī...» will of necessity require a verb in the past, and the verb will end in «-nt». If the expression is expanded thus, «Mīlitēs bonī herī cum» the student should be taught to react to the «cum» as expressing time rather than causality or concession since in ordinary prose this conjunction indicates time more frequently than both of the other usages combined.

The principle of expectancy can also be used in the interpretation of case usage. When the student meets an ablative without a preposition he should react to it as answering the question «quōmodo». Similarly «cui» will help with the dative and «cūjus» with the genitive.

9 Keeping the interest of students in the study of Latin is important. The surest way to keep this interest is to make certain that the student's power over the language grows constantly. If he continues to grasp the meaning of the Latin as he progresses through more and more complicated Latin, then his interest will be sustained. We might call this the principle of intrinsic interest as opposed to the extrinsic. Pictures, games, slides, and movies are extrinsic stimuli but these will have only a passing effect upon the student. His own consciousness of his power in comprehending the language is enduring and satisfying. When this intrinsic interest is present the student is only too willing to continue to subject himself to the discipline of the hard work that is entailed in learning another language.

10 Most teachers are familiar with the student who correctly parses a form, but does not use it properly in a sentence or give its correct meaning. To obviate such situations teachers should make use of the principle of teaching in context.

Contextual teaching is important in the learning of vocabulary and is directly opposed to the disparate lists that have upon occasion been presented to students. The context provides associations that help the student remember the meaning of the word; if the context is repeated many times the student will come automatically to associate the proper words with this context and the words will remain his permanent possession.

Forms too should be taught in context and then drilled in context. Even if the context is no more than a sentence, it is far superior to the rote recitation of the endings of the declensions.

Grammar too must be taught in context for it is only the context that will clearly indicate to the student how this or that usage functions.

11 The foregoing principles have their bearing upon testing. Test the student's language skill, not his memory. Most teachers are familiar with the procedure whereby students laboriously mastered a small amount of text, diligently reviewed it before an examination, and then in the examination parroted what they heard in class. Such testing does not test language skill, though it might indicate the student's ability to recall.

Testing a student's language skill consists essentially in determining whether he can understand the content of a communication. Hence the ideal in testing is sight comprehension. To be sure, such a passage should remain within the framework of the student's experience with the language thus far, but it should not be the same text that he read before.

Testing the student's language skill also eliminates the all too familiar type of question in which grammar analysis is required by way of an answer. Testing the meaning of isolated forms and asking for parsing is not consistent with the ideal of comprehension.

12 A final principle may in a way sum up all that has been said. Make everything in the class contribute to the final goal — comprehension of the Latin as Latin.

All the external activities of the class must contribute to the student's internal activity. Hence it follows that they are useful only to that extent. Ruled out then are those activities that are merely entertaining. Entertainment has its place of course but that place is strictly outside the classroom and outside of class time. Such an activity is usually passive and hence has little value for the student who wishes to actively master the language.

All the internal activities of the student must contribute to a growth in the power of comprehension. Growth in the power of comprehension will in turn stimulate the student's internal activities and the mutual interplay of these two forces cannot but lead to final success in the learning of Latin.

Chapter 3

The teaching of morphology

The declensions

Order of cases

The first thing that is likely to impress a teacher when he pages through some of the modern textbooks of Latin is the unusual order of the cases. This order for the cases offers, it is true, some difficulty for the teacher who has been trained in the traditional way; but it offers no difficulty to the students for they have never seen the traditional order of the cases. Moreover, the teacher in a short time gets used to the new order — we might say that he learns along with the students but much faster since he is already acquainted with the language.

The traditional order of the cases does not present them in the order of importance. Tabulations of the occurrences of the cases in Latin authors will soon convince us of this. Basing our figures on the proportion of 100 we find that the ablative occurs 39 times, the accusative 37, the nominative 15, the dative 6, and the genitive 3.

It would seem then that we should give the cases in this order: ablative, accusative, nominative, dative, and genitive. One very obvious advantage would be the relative ease of classifying the words according to declensions since the first form the student would memorize would be the one that gives the clue to the declension. But under present circumstances where textbooks have been written and dictionaries compiled with the assumption that the nominative is to be given first, it is advisable that in any presentation of Latin nouns the nominative be retained.

Many modern texts give the nominative and then the ablative. This has advantages since the accusative singular can be formed by the addition of "m" and the accusative plural by the addition of "s" provided one is careful of quantities in the accusative singular. Classifying nouns by using the nominative and the ablative does involve difficulties when the student consults dictionaries and for that reason some textbooks do not retain this scheme throughout but revert to the traditional nominative and genitive once the student is thoroughly familiar with nouns.

Considering all the problems the ideal order seems to be: nominative, accusative, ablative, dative, and genitive. A brief glance at the paradigms when they are drawn up in that order reveals several advantages over the traditional presentation. For example, the dative and ablative plural are placed close to each other as are the nominative and accusative plural. These latter are identical in form in most declensions.

Number of cases to be presented

Some authors present only the nominative, accusative, and ablative at first and then much later bring in the remaining two cases. This has its problems since students are not likely to ever get the various declensions straight without a great deal of effort. Hence it would seem advisable that all five cases be given within a relatively short period of time. We do not mean that in the very beginning the teacher should present the entire paradigm of the first declension, but we do feel it is difficult for the student at a much later date to add the two remaining cases.

Nor should the plural of the individual declensions be unduly delayed. As soon as students have the singular fairly well in mind the plural should be presented in order that drills may be varied and in order that students have an equal opportunity for learning the plural.

The function of the cases

Since English is a language that signals meaning by the position of the words and Latin is an inflectional language, the student must learn to comprehend the meanings of the endings of words. This is possibly the greatest contrast between the two languages. Hence the students must be drilled until they instinctively react to the endings of words no matter what the position of the words is in the sentence.

Since, too, the number of cases in Latin is greater than the very rudimentary case forms that we have in English, chiefly in pronouns, it will be a help for the teacher and the student alike to keep the following outline in mind. It can be completed as the various cases are taught.

14

The five linguistic functions are:

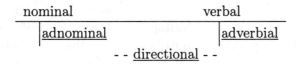

	nominal		verbal
	adnominal		adverbial
	- - directional - -		

Under the nominal we include the nominative and accusative cases. Under the adverbial are included the ablative and dative cases, as well as a few special usages of the accusative. The genitive case functions adnominally. Later in the course this same diagram can be used to show the functions of clauses. Under directional we list the conjunctions and connecting words.

Horizontal presentation of the declensions

The traditional system presents the declensions vertically and usually one at a time. In the newer approaches this is done horizontally and with obvious advantages. For example, it permits the teacher to use an inductive approach that will from the outset stress the similarities in the paradigms rather than those elements that make the declensions distinct. With but a few simple directions such as "m" signalling the accusative, "t" indicating the verb, and all other endings indicating the nominative case, the teacher can drill the students and use nouns of any declension. Then when he later classifies the nouns the student will already have some acquaintance with each of the declensions, and the similarities will remain fixed in his mind.

Let's look at the horizontal presentation for a moment.

	Nom	Acc	Abl	Dat	Gen
1	rosa	rosam	rosā	rosae	rosae
2	servus	servum	servō	servō	servī
3	lēx (gs)	lēgem	lēge	lēgī	lēgis
4	portus	portum	portū	portuī	portūs
5	rēs	rem	rē	reī	reī

The nominative ends in "s" except in the first. The accusative has "m" in all declensions. The ablative has the declension marker only. Three of the declensions have "i" in the dative.

15

	Nom	Acc	Abl	Dat	Gen
1	rosae	rosās	rosīs	rosīs	rosārum
2	servī	servōs	servīs	servīs	servōrum
3	lēgēs	lēgēs	lēgibus	lēgibus	lēgum
4	portūs	portūs	portibus	portibus	portuum
5	rēs	rēs	rēbus	rēbus	rērum

The nominative and accusative are alike in the third, fourth, and fifth declensions and all end in "s". The accusative plural for all can be formed by adding "s" to the ablative singular. The dative and ablative cases are always alike. The genitive plural ends in "um" with some variations in the preceding syllable.

These are but some of the obvious similarities that can be easily taught to students. The structural linguist no doubt will point out others that are not so apparent.[1]

Teaching the five declensions

After a brief study of the horizontal presentation of the declensions it will be evident that the nominative and accusative cases should be the first to be presented to the student. Moreover, these cases present but little contrast with the English. The following presentation might be used.

Tell the students that Latin has the following signals: words that end in "s" or "a" indicate the subject; those that end in "m" signal the object; while the verb can be easily recognized from the "t" ending.

To get a start with vocabulary the teacher passes out a page of pictures that have the Latin terms for the objects in those pictures. Or he may wish to write out a list of words such as the following:

calumnia	injūria	accūsat	exercet
candēla	sententia	honōrat	terret
causa		invītat	silet
corōna	dominus	jūdicat	urget
culpa	lēgātus	labōrat	spernit
fābula	medicus	recuperat	
fēmina	populus	stimulat	
herba	cīvis	tolerat	

---

[1]For a similar but more exhaustive treatment the teacher is referred to the «Classical Weekly» for January 23, 1950. An excellent presentation is to be found in «Latin: A Structural Approach», pages 67–69, by Waldo E. Sweet, University of Michigan Press, Ann Arbor, 1957.

Before proceeding further the teacher explains that «quis» will want the subject for an answer, «quem» or «quid» will require the object, and «quid agit» will ask for the verb.

Now the teacher has enough marerial to conduct considerable drill on the contrast between English and Latin, the difference between a language that signals meaning by the position of words and one that indicates meaning by inflectional endings.

A word of caution is in order. The students learn quickly enough to respond to the signals. Hence they can give the subject in quick reply to «quis» but they can do this without knowing the meaning of the word that they give in reply. This is not a serious problem at this point in their training since the teacher wishes the students to become familiar with the sounds and to respond to the signals that are given in the endings of the words. Fuller comprehension can come later when the lexical items are stressed.

Once the students are familiar with the nominative and accusative cases the teacher introduces them to the use of the ablative. He indicates its function by putting it in the proper place in the diagram on page 15. The prepositions «in» and «sub» are convenient for introducing the ablative.

The ablative will cause no trouble since the teacher can tell them that in addition to the presence of «in» and «sub» they can recognize an ablative by the vowel ending of the word. The only vowel that needs special care is "a" which should have a macron when it indicates the ablative case.

To facilitate the drill of the ablative it is desirable that the students be taught the passive ending for the verb, «-ur». Then give the simple distinction that the preposition «ā» or «ab» is used with persons but not with inanimate things. There is no need to refer to the ablative of agent and the ablative of means at this point. Such terms can come later.

Once the students have mastered the first three cases of the first declension, the teacher gives the genitive and dative cases. He indicates where they fit in the diagram on page 15. The genitive will indicate possession, and the dative will give the indirect object usage of English. The question words «cui» and «cūjus» are given. Now the teacher can drill the entire singular of the first declension.

Following much the same procedure the teacher presents the second declension including the neuter forms.

When students have indicated a fair mastery of the cases in the singular for the first and second declensions the teacher should introduce the first- and second-declension adjectives. Besides making them familiar with the type of adjective that accounts for about seventy-five per cent of Latin adjectives

17

the introduction of the adjective permits an expansion of the expression of ideas.

Following the introduction of the adjective the teacher should proceed at once to the teaching of the plural. Give the Latin words that will signal the plural and then drill. The plurals will be mastered in a shorter period of time since students are already familiar with the usage of the cases and so can concentrate on the meaning of the endings.

Now is the time to teach the third declension in much the same way, but teach it in conjunction with the third-declension adjectives in order that similarities can be stressed and contrasts pointed out.

Little time need be spent on the fourth and fifth declensions, especially the latter since it is represented in Latin mostly by two words, «rēs» and «diēs». Moreover, a check of the horizontal presentation of the declensions will indicate how regular the fourth declension is. The neuter nouns of the fourth can be omitted entirely since they are represented chiefly by «cornū» and «genū», and these do not occur frequently.

For each of the steps outlined above it is desirable that the forms be met in reading before they are fully catalogued and reduced to the order of a formal paradigm. Unfortunately we do not have a great amount of such simplified reading and so the teacher will probably have to compose such materials. A little practice in simplifying stories will give the teacher facility. Then there remains the task of duplicating it. It is to be hoped that Latin teachers will pool their efforts and publish an abundance of simplified stories for beginners in Latin.

It should be noted that the restriction to the third person singular of the present tense of the verb is not necessarily to be followed. Teachers will find it profitable to introduce the plural of the verb as soon as they teach the plural of the noun. An early introduction to the imperfect, the future, and even the perfect tenses will be profitable as it will fashion a framework upon which the student may later build when he takes the verb in detail.

The presentation of adjectives

The traditional way of presenting the cases and genders of the adjective does not emphasize the forms that are similar. Just as the traditional order of the cases was abandoned, so now the traditional order of the genders is changed in order to secure greater emphasis on similarities.

Here is how the adjectives of the first and second declensions appear in the new paradigms.

	Fem	Masc		Neut	
Nom	alta	altus		altum	
Acc	altam	⟶	altum	⟵	
Abl	altā	⟶	altō	⟵	
Dat	altae	⟶	altō	⟵	
Gen	altae	⟶	altī	⟵	
Nom	altae	altī		alta	
Acc	altās	altōs		alta	
Abl	⟶	altīs		⟵	
Dat	⟶	altīs		⟵	
Gen	altārum	⟶	altōrum	⟵	

Even a cursory glance at the above table of forms will clearly reveal to the student that in the singular the masculine and neuter forms are alike except for the nominative singular. A study of the plural will clearly reveal the identity of form for the ablative and dative, as well as agreement between the masculine and neuter genitive.

Adjectives like «gravis, grave» look like this in the new paradigm.

	Fem	Masc		Neut
Nom	⟶	gravis	⟵	grave
Acc	⟶	gravem	⟵	grave
Abl & Dat	⟶	gravī		⟵
Gen	⟶	gravis		⟵
Nom & Acc	⟶	gravēs	⟵	gravia
Abl & Dat	⟶	gravibus		⟵
Gen	⟶	gravium		⟵

Irregulars in the dative and genitive singular appear thus in the new paradigm.

	Fem	Masc		Neut	
Nom	sōla	sōlus		sōlum	
Acc	sōlam	⟶	sōlum	⟵	
Abl	sōlā	⟶	sōlō	⟵	
Dat	⟶	sōlī		⟵	
Gen	⟶	sōlīus		⟵	

The relative pronoun presents this picture in the new arrangement.

19

	Fem	Masc		Neut	
Nom	quae	quī		quod	
Acc	quam	quem		quod	
Abl	quā	⟶	quō	⟵	
Dat	⟶	cui		⟵	
Gen	⟶	cūjus		⟵	
Nom	quae	quī		quae	
Acc	quās	quōs		quae	
Abl & Dat	⟶	quibus		⟵	
Gen	quārum	⟶	quōrum	⟵	

Teachers who have learned the traditional paradigms will be frightened, no doubt, at the above presentation but they need not be. They will not need to spend time relearning the declensions. For the most part they can do this relearning as they teach the matter, and since they are familiar with the Latin they will learn much more rapidly than the students.

The order of the genders does not create difficulties for the student because he is not likely to consult the dictionary. Later, when the forms of the nouns and adjectives are mastered, the student will readily enough adjust to the dictionary listings.

Drilling the declensions

Some amount of vertical drilling of the declensions can be used in order to check the student's knowledge of the endings for the separate declensions. But this should be used sparingly. In order to drill within some context the teacher can compose sentences such as these that will indicate the usages of the cases.

> Mariā est māter Deī.
> Mariam, mātrem Deī, laudāmus.
> Ā Mariā, mātre Deī, adjuvāmur.
> Mariae, mātrī Deī, dōna magna data sunt.
> Mariae fīlius est Chrīstus.

After some amount of drill students might be given an assignment that will require them to compose several series of similar sentences.

Obviously much drill must be given the students but this drill should always be done in the context of sentences at least. Sentences are the minimum unit that will help students arrive at an automatic reaction to language situations. If the teacher has given the third person singular of verbs then he is in a position to drill the declensions. Here are some practical schemes for such a drill.

Completion drill

Write out the following scheme on the chalkboard, or give the students duplicated pages that contain the scheme.

    Marī___ amat puell___
    Marī___ amātur ā puell___
    Marī___ dat ros___ puell___
    Marī___ videt ros___ puell___

Call upon the students to read the sentences aloud completing the words with the proper case endings. Once students have mastered the singular, proceed to the plural. Be sure to change the word order in succeeding sentences in order to make the students fully aware of the function of the endings as opposed to position.

A progressive completion drill

The completion drill can be used with the individual declensions, but as progress is made, the drill should be used to contrast the forms of the various declensions and the sentences themselves should be expanded to include other items as they are learned.

1 juxtapose the cases for contrast
    ā puell___ amātur Marī___
    ā serv___ vidētur lēgāt___
    ā serv___ et ā mīlit___ vidētur puer
    dōna rēg___ et domin___ sunt bona

2 vary the declensions
    ā serv___ amātur vīt___
    ā rēg___ amātur fēmin___
    tēl___ host___ urb___ oppugnant

3 expand with various parts of speech
    adjectives
    ā bon___ serv___ amātur vīt___ long___
    adverbs
    ā bon___ serv___ avid___ amātur vīt___ long___

As the students progress in their knowledge of Latin, the teacher can use the various degrees of comparison of both the adjective and the adverb to review the declensions.

Flashcards

Flashcards that have words in definite cases, for example, «servō», can be used readily for drill. The teacher exposes the card to the class, then calls on a specific student. (He should allow some time before naming the student in order to allow all to think.) It is the task of the student to form a complete sentence using the word on the card. For example, «Servō dat rosam Marīa.»

This scheme may seem to go slowly but if the cards have words that the students have seen in their reading, then sentences can be formed rather quickly as the context is familiar.

Cards with endings only, for example, ...ō, can be used by way of variation. The student in this case supplies the word and then uses it in a sentence. If he errs, the teacher calls upon another student and if he answers correctly then the first student should repeat the answer.

If the teacher has a good supply of such flashcards, he can easily conduct contests between the various rows of the class. After appointing a scribe to keep the record of correct responses, the teacher shuffles the cards. He indicates, for example, that the first row is to answer; if they miss, then the second row has the opportunity of answering. Points are kept for correct scores. Rewards, such as a perfect score for a daily quiz, can be added to the record of the students in the winning row.

Teachers should keep in mind that drills such as those outlined here also reveal the student's knowledge of vocabulary.

Circle drill

Send a student to the board to write six nouns of the first declension; send another for nouns of the second declension, and so forth. When this is completed the teacher goes to the board and draws a big circle and at parts of the circle he puts down the endings of the words. With a pointer the teacher indicates the noun, then points to an ending. The student gives the form and then uses it in a sentence. If a student has been called upon previously to put down six or more verbs on the board, the students will find the drill easier.

This drill can be used for contests just as in the case of flashcards. Again, it may seem to go slowly but the students are working with the language in meaningful situations and not just with isolated forms.

It will happen in the course of the drill that the teacher will point to an impossible combination, for example, «nauta» and then «-ōrum». In this case the students can be instructed to simply indicate that the form is an impossible one. He should, of course, be given credit for a correct answer.

Questions

Proper questioning can force the student to give any case that the teacher wants. When asking the questions the teacher should always insist upon the answer being a complete sentence. Only complete sentences will fix the patterns in their minds. Here are some suggestions for eliciting the various cases.

Ā bonō servō līberē datur rosa pulchra puellae.

Nom	Quis dat rosam?	Servus bonus dat rosam.
Acc	Quid dat servus puellae?	Rosam dat servus puellae.
Abl	Ā quō datur rosa?	Ā bonō servō datur rosa.
Dat	Cui datur rosa?	Puellae datur rosa.
Gen	Cūjus rosa datur?	Servī rosa datur.

The various parts of speech can be elicited by proper signals.

Adj	Quālis rosa datur?	Pulchra rosa datur.
Verb	Quid agit servus?	Dat rosam puellae servus.
Adverb	Quōmodo ā servō datur rosa?	Līberē datur rosa puellae.
	Quōmodo dat servus rosam?	Līberē dat servus rosam.

It must be noted that in replying to the questions the student frequently answers without knowing the lexical item. Such a lack of knowledge should not worry the teacher at this point since he has at his disposal other ways of arriving at the student's comprehension of the text. We shall discuss these later.

Teachers who have not used the questioning technique in class need not be alarmed at their lack of experience. At first the questioning may be a bit slow but very soon the teacher finds himself very apt in this art, so much so that he can conduct a very rapid drill that will keep each of the students in the class on the alert.

Drilling the individual cases

Nominative The easiest way to drill the nominative case is to change a sentence from the active to the passive.

Fēmina amat puerum.   Puer ā fēminā amātur.

Fēminae amant puerōs.   Puerī ā fēminis amāntur.

Accusative The accusative can be easily drilled by changing a sentence from the passive to the active.

Puer ā fēminā amātur.   Puerum amat fēmina.

Puerī ā fēminīs amantur.   Puerōs fēminae amant.

Ablative There are many ways of drilling the ablative. Here are some suggestions.

1 changing a sentence from the active to the passive

    Fēmina amat puerum.   Ā fēminā amātur puer.

    Fēminae amant puerōs.   Ā fēminīs amantur puerī.

2 use the prepositions «in» and «sub» in conjunction with the direction that the student is to indicate where the person or thing is at the present time

    Caesar vēnit in urbem.   Caesar nunc est in urbe.

    Puer cucurrit sub arborem.   Puer nunc est sub arbore.

3 use the ablative of comparison

    Patria mihi carior est quam vīta. Patria mihi carior est vītā.

    Diēs est clarior quam nox.   Nocte diēs est clarior.

4 employ the ablative of respect

    Fortissimī omnium sunt.   Omnēs fortitūdine superant.

    Optimī omnium sunt.   Omnēs bonitāte superant.

5 make use of the ablative of accompaniment

    Lēgātus et Caesar veniunt.   Lēgātus cum Caesare venit.

    Dux et lēgātī veniunt.   Dux cum lēgātīs venit.

6 use the ablative of cause

    Propter victōriam gaudet.   Victōriā gaudet.

    Ob mortem fīliī dolet.   Morte fīliī dolet.

Dative Here are some ways of drilling the dative.

1 Use the verb «habet» in the first sentence and instruct the students to change the construction to «est» and the dative in order to show

possession.

Puer librum habet.   Puerō est liber.
Puerī librōs habent.   Puerīs sunt librī.

2 The construction «prope» and the accusative can be changed to «prox-imus» and the dative.

Puer est prope arborem.   Puer est arborī proximus.
Puerī sunt prope arborēs.   Puerī sunt arboribus proximī.

3 Use adjectives such as «amīcus».

Est meus amīcus.   Est amīcus mihi.
Est amīcus mīlitum.   Est amīcus mīlitibus.

4 Use verbs that take their object in the dative case.

Mē adjuvat.   Mihi auxiliātur.
Tē adjuvat.   Tibi auxiliātur.

Genitive There are a number of ways of drilling the genitive and here are some suggestions.

1 Use a circumlocution and ask the students to use a verb whose object is in the genitive case.

In memoriā mīlitēs habeō.   Mīlitum meminī.
Dēbēmus arma habēre.   Armōrum indigēmus.

2 Adjectives can be used effectively.

Inter hōs mīlitēs fortissimus   Hōrum mīlitum fortissimus
est.   est.
Bellum multa perīcula habet.   Bellum est perīculōrum plēnum.
Caesar glōriam cupit.   Glōriae cupidus est Caesar.

3 Use the predicate genitive to indicate that someone has a duty, right or property. It can be used in conjunction with such verbs as «dēbeō».

Mīlitēs urbem dēfendere dēbent. Mīlitum est urbem dēfendere.
Patrēs fīliōs custōdīre dēbent. Patrum est fīliōs custōdīre.

4 The partitive genitive can be used effectively for drill.

Nōn omnēs (nōn multī) mīlitēs   Pars mīlitum pugnāre recūsant.
pugnāre recūsant.

25

5 The genitive of charge also provides material for drill.

    Propter fūrtum mē accūsat.   Fūrtī mē accūsat.

6 Participles afford drill material also.

    Mīles patriam amat.   Mīles est amāns patriae.

Drilling the comparison of adjectives

Superlative degree

1 The superlative forms of the adjective are the easiest to drill. By using the preposition «super» with the accusative the teacher can elicit from the student the superlative degree of the adjective.

    Puer super omnēs bonus est.   Puer optimus est.
    Puer super omnēs malus est.   Puer pessimus est.

2 The ablative of respect can also be used.

    Omnēs fortitūdine superant.   Fortissimī omnium sunt.
    Omnēs bonitāte superant.   Optimī omnium sunt.

3 And here is another scheme that can be used.

    Puer nimium malus est.   Puer pessimus est.
    Mōns nimium magnus est.   Mōns maximus est.

Comparative degree

1 The comparatives can be drilled easily by making use of «alter... alter», the one, the other, when speaking of two. Students are given the directions that they are to complete the second part of the sentence by adding the comparative of the adjective that appeared in the first clause.

    Alter est sanctus.   Alter est sanctior.
    Altera fēmina est humilis.   Altera est humilior.
    Alterum munus est bonum.   Alterum est melius.
    Alterī sunt bonī.   Alterī sunt meliōrēs.

2 Completion drills are handy for comparatives.

    Brutus est fortis sed Caesar est _____.
    Nauta est bonus sed mīles est _____.
    Ex hīs duōbus sanctīs, alter est _____.

3 The ablative of comparison is also excellent for drilling the comparatives.

Paulus mē audāciā superat.   Paulus mē audācior est.
Cīvis eum sapientiā superat.   Cīvis eō sapientior est.

Drilling the comparison of adverbs

Superlative degree

1 The superlative of the adverb can be drilled in the same manner as the superlative of the adjective by using «super» and the accusative case.

Super omnēs fortiter pugnat.   Fortissimē pugnat.
Nimium fortiter pugnat.   Fortissimē pugnat.

2 Questions can be used effectively for drilling the adverb.

Quōmodo vīvit vir fortissimus?   Fortissimē vīvit vir fortissimus.

Comparative degree

1 The use of completion sentences is handy.

Brūtus fortiter pugnat sed Caesar pugnat _____.
Puer bene vīvit sed sanctus vīvit _____.
Ex hīs duōbus sanctīs, alter vīvit _____.

2 Questions too can elicit the comparative degree of the adverb.

Quōmodo vīvit vir fortior?   Fortius vīvit vir fortior.
Quōmodo agit cīvis sapientior?   Sapientius agit cīvis sapiēns.

3 «Alter...alter» elicits the comparative of the adverb.

Alter fortiter pugnat.   Alter fortius pugnat.
Alter puer sanctē vīvit.   Alter sanctius vīvit.
Alterī celeriter currunt.   Alterī celerius currunt.

Drilling the numerals

In general students find the drills on numerals interesting and challenging. Here are some schemes that have been used successfully in the classroom.

Addition

1 Oral drill

Septem et septem sunt _____.
Trēs virī et trēs virī sunt _____.
Sī tribus virīs trēs accēdunt, adsunt virī _____.
Sī duōbus nummīs quīnque adduntur, habet ille nummōs _____.
Sī tribus virīs trēs accēdunt, quot adsunt virī?
Sī duōbus nummīs quīnque adduntur, quot habentur?

2 Written drill

The teacher writes the sentences on the board or gives out duplicated pages that contain sentences such as the following. Students are asked to read them aloud.

VII et VII sunt _____.
III virī et III virī sunt _____.
Sī tribus virīs III accēdunt, adsunt virī _____.
Sī II nummis V adduntur, quot habentur?
Sī III virīs III accēdunt, quot adsunt virī?

3 Chalkboard drill

The teacher writes the Roman numerals from one to ten on the chalkboard. With a pointer he indicates which two or three numerals are to be added. Students give the total, either aloud or in writing.

Subtraction

Subtraction can also be used for the drilling of numbers. And the same divisions of written and oral can be used that were used in addition. To indicate subtraction several ways may be adopted.

Sī ex septem mulieribus eximiuntur trēs, adhūc restant _____.
Adsunt vīgintī hominēs. Demptīs quattuor, adhūc restant _____.
Sī dē septem puerīs discēdunt trēs, manent _____.
Sī dē quīnque pānibus sūmuntur trēs, manent _____.
Sī ex septem mulieribus eximiuntur trēs, quot adhūc restant?
Adsunt vīgintī hominēs. Demptīs quattuor, quot restant?
Sī dē septem puerīs discēdunt trēs, quot manent?
Sī dē V pānibus sūmuntur III, quot manent?

Multiplication

Multiplication will help the teacher drill the students in the adverbial numbers.

Bis bīna sunt quattuor.

Ter terna sunt novem.

The adverbial numbers will not occur too frequently in their reading and consequently students need not be drilled as thoroughly in these forms as in the ordinal and the cardinals. Once they have drawn up a multiplication table or two for homework, little further work need be done. This is particularly true with the higher numbers where the typical endings will always indicate the adverbial numbers. What has been said about the adverbials is also true about the distributives.

By way of external interest the teacher may wish to draw a tombstone on the board and then write in the following:

```
   ra       ra     ra     (ter 'ra' — terra)
         es  et  in
   ram      ram    ram    (ter 'ram' — terram)
          ī     ī          (bis 'i' — ībis)
        quod sum mox eris
```

Drilling of pronouns

Students readily enough learn the third person pronouns along with the presentation of the third person of the verb. First and second person pronouns can best be taught in conjunction with the corresponding verb forms. The various cases can be drilled as follows.

Nominative	Ego adsum.	Nōs adsumus.
	Tū ades.	Vōs adestis.
	Is adest.	Eī adsunt.

Students would be asked to change from singular to plural or vice versa.

Accusative	Videt mē.	Videt nōs.
	Videt tē.	Videt vōs.
	Videt eum.	Videt eōs.

Again students will be asked for plural if the singular is given and vice versa.

Ablative	Ego eum amō.	Is ā mē amātur.
	Tū eum amās.	Is ā tē amātur.
	Ille eum amat.	Is ab illō amātur.

This is nothing else than the familiar change from active to passive. Again, singular and plural can easily be used in the drill.

Dative	Dat mihi librum.	Dat nōbīs librum.
	Dat tibi librum.	Dat vōbīs librum.
	Dat eī librum.	Dat eīs librum.

This is the familiar indirect object usage which students find rather easy to master.

Genitive	Meī servandī cupidī sunt.	Nostrī servandī cupidī sunt.
	Tuī servandī cupidī sunt.	Vestrī servandī cupidī sunt.
	Illōs servāre cupiunt.	Illōrum servandōrum cupidī sunt.
	Mulierēs sē servāre cupiunt.	Mulierēs suī servandī cupidae sunt.

Possessive pronouns can be drilled as if they were adjectives, except that the question words «cūjus, quōrum, quārum» will be used to elicit the forms.

Mea māter est bona.	Cūjus māter est bona?
Tua māter est bona.	Cūjus māter est bona?
Noster pater est bonus.	Quōrum pater est bonus?

The demonstrative and intensive pronouns can also be drilled as adjectives. They need but to be added to a noun and the individual case can be drilled as indicated earlier for nouns.

The relative pronoun «quae, quī, quod» can be drilled by means of relative clauses. Give two statements and ask the students to turn the first into a relative pronoun.

> Marīa est bona. Marīa est māter Deī.
> Marīa, quae est bona, est māter Deī.
> Marīam vidēmus. Marīa est māter Deī.
> Marīa, quam vidēmus, est māter Deī.

Or the teacher may wish to drill the relative pronoun by means of completion sentences.

> Vir _____ adest, est creātūra Deī.
> Vir _____ videō, est creātūra Deī.
> Vir dē _____ loquor, est creātūra Deī.

Some helps for drilling declensions

Since teachers will want to drill their students by means of sentences (the minimum contextual situation), it is essential that they have a good stock of sentences ready at hand. It is possible, of course, to duplicate a page of sentences and then distribute them to the students for drill purposes. This does not seem the best plan, however, since the teacher cannot then take the sentences in order as the students will be preparing the next sentence rather than working on the one that the teacher has called for.

In order to try to make certain that all the students are working on the same sentence at the same time I suggest the following:

1 Write the sentences on the chalkboard as you need them. But this is slow work and might well retard the interest of the student as well as cause obvious discipline problems in many instances.

2 If you are so fortunate as to have access to a tachistoscope, flash the sentence on the screen for a definite period of time. Such drill is satisfactory provided that the students are familiar with the content of the sentence through their reading. Otherwise it may put too great a burden on the memory and not definitely indicate the knowledge the student has of the forms and how to manipulate them in given language situations.

3 Perhaps a simpler method is to use a slide projector and leave the sentence on the screen during the entire drill. This permits the student to concentrate on the question and on the processes he must go through in order to answer satisfactorily.

4 But if teachers do not have mechanical aids at their disposal they can still conduct a drill rather effectively and quickly in the contextual situations. Prior to class the teacher writes the sentence on a strip of cardboard. This he affixes to hooks just above the chalkboard as he needs it. This scheme permits the teacher to prepare the sentences in advance and it does not require a large expenditure of money and it is as fast in the making as is the preparation of slides.

In order to make slides rapidly, teachers can secure from school supply houses a special carbon and transparent material. Thus the teacher can type the material, remove the carbon, fix the transparency to a frame and his slide is ready for classroom use.

5 For the teacher who wishes to prepare the material before class there is the blackboard cloth that can be purchased from school supply houses. If this is on a roller, the teacher merely pulls the cloth down in order to expose a sentence at a time for drill.

Even the old fashioned window shade, especially the deep green ones, can be used for a cloth blackboard. This, of course, is not as satisfactory as the ones that are sold commercially.

6 The use of tapes is perhaps the most efficient way to drill the students both in and out of class. The publishers of most modern textbooks will furnish master tapes from which copies may be made. In order that students may

work rapidly, it is best to use sentences with which they are familiar, or better still, sentences that they have met in their reading or have memorized. If they have memorized the sentences then the student's concentration can be directed toward the formulation of the answer and no time is lost. In any case, except possibly in test situations, the students should have been given the opportunity to study the sentences the night before. The oral work with the tapes will thus reinforce their visual learning.

Use of the chalkboard in drills

The chalkboard can be used very effectively in the drilling of the declensions as every experienced teacher knows, but it is not out of order to mention some schemes that may be used when drilling the forms in the context of sentences. Note how the schemes make use of the aural-oral approach in order to reinforce and vivify the visual presentation.

1 Dictate a sentence and then ask for definite changes. For example, active to passive, passive to active, singular to plural, and so forth. Again, the sentences should be taken from the reading if possible in order that students may be familiar with the language situation created by the sentence.

2 Dictate a simple sentence and allow the students to expand it by the addition of adjectives wherever possible or by the insertion of suitable adverbs.

3 Dictate part of a sentence, for example, «Bonus mīles in …». After calling on a student to indicate all that is known about the sentence thus far, call upon another to indicate what can be expected in the remainder of the sentence, call upon a third to insert the next word, then proceed to finish the sentence.

Occasionally the teacher can allow the students to make a game of such a drill. The student must endeavor to insert a word that will fit into but at the same time will not complete the sentence. It is surprising how students enter into such a drill and some lengthy sentences are the final result. Should the teacher doubt about the correctness of a word he can check with the student privately (in order not to give too much of a clue to the rest of the students).

4 It is not out of order occasionally to ask a student to go to the chalkboard and decline a word vertically. Make it more difficult by adding an adjective. When this is completed, allow another student to make the forms part of a complete sentence.

5 The cooperative plan works well. Send a student to the board to write a sentence. Call upon others then to draw it up into a drill similar to the pattern practices or drill masters that they have in their texts.

6 Send a student to the board and allow him to write a sentence that contains a nominative. Send another to change the sentence so that the nominative becomes an accusative. Continue the process through the various cases.

Robertus est servus dominī.

Robertum, servum dominī, laudāmus.

Ā Robertō, servō dominī, opus perficitur.

Robertō, servō dominī, nōs dōna damus.

Robertī opus nōn celeriter perficitur.

This drill can be used as a contest between rows. Each row sends a representative to the chalkboard to write a model sentence. Succeeding representatives make the changes that are required to illustrate the forms of the five cases.

Homework

Homework, if it is to have any value, must reinforce what the student has learned in class, or it must prepare him for things that he is to learn in class. Here are some suggestions for helping students to profitably study outside of class time.

1 Duplicate pages that contain sentences but leave off the endings of the words. Allow the students to complete them outside of class time.

As the student's knowledge of vocabulary grows and his knowledge of forms increases the teacher should choose paragraphs that tell a story rather than disconnected sentences.

2 Indicate that the students are to draw up sets of sentences that will use the same word in the various cases of the declension (see page 33).

3 Memorize sentences that will be used for drill the following day.

4 Read the story in the lesson many times trying to understand it as they read. If the story becomes so familiar that they have practically memorized it, well and good. Such memory fixes the patterns in their memories. This is similar to the situation in which children in the lower grades memorize the reading simply from hearing it. Who has not seen such a student do the reading even when the book is handed to him upside down?

5 Give a page of simple sentences and have the students expand them by suitable adjectives and adverbs; this scheme can be used effectively throughout the year as the students progress through a study of prepositional phrases, relative clauses, subordinate clauses, and so forth.

6 Give a series of incomplete Latin sentences. Instruct students to write what is known about the sentence thus far, what it is they can predict will

33

occur in the remainder of the sentence. They should then complete the sentence in their own words. Such a task is not too difficult but it is time consuming. If the teacher is satisfied that students will do such work orally, then this is the better way. Check on it the next day in class.

7 Occasionally it is profitable to assign the diagramming of some sentences.

8 If the teacher wishes students to study vocabulary, he may give as an assignment the preparation of a list of English derivatives.

9 Give the students several sentences and ask them that night to indicate the questions (writing them out in full) that will elicit each of the words in the sentences. This scheme is particularly helpful if you wish to find out their knowledge of the grammar, for example, the difference between the ablative of agent («ā quō, ā quibus») and the ablative of means («quibus auxiliīs, quō īnstrūmentō»). Needless to say, it is not necessary to assign the making of questions for each word. At one time the teacher may wish to find out their knowledge of conjunctions, at another their knowledge of adverbs, and so forth. The assignments are made accordingly.

10 Using the story that was read in class, the students are to draw up questions about the forms, for example, questions on structure, «Quis domum īvit?»

At other times the teacher can instruct them to draw up comprehension questions. When these are turned in the following day, some are selected for the daily quiz.

11 At other times the homework of the students may consist in their filling in certain parts of their notebook, for example, model declensions, model sentences, certain uses of the ablative, and so forth.

Notebooks

It is advisable that teachers require students to keep notebooks. Particularly is this true in freshman year. In the notebooks the students enter the things that the teacher thinks will be helpful such as model declensions, lists of words that are exceptions to the gender rules, model sentences that are to be memorized, model paradigms of the verb, and so forth. The work involved in completing the notebook is salutary review and provides the student with readily accessible paradigms whose meaning is the greater since it is their own work. Many students continue to use such notebooks in succeeding years.

In the notebook it is advisable to have a grammar section. As the students meet the various uses of «cum» for instance, these are added. Thus a cumulative review is handy at all times. Such work helps their reading. They easily visualize the various uses for «cum» that they noted in their notebook.

If the teacher decides that students must keep a notebook, then several things must be kept in mind if such work is to be effective. All should have uniform notebooks and the pages should be numbered consecutively. All students should enter the same material on the same pages. This can be achieved if the teacher indicates, for example, that a fourth declension model is to appear on page 15 of the notebook.

If the teacher himself has drawn up his own notebook in advance, then the notebooks of the students will be orderly and well planned.

Needless to say such notebooks should be checked by the teacher from time to time. This can be done rapidly at the beginning of class. Tell the students to open their notebooks to page 20. As they read the story in the text privately the teacher goes about the room checking the notebooks and conferring with students whose books contain errors.

Concluding remarks

Teachers who have been trained in the traditional way will, no doubt, miss the familiar exercise of translation. Schemes that involve translation have been omitted advisedly since translation is usually to be the last resort to determine whether or not the student has comprehended the passage or the sentence. Latin questions, diagramming, and other devices of the teacher's own choosing will find out whether the students have understood what the Latin wished to communicate. The use of such questions in Latin is in itself a constant test of comprehension and provides the student with greater opportunities for becoming familiar with the Latin.

Many teachers, too, will miss the drills that involve English to Latin. But it must be remembered that we are trying to teach them to comprehend the Latin, not to write it. Some production of the language is in order but this should come after the mastery of the construction as it appears in the readings. Formal translation in any quantity should be left to the third and fourth years of the study of the Latin.

There can be some production of the language even in first year provided that this is on an elementary basis and involves situations with which the students are familiar, for example, some simple sentences that are based on a reading that the students have mastered.

To stimulate a beginning in the production of the language the teacher may give out pictures and ask students to write sentences about the objects in the picture. He might allow them to choose a picture from the Sunday newspaper and write a short paragraph about it. Students will quite naturally choose pictures about which they feel they can write fairly well. Such a scheme allows for individual differences and interests.

None of the foregoing suggestions treat of parsing. The omission of this overworked scheme is omitted advisedly. The ability to correctly parse a word does not indicate real knowledge of the use of a form. Students can indicate that a form is the third person singular of the pluperfect indicative active but they cannot use it properly in a sentence and frequently they cannot give its English equivalent. The emphasis then should be on the correct use of the form. For example, the student knows that when he meets expressions such as «tertiō diē postquam» the verb will ordinarily be something like «laudāverat», and this form will indicate an action that has occurred in the past before another action that has been completed. He also knows that English uses the auxiliary "had" to express a similar idea.

Drilling the declensions as we have envisaged it here will take out of it some of the rote and dullness with which both teachers and students are familiar. Learning the declensions can be at least somewhat interesting. Football teams do not just learn the signals for the plays, but they use them constantly in practice in order to make the play function smoothly. Latin students too will want to know the signals but they will also wish to use them in order to understand what the Latin says.

The verb

Frequency counts

While realizing that frequency counts are good only for the authors that were used while making the count and that consequently no general conclusions can be drawn that will necessarily fit all the circumstances in the language, yet such frequency counts can be of service. If the count is based on a large amount of the literature of the language and if all types of that literature are included, then the frequency count can be of service in helping the teacher determine to some extent at least what is to be the emphasis in his teaching.

Let us briefly list some of the frequencies for the verb. For a fuller treatment the teacher is referred to the «Classical Journal», volume 33, page 18.

Person		Voice	
3 – 85 per cent		Active	– 88 per cent
2 – 9		Passive	– 12
1 – 6			

Tense		Conjugations	
Present	– 40 per cent	Third	– 35 per cent
Perfect	– 32	First	– 21
Imperfect	– 13	Sum	– 14
Pluperfect	– 7	Second	– 13
Future	– 4	-iō	– 10
Fut. Perfect	– 1	Fourth	– 5

The most frequently occurring verbs in order are:

possum	sum	dō	putō
videō	habeō	volō	ferō
faciō	dīcō	veniō	

Conclusions for the teacher

In term of teaching emphasis we can note the following with regard to the verb.

1 The third person, singular and plural, of the present tense in the active voice is by far the most frequently used form of the verb. The third person outnumbers the other two by about five to one.

2 The active forms outnumber the passive by about eight to one.

3 The present and perfect tenses amount to more than 70 per cent of all the uses.

4 Twelve of the possible one hundred and thirty-four forms of the verb will give about 70 per cent of the use of the verb. These forms are: third singular and plural of the present, imperfect, perfect, pluperfect indicative active, the present active and passive infinitives, the present and perfect participles.

The principal parts of verbs

The traditional way of giving the principal parts of verbs, for example, «moneō, monēre, monuī, monitus» is perhaps the best since it helps students easily distinguish to what class the individual verb belongs and, moreover, dictionaries, grammars, and other books in Latin use this method. However, some consideration should be given to possibly changing this traditional way, at least in part and for a time in the learning of Latin.

Since the third person appears about five times more frequently than the first and the second combined, as our own reading of Latin testifies, some

37

consideration should be given toward adopting the third person instead of the first when giving the principal parts of the verb.

Pedagogically, too, we should be induced to adopting the third person for the principal parts. Students can be gently introduced to the complexities of the Latin verb by telling them in the beginning that «-t» and «-nt» endings will signal the verb in any sentence. Nothing need be said about the various classes of verbs until much later. Note that the «-t» and «-nt» rule holds for the perfect tense as well. As students make progress in their reading, the various tenses can be introduced. Once they have seen and learned to use all the tenses, the teacher can use this framework for building all the forms of the verb.

If the third person is used for the principal parts, there is but one difficulty, the «-iō» verbs. This class of verbs accounts for about ten per cent; so it is a sizeable number. The difficulty can be avoided if some arbitrary signal is adopted to distinguish them, such as «capit (-iō), capere, cēpit, captus».

Some consideration might be given too to the dropping of the first of the principal parts. In the traditional building of the verb the infinitive is used for the formation of the present system (present, imperfect, and future). Hence, it would seem that listing the first of the principal parts is helpful only in the case of «-iō» verbs.

In the early stages of learning Latin the principal parts of the verbs should be given in the third person instead of the first. This scheme obviates giving the student the entire verb at the beginning, makes it easy to teach the tenses (expand «laudat» by putting «-ba» before the final «t» for example), and permits the student to begin learning the principal parts at an early stage in his learning of Latin. This last is important because the principal parts must be learned from the dictionary — there is no way of arriving at them by rule. If he learns the principal parts at the beginning, there will be little need later to add the remaining parts since he has already memorized them.

Some modern texts do use the third person in giving the principal parts. Once the student has learned all the forms for the verb, these texts usually revert to the traditional first person in order to minimize difficulties when consulting the dictionary or when using books that list them in the traditional way.

Presentation of the verb

The third person singular and plural of the present tense of the verb can be given to the students from the very beginning. This permits the telling of stories and the use of the cases in real language situations. The various tenses should be introduced periodically in order to give the student time to assimilate the forms and meet them often enough in the reading so that he becomes thoroughly familiar with them.

The verb should be presented inductively. Only a brief explanation is given as the various tenses are introduced. Once all the tenses have been seen in the readings the teacher can present the entire conjugation.

All the conjugations should be presented simultaneously. This permits teacher and students to note the similarities and the differences. Such a presentation is not overwhelming for the student, provided the teacher presents a tense at a time for learning.

Once the students have seen the third person forms for all the tenses of the indicative, the teacher should give a reading that will include all the classes of verbs. Together with the students the verbs are listed, and under the teacher's direction these are sorted into classes. The long "a" and the long "e" classes will be evident at once. Then there remain those that end in "it" in the present.

Order can be brought into these if the student checks the imperfect and the future tenses of these three classes. One class has «-iēbat» and the other class has only «-ēbat». There remains but the dubious «-iō» verbs and these the teacher explains to the students.

As soon as the students are familiar with the various classes of verbs and know the paradigm for the third person of all tenses of the indicative, the teacher can proceed to the presentation of the first and second person pronouns. These are taught in order to facilitate drill of the verb.

After the presentation of the pronouns the teacher proceeds at once to the presentation of the various persons of the present tense of the verb. He thus fills out the skeleton of the present tense. After the present tense is mastered, the other tenses are taken in order.

The Latin verb vs the English verb

The formation of the Latin verb means more to the student if he understands how the Romans approached the verb. In English we start with the person, then give the time signal, and then the main verb idea as in the expression, "I was singing". Latin does just the reverse. They think of the verb action, then the signal for time, and finally the person involved, for example, «laudābat». The Latin says equivalently, "Praising was he."

Contrast teaching

Throughout the presentation of the verb the teacher will be careful to drill the forms that are in strong contrast. The forms «regit, reget, regat» will need much drilling in order to fix their function in the minds of the students. The same principle affects the presentation of the present subjunctive: the "e" of the first and the "a" of the remaining conjugations. Since the first is the long "a" conjugation, students readily enough see that "a" could not be the distinguishing feature of the present subjunctive because it could not then be distinguished from the present indicative.

Teaching the formation of the verb forms

1 The traditional presentation of the verb involves the use of various stems for the formation of the tenses. These are three in number: the present which is derived from the second principal part by dropping the ending «-re»; the perfect which is secured by dropping the final «-ī» of the third principal part, and the final stem, the perfect passive stem which is identical with the last of the principal parts. The present stem yields the present, imperfect, and future tenses of the indicative as well as the present and imperfect of the subjunctive; the perfect active stem yields the tenses of the perfect system in the active while the last principal part is the basis for the perfect system passive.

2 The expansion system of teaching the verb agrees with the traditional in the formation of the perfect system both active and passive. For example,

> «laudāv-» (perfect stem) plus «-erat» (imperfect of the verb «sum») when combined give «laudāverat» — the pluperfect indicative active.
> «laudātus» (perfect passive stem) plus «erat» (imperfect of «sum») when combined give «laudātus erat» — the pluperfect indicative passive.

The expansion system offers nothing new in the perfect system but it does affect the present system of the verb: present, imperfect, and future of all moods and voices.

In the expansion system the tenses of the present system are formed by infixes, certain letters or combinations of letters that are inserted between what would ordinarily be called the stem and the personal ending. The first principal part, for example, «amat», is used as the base. Then by a series of expansions the various tenses of the verb are formed.

40

This expansion system is in accord with Latin thinking but not with English. In English we start with the particular and go to the more general, "I was going". Latin starts with the general and gradually modifies the thought down to the particular, «ī-ba-m». This system seems to be in accord with the reading goal. Hence further study is in order.

The first conjugation is an easy one to work with in the expansion system of presenting the verb.

ama-t	–	the base form and the first of the principal parts.
amā-ba-t	–	add the infix -ba- to form the imperfect tense.
amā-bi-t	–	add the infix -bi- to form the future tense.
am-e-t	–	ordinarily the signal for the present subjunctive is "a" but since this is the long "a" conjugation the signal "e" is used.
amā-re-t	–	add the infix -re- to form the imperfect subjunctive or add the personal endings to the second principal part.
amā	–	drop the "t" to form the imperative singular.
amāt-e	–	add "e" to form the imperative plural.

The second conjugation works better than the first: «mone-t, monē-ba-t, monē-bi-t, mone-a-t, monē-re-t, monē, monēt-e». There is some difficulty with verbs of the third conjugation because letter changes are involved rather than mere expansion but students readily enough learn the difference between «regit, reget and regat». Quantities too pose something of a problem for the various forms but again a little study will help students master this. The fourth conjugation poses no problem as everything follows the pattern just as «moneō» does. In the -iō conjugation everything is formed regularly except for the imperative.

The plurals present no problem except the one difficulty that is present in any system of teaching the verb — the «-bunt» of the future in the first and second conjugations.

The variation between «-ō» and «-m» as the signal for the first person singular is a difficulty too when teaching all the forms of a tense, but again that is common to any system for teaching the verb.

The passive forms present no problem especially when only the third singular forms are involved. For the rest the passive endings are substituted for the active.

The four conjugations

There are some interesting generalities about the various conjugations that are not usually given to the students but are used by the teacher as something of a guide for the emphasis that he will use in his teaching.

The first conjugation

The vast majority of verbs in this conjugation are transitive and quite generally express an idea of making, causing, or reducing something to a state or condition.

This conjugation has the largest number of uncompounded verbs, slightly in excess of three hundred and fifty. Most verbs that were borrowed from other languages were put in this conjugation. About one-half of the deponents belong here and most of them are regular.

The chief irregularities of this conjugation are the verbs «dō, stō, and adjuvō». A few verbs like «secō» and «vetō» have perfects in «-uī».

The second conjugation

The majority of verbs in this class are intransitive and indicate a condition or state of being. There are relatively few verbs in this conjugation, something more than a hundred. Many of these are derived from nouns such as «terror, valor, horror, rubor, stupor». Quite a number of verbs lend themselves to the unit teaching of vocabulary. For example, «horreō, horror, horridus, horrēscō, horribilis, horrendus».

Most of the irregularities appear in the perfect active where the forms vary between the patterns of the first and the third.

The third conjugation

Since this conjugation contains the greatest number of verbs (about eight hundred, only two hundred of which are uncompounded), it is the most frequently used.

The perfects of this conjugation seem to contain irregularities. Actually these so-called irregularities follow definite patterns since the letter "s" combines with the mutes in definite patterns. For example, «regsit» becomes «rēxit», «scribsit» becomes «scrīpsit». Other variations in the perfect include reduplication («pependit»), the use of the present stem («dēfendit»), vowel changes («ēgit»), and the «-īv» ending («petīvit»). The inceptives have their perfect in «-īv» for the most part.

The fourth conjugation

This conjugation has the fewest verbs (somewhat in excess of fifty uncompounded and a fair number of derivatives). Many of the verbs of this conjugation are derived from nouns: «vestis, vestiō; sitis, sitiō». Very many of the verbs in this class describe a bodily or mental state: «sciō, sentiō, ēsuriō, saliō, comperiō, audiō, dormiō».

This conjugation has the fewest deponents, with «mentior, orior», and «assentior» being fairly common. So far as number of deponents is concerned the conjugations line up thus: first, third, second, and fourth, with the last two having an almost equal number.

The fourth is the most regular of the conjugations, possibly because it was the least used. Most of the irregularities are in the perfect active, or third principal part. These vary between the second («aperuī») and the third («vēnī»).

The irregular verbs

Some texts do not teach the irregular verbs in first year. Since most of the irregulars are rather frequently used it would seem better to teach at least the more commonly used irregulars in first year. This can be done readily enough if the reading of Latin is the goal, since students soon come to recognize the forms they meet in their reading and learn to interpret them. It seems that the more frequently used words tend to become irregular.

In the first year students should become acquainted with at least «possum, sum, volō», and «ferō». Actually these do not have too many forms that may be classed as irregular. For example, «volō» is irregular only in the present indicative and the present subjunctive. The imperfect «volēbam» and the future «volam» follow the regular rules for the formation of tenses. If students have been taught to form the imperfect subjunctive from the second principal part then «vellem» and the other forms are not irregular. All the perfect tenses of these verbes are regular. The verb «possum» is not irregular if one considers that is a combination of «potis, pote» and «sum», and knows how these are combined.

The subjunctive mood

Many texts defer the teaching of the subjunctive until the second year in the study of Latin. This need not be. The use of the subjunctive is helpful in teaching the students to read the language, for its use permits the subordination of ideas in greater variety than the use of the indicative alone.

43

Students readily enough understand that the subjunctive mood represents a state or action as something that is possible, conditional, or doubtful. Some authors refer to it as the mood of non-assertion. This helps the student to understand why subordinate clauses in indirect statements (accusative with the infinitive) are put into the subjunctive mood; they are once removed from the actual assertion. Some teachers explain the subjunctive as expressing the conceptual or ideal order as opposed to that of reality, and hence they speak of the subjunctive as expressing that which is once removed from reality.

For drill purposes teachers sometimes assign rather arbitrary English equivalents for the subjunctive such as "may", "can", "might", "should", and "would". These may be misleading for the student. It would seem that the subjunctive should be taught in meaningful situations such as purpose clauses. The forms can then be drilled without the help of the English and such a procedure is more in keeping with teaching the student to comprehend the Latin directly.

Actually, if we keep in mind that students are being taught to read the language and understand it without the help of English, most of the difficulties with the subjunctive vanish. With the reading goal in mind students can readily classify many distinct usages of the subjunctive. For example, even students of first year Latin can learn the uses of «cum» and the subjuntive if they know what to expect in their reading. A simple outline such as the following helps them to understand.

cum

preposition – a noun or an adjective will be in the immediate vicinity, generally following the «cum» and this noun or adjective will be in the ablative case.

conjunction –
if there is no noun or adjective in the ablative then we know that «cum» functions as a conjunction.
if it appears at the beginning of a sentence we have to suspend judgment about its usage until we have read the main clause unless the verb is in the subjunctive in which case it will most likely give a time relationship generally equivalent to our English "when".

if it comes later in the sentence, generally after a main clause, we have to keep three possiblites in mind: time, cause, and opposition, and in that order since time occurs about twice as often as the other two combined.

Frequently enough the context more or less forces the reader into one or other meaning of «cum» even before he comes to the end of the sentence. For examples we use the following.

«Fēlīx nōn est cum...» in this instance we quite naturally expect the adversative idea and can complete the sentence with «dīves sit».
«Superātus est cum...» because of the idea of the main verb we expect causality and so can complete the sentence with «copiae dēfuissent».
«Fatīgātus domum rediit cum...» because of the idea in the main part of the sentence we expect a time relationship and complete the sentence with «sōl sē praecipitāret».

In the teaching of the perfect subjunctive many teachers do not require the students to distinguish between these forms and those of the future perfect indicative. Such a procedure fails to call attention to a signal that will in many instances tell the student immediately which mood is involved. And this signal is the quantity of certain vowels. Note the tenses as presented here.

monuerō	monuerim
monueris	monuerīs
monuerit	monuerit
monuerimus	monuerīmus
monueritis	monuerītis
monuerint	monuerint

Actually there is a possibility of confusion only in the third singular and the third plural. In all other instances the Latin distinguishes.

The independent subjunctive

A little explanation about the use of «utinam» and the various forms of wishes, especially if this is taught in connection with conditional sentences in their simpler forms, will give possibilites for teaching the subjunctive forms within the framework of actual usage. This will give a greater power

45

for reading than just learning isolated forms. It will also help the student later when he wishes to produce the language as usage already been drilled along with the forms.

Similary, the teaching of the exhortatory subjunctive and the jussive subjunctive affords ample means for drilling the students in form and usage, especially if these two independent usages of the subjunctive are taught in conjunction with the imperative. Many simple sentences can be drawn up and the students told to change them from one to the other construction. For example, «animum mūtāte» can be changed into «animum mūtētis» and vice versa. It might be noted here that if exhortations are taught in conjunction with the imperative, students should understand that since we cannot give a command to ourselves, the next best thing we can do is to use an exhortation.

The sequence of tenses

Keeping in mind that we are ultimately teaching the students to read the Latin as Latin we will find that the difficulties of this usage in Latin are greatly minimized.

If the students can be brought to realize that indicative is the mood of reality or statement, and that the subjunctive is the mood for many subordinate clauses, then there remains only the problem of remembering which tenses of the subjunctive follow the various tenses of the indicative. Moreover, most of the difficultes in sequence arise when there is question of the production of the language. In the reading it will be presumed that the author took care of the problem of sequence.

To bring out clearly the stage of action involved in the tenses of the subjunctive, it is sufficient to tell the students that the present and the imperfect indicate action at the same time or after the main verb; the perfect and pluperfect give an action as completed before that of the main verb.

To help them remember the distinction between primary and secondary tenses, students can be told that the primary tenses of the indicative deal with present and future time (the nonpast tenses), while the secondary tenses refer only to the past.

The imperative

Little need be said about the imperative as most students have no difficulty in learning it since all the conjugations follow the same pattern so far as formation is concerned. Generally students are taught to drop the «-re» of the second principal part in order to get the imperative singular active, and add «-te» for the plural active. The singular passive is the same as the second principal part, while the plural is identical with the second person plural of the present indicative passive. The future imperative need not be taught until the second or third year of Latin. If the teacher follows the expansion system of building the verb form outlined earlier, students drop the «-t» of the third singular and make the necessary adjustments in the quantily of the vowel in order to secure the singular imperative; they add «-e» in order to form the plural. The passive imperatives are taught as indicated in the previous paragraph.

The infinitives

The only problem that arises in the teaching of the infinitive is that of faulty denomination. It is a misnomer to speak of present, future, and perfect infinitives since they do not express time but rather a stage of action, prior, subsequent, and contemporaneous with reference to the main verb.

Here is a scheme that has been found helpful in teaching the student that infinitives indicate stage of action.

Monday:	Dīcō mē flēre.	Vult flēre.	Cupit īre.
Tuesday:	Dīxī mē flēre diē Lūnae.	Voluit flēre.	Cupīvit īre.

By contrasting the literal translation with what we ordinarily say in English, students will readily see that «flēre» means "am weeping" or "was weeping" depending entirely upon the time as indicated by the main verb.

The present participle

Once the students have learned the third person plural of the verb they can easily learn the present participle. For the nominative they add «-ns» to the present stem.

In order to help the students check for the ablative singular the teacher can give this scheme.

The ablative singular of the present participle of the first and second conjugations can be formed by adding «-ī» or «-e» to the third person plural of the present indicative.

amant – amantī, amante   docent – docentī, docente

The ablative singular of the present participle of the third and fourth conjugations can be formed by adding «-ī» or «-e» to the third person plural of the future indicative.

47

regent – regentī, regente   audient – audientī, audiente
capient – capientī, capiente

The gerund and the gerundive

A simple explanation of the formation of these will make it possible for students to note them in their reading.

In order to drill the forms, adjectives like «cupidus», the purpose construction of «ad» and the accucative will suffice for the gerund. For the gerundive the teacher can use any expression that indicates necessity or obligation such as the verb «dēbet».

Morphology and grammar should not be separated

By this time the reader has probably concluded that the author has wandered far afield. He has talked much about grammar while talking about the teaching of forms. Actually this but proves that morphology cannot be taught independently of grammar if the morphology is to be taught in meaningful situations.

Teaching the morphology in context is the quickest and most reliable way of securing automatic use, and this automatic use involves grammar because grammar is nothing else than a formulation of usage. Students do not necessarily need to know the terms for all the uses of the ablative, but they should be able to understand what the ablative wishes to communicate. If they understand the communication, but cannot "tag" the exact grammatical usage, the goal of teaching has nonetheless been secured.

In teaching the forms in first year, most of the structure of the language has been seen, not that it has been mastered (for that is a lengthy process), but an acquaintance has been made with it — an acquaintance that must be renewed and strengthened in the succeeding years of study.

Drilling the verb

Considering that the goal is the reading of Latin it should be evident to all that the drilling of the verb which consisted in giving forms in isolation will contribute but little. Even if students give the English meaning as they give the Latin form, this will not help toward the goal since English is constantly being made the reference point for the understanding of the Latin.

Parsing of a verb, that is, giving person, number, tense, mood, and voice, will likewise not contribute to the reading ability. Students can frequently give this classification quite perfectly but they cannot give the meaning of the form.

Good teachers have always been teaching the students that «-ba» indicates the imperfect, and «-bi» marks the future for the first and second conjugations, and that «-e» indicates the future in the third and fourth. Why then did it not help toward the reading of Latin? Possibly because teachers were too interested in the use of tags and the rote recitation of the forms. Moreover, many thought that until all the forms were learned perfectly it was impossible to do any reading. Teachers now still do the drilling, but it is done in context in order to have the students achieve a sort of "feeling" for what the various signals of the Latin verb convey.

Instead of telling students that «-ba» indicates the imperfect and then drilling the forms of the imperfect tense, the teacher should rather put the forms in a meaningful context. This can be done easily in individual sentences (the minimum unit of context). For example, if the student knows the meaning of «Ego puellam amō», he can be given the meaning of the adverb «herī». This adverb is then put into the sentence and the requisite change made in verb, «Herī ego puellam amābam.»

Many of the techniques of drill that teachers have been accustomed to using in their teaching of Latin can still be used to advantage but they must be modified. Keeping in mind the goal of reading Latin, the author submits the following ways of drilling the verb in meaningful situations. Note that as the verb is drilled, many grammatical usages are learned simultaneously. Thus patterns of usage are learned which should speed the process of learning how to read Latin.

The alert reader will notice that most of the examples in the following suggestions will be given in the active voice. This does not mean that the passive cannot be used or should not be drilled, but to give all the possibilities would needlessly lenghten this treatment of drill. It should be remembered that deponents are handy for drilling the passive forms.

Before proceeding to specific methods for drilling the verb, it might be remarked that it is presupposed that students have been reading Latin prior to a formal presentation of the verb. During the reading the students should have become acquainted with the «-t» and «-nt» as well as the «-tur» and «-ntur» of many verbs, and even some tenses other than the present.

Using readings the students have already seen

1 Change of tense

If the readings with which the students are familiar have been using the present tense forms of the verb, then when the imperfect is taught, it will be profitable to go back to the readings. This time, though, students will read them and as they read they will change the verbs to the imperfect.

If adverbs of time are present, it will be necessary to change these but this will only reinforce the meaning of the imperfect.

Since the students are acquainted with the reading and have understood the story as told in the present, it is easy for them to think of it in the past. Discretion must be used, of course, since the imperfect tense might not fit every verb in the story. Possibly a present must be retained or a perfect inserted. If a perfect must be inserted, the teacher can give the form with but a brief explanation. If the students themselves are able to note that the imperfect does not properly fit the context, then the teacher knows that they are understanding the reading as well as understanding the use of the imperfect.

Besides learning the new forms of the verbs, this rereading provides a good opportunity for practice in learning how to get the thought as the Latin proceeds.

2 Change of number

Again, refer the students to some familiar reading. Tell them that as they read they are to change singulars to plural and plurals to singular wherever possible, that is, without violating the general meaning. This cannot be done without comprehension on the part of the student.

The change in number in the nouns will necessitate a change in the verb. It is thus that you secure the drill you wish, and you are securing it in meaningful language situations.

3 Change of person

Select passages in the third person with which the students are familiar and ask them to read the story but to change to the first person. Then vary the drill by changing to the second person. Sometimes there may be hilarious results but that will only the more surely indicate to the teacher that the students are comprehending the Latin.

Using individual sentences in drill

Individual sentences do provide a bit of context for drilling the verb but these should if possible be taken from readings with which the students are familiar.

Drilling the indicative

Just as questions were used to elicit the various cases of nouns and their function, so in the case of the verb various expressions will be used to elicit from the students the tense that is desired in any given situation. For example, suppose we have the sentence «Rōmānī hostēs superant.»By using expressions such as «Quid agit, quid agēbant, quid aget» we can elicit the singular or the plural of any tense of the indicative. The passive forms can be elicited by using expressions such as «Quid patitur, quid patiēbantur» and so forth. These expressions or signals can be used for drill in class, for homework, and for drill on tapes.

The drill sentences can be written on the board, flashed on the screen with a tachistoscope, kept on the screen by using a slide projector, or they can be given on tapes.

Adverbs

Adverbs are a simple way of drilling the various tenses. Once the teacher has indicated the meanings of «hodiē, herī», and «crās», he is in a position to drill the tenses of the present system of the indicative. The student sees the sentence or hears it, then hears the adverb and makes the requisite changes as he repeats the sentence.

> Puer librōs portat.
>> Crās   puer librōs portābit.
>> Hodiē puer librōs portat.
>> Herī   puer librōs portābat.

Once the students know the third person, other persons can be indicated by using as a signal «crās ego, herī tū», and the other combinations that are possible.

Adverbial expressions

Adverbial expressions can also be used to drill the various tenses. The drill is identical with the one that was just described and the only change is in the signals. Here is an example of the drill.

51

Puer librōs portat.

Tempore praesentī	puer librōs portat.
Tempore imperfectō	puer librōs portābat.
Tempore futūrō	puer librōs portābit.
Tempore perfectō (praeteritō)	puer librōs portāvit.
Tempore plūs quam perfectō	puer librōs portāverat.
Tempore perfectō (praeteritō) in futūrō	puer librōs portāverit.

Before conducting such a drill the teacher must make certain that the students understand the signals. It will help if they know the meaning of the compound «perficiō».

It may be objected that these expressions of time are dangerously close to the asking of forms in isolation. It would seem better then to use the above type of drill sparingly.

Further suggestions for drill

1 Completion exercises

Completion exercises are generally thought of as being more suitable for written work, but they can be equally serviceable in oral drill. The use of a tachistoscope or a slide projector facilitates the presentation of the sentences. It is better to use entire paragraphs than individual sentences provided the material is not beyond the reading level of the students. Here is a sample of what a drill might look like.

Puer Deum amat.

Puer Deum hodiē...	amat.
Puer Deum crās...	amābit.
Puer Deum herī...	amābat.
Ego Deum hodiē...	amō.
Tū Deum herī...	amābās.
Ille Deum crās...	amābit.

2 Drilling the future perfect tense

«Cum» temporal clauses are helpful for drilling the future perfect tense of the indicative. Simply duplicate a large number of sentences or prepare a number of slides, and then call upon the students to complete the sentences with a suitable verb.

The teacher should beforehand explain to the students that Latin is very careful to observe the relationships between the two clauses. In the English sentence, "When I arrive home, I'll study", the action of the first clause is completed before the action of the second begins, but in English we are not forced to state the time relationships so accurately. In Latin, however, the time relationship must be accurately expressed so that the Latin says equivalently, "When I shall have arrived home, I'll study." With that much explained to the students, the teacher is ready to drill. Note that the future tense is also reviewed.

Cum Rōmam vēn ___, tē vidē___.
Cum Caesar pervēn ___, mīlitēs fortiter pugnā___.

3 Drilling the perfect and the pluperfect

Clauses introduced by «postquam» provide a means of drilling the perfect and the pluperfect tenses of the indicative. Besides learning the forms the students will have been thoroughly drilled in the uses of «postquam», and are not likely to forget that this conjunction takes the pluperfect when an exact interval of time appears with it.

Perfect: Postquam Caesar vēn___, mīlitēs fortiter pugnā___.
Pluperfect: Tertiō diē postquam Caesar vēn___, hostēs fūg___.

4 Drilling the irregular verbs

Causal clauses introduced by «quod, quia», or «quoniam» followed by the indicative can be used to drill the various tenses of the indicative. These are particularly helpful for some of the irregulars like «volō, nōlō, and mālō».

Caesar venit quia vult.
Hodiē   Caesar venit quia vult.
Herī   Caesar vēnit quia volēbat.
Crās   Caesar veniet quia volet.
Hodiē ego   veniō quia volō.
Crās tū   veniēs quia volēs.
Hodiē nōs   venīmus quia volumus.

5 Drilling the persons in a given tense

The persons of any tense may be drilled in sentences also and in that way the teacher can avoid drilling isolated forms. The teacher can use any of the six tenses of the indicative in the sentence that will be used for the drill.

53

He should not, of course, take the persons in order as they occur in the paradigm. He might do this for one or two sentences but then they should be given more or less at random. Here is how the present might be drilled.

Ego agricolae equum videō.
Tū   agricolae equum vidēs.
Nōs   agricolae equum vidēmus.
Illī   agricolae equum vident.
Vōs   agricolae equum vidētis.
Ille   agricolae equum videt.

Drilling the subjunctive

Purpose clauses would seem at the first glance to be a handy way of drilling the various tenses of the subjunctive. But since purpose clauses also involve the teaching of sequence, it will probably be better at the beginning to make use of the independent subjunctive for the drills.

Drilling the present, imperfect, and pluperfect

Wishes can be used to drill the present, imperfect, and pluperfect subjunctive tenses. Such a drill will need to be prefaced by a short explanation of the grammar involed. It might be done thus.

Wishes are always introduced by the word «utinam». Later the students can learn when «utinam» is omitted.

Wishes whose fulfillment is still possible (I wish he would come), always refer to the future and for these Latin uses «utinam» and the present subjunctive. Later they can be told about the possibility of using the perfect without difference in meaning.

Wishes that are impossible of fulfillment here and now (I wish he were here), are expressed by «utinam» and the imperfect subjunctive.

Wishes whose fulfillment was impossible in the past (I wish he had been here), are expressed by the pluperfect subjunctive.

Following the brief explanation of the grammar the teacher is ready to drill. He should after the first few sets of drills vary the order. Here is a sample drill.

In the following drill you are expected to change the sentence you see (hear) into a wish. The tense of the indicative will be a clue to the type of wish that must be used.

Nauta amābit mare.	Utinam nauta mare amet.
Nauta amat mare.	Utinam nauta mare amāret.
Nauta amāvit mare.	Utinam nauta mare amāvisset.
Nōn adest.	Utinam adesset.
Nōn adfuit.	Utinam adfuisset.
Aderit.	Utinam adsit.

Drilling the present and perfect subjunctives

Negative commands can be used to drill the present and the perfect subjunctives but only in the second person.

Nōlī flēre.	Nē flēverīs (nē fleās).
Nōlī pugnāre.	Nē pugnāverīs (nē pugnēs).
Nōlīte flēre.	Nē flēverītis (nē fleātis).
Nōlīte pugnāre.	Nē pugnāverītis (nē pugnētis).

To drill the present and the perfect subjunctives the teacher may wish briefly to explain what a concessive subjunctive is and then proceed to the drill.

The explanation might go like this. The subjunctive can be used to show that something is granted or conceded. The present tense is used for present time, and the perfect tense for past time. The conjunction «ut» is frequently used to introduce such a construction.

In the following drill change the statement into a construction that will indicate a concession, something granted for the sake of argument.

Est vērum.	Sit vērum (Ut sit vērum).
Fuit vērum.	Fuerit vērum (Ut fuerit vērum).
Tū fortiter ēgistī.	Tū fortiter ēgerīs (Ut tū fortiter ēgerīs).
Lēgātus cum Caesare vēnit.	Lēgātus cum Caesare vēnerit (Ut lēgātus cum Caesare vēnerit).

The perfect subjunctive can be drilled more easily once the students are familiar with the sequence of tenses.

Drilling the present and imperfect subjunctive

Deliberative questions are helpful for drilling the present and imperfect subjunctive. A very brief explanation of what a deliberative question is and the tenses that are involved must, of course, precede the drill. Some examples from English with the proper intonations will readily indicate to the students the difference between direct and deliberative questions. Here is a sample of what a drill might look like.

Change the direct question you see (hear) into a deliberative question. The tenses of the indicative are a clue to the tense that is to be used in the subjunctive.

Quid facit?	Quid faciat?
Quid faciēbat?	Quid faceret?
Quid facimus?	Quid faciāmus?
Quid faciēbant?	Quid facerent?

Once a few sets such as the above are given, the sentences might be lengthened to include circumstances that will warrant a deliberative question.

Drilling the third person of the present subjunctive

Should the teacher wish to present the third person forms of the present subjunctive before proceeding to the other forms he can profitably start the jussive subjunctive. He can indicate briefly that Latin can soften a command as we do in English. "Let Johnny do it" is expressed in Latin by «Joannēs faciat». Here is a sample drill.

In this drill change the direct statement to a softened command.

Mīles pugnat fortiter.	Mīles pugnet fortiter.
Mīlitēs impetum faciunt.	Mīlitēs impetum faciant.

Drilling the infinitive

The easiest way to drill the infinitive is to make use of indirect discourse. To simplify the drill it is better to have the statements introduced by the present tense only of verbs like «dīcō». After a brief explanation of the usage for indirect statements, the drill might take a form such as this.

Change the statement you see (hear) into an indirect statement dependent upon the verb «dīcō».

Homō est bonus.	Dīcō hominem esse bonum.
Homō erat bonus.	Dīcō hominem fuisse bonum.
Homō erit bonus.	Dīcō hominem futūrum esse bonum.

After a few simple sentences such as the above, the introduction of adjectives and adverbs will help to vary the drill as review the elements of agreement and the usage of adverbs and adjectives.

56

The drill will be less complicated if the sentences contain intransitive verbs and subjects that are masculine gender. Later in the drill transitive verbs and subjects that are feminine and neuter should be introduced. The passive infinitives can be drilled by transitive verbs. At first the sentence to be changed should be in the passive voice; later the sentence should be given in the active in order to force the student to make the changes from active to passive.

Deus ā nōbīs amātur.	Dīcō Deum ā nōbīs amārī.
Nōs amāmus Deum.	Dīcō Deum ā nōbīs amārī.

Drilling the gerund

With only brief explanations concerning procedure the gerund can be drilled rather easily. It is best to use only intransitive verbs since the gerundive construction is generally preferred in place of the gerund with a direct object in the accusative case. Here are some suggestions for drilling the various cases.

genitive

Cupiō pugnāre.	Cupidus sum pugnandī.
Cupiō fugere.	Cupidus sum fugiendī.

dative

Semper scrībēbat.	Semper sē scrībendō dedit.
Semper plangēbat.	Semper sē plangendō dedit.

accusative

Vēnit ut pugnāret.	Vēnit ad pugnandum.
Exīvit ut vidēret.	Exīvit ad videndum.

ablative

Sibi glōriam acquīrit quia pugnat.	Pugnandō sibi glōriam acquīrit.
Sibi glōriam acquīrit quia bene currit.	Bene currendō sibi glōriam acquīrit.

Drilling the gerundive

The easiest way to drill the gerundive is to use an expression that will force the student to produce the gerundive of necessity. The drill should proceed in stages though in order to help the student become familiar with the various constructions. Here are some suggestions.

First use the simpler forms.

57

Deus dēbet laudārī.	Deus laudandus est.
Vōs dēbētis accūsārī.	Vōs accūsandī estis.
Virī dēbent salvārī.	Virī salvandī sunt.
Exercitus dēbet vincī.	Exercitus vincendus est.

We then expand with the dative of agent, thus contrasting the dative with the ablative of agent.

Virī dēbent salvārī ā mīlitibus.	Virī mīlitibus salvandī sunt.
Vōs dēbētis accūsārī ā servīs.	Vōs servīs accūsandī estis.

Next use a sentence in the active voice which will need to be turned into the passive and thus emphasize that the gerundive is a passive verbal.

Dēbēmus Deum laudāre.	Deus nōbīs laudandus est.
Servī dēbent dominōs accūsāre.	Dominī servīs accūsandī sunt.

If the teacher is intent upon drilling the gerundive, he need not, at least in first year, use verbs whose objects are in a case other than the accusative. However, if the teacher wants them to know the uses of the gerundive as well as the forms, he might give some drill in intransitive verbs whose object is in a special case. In any drill, however, the impersonals should be kept until the last.

Drilling the participles

Participles may be drilled easily by the use of sentences that involve a subordinate clause. The teacher asks the student to change the subordinate clause to a participal construction. Here are some suggestions for the present and the perfect passive participles.

Present participle

Dum pugnat, occīsus est.	Pugnāns occīsus est.
Rēgem, dum proficīscitur, occīdērunt.	Rēgem proficīscentem occīdērunt.
Dum iter faciunt, omnia vident.	Iter facientēs omnia vident.
Dum proficīscuntur, eīs dōna dedērunt.	Proficīscentibus dōna dedērunt.
Sī vir pugnat, quālis vir est?	Vir pugnāns est.
Sī vir patriam amat, quālis vir est?	Vir amāns patriae est.

Perfect passive participle

Gallōs quōs cēpit interfēcit.	Gallōs captōs interfēcit.
Gallīs quōs cēpit frūmentum dedit.	Gallīs captīs frūmentum dedit.
Caesar, quia lēgātī occīsī sunt,	Caesar propter lēgātōs occīsōs

bellum gessit.   bellum gessit.

Mīlitum quī occīsī sunt virtūtem   Mīlitum occīsōrum virtūtem
laudāvit.   laudāvit.

Rēgem postquam profectus est,   Rēgem profectum interfēcērunt.
interfēcērunt.

Sī vir laudātus est, quālis vir est?   Laudātus vir est.

Sī vir quem videō laudātus est,   Laudātum virum videō.
quālem virum videō?

Future participle active

The future participle hardly needs a separate drill as it can more easily be drilled along with the infinitives where there is question of indirect statements after verbs like «dīcō». If some drill is desired the teacher might make use of these suggestions.

Paulō antequam mortuus est,   Moritūrus haec dīxit.
haec dīxit.

Paulō antequam vulnerāvit mīlitem, Vulnerātūrus mīlitem haec fēcit.
haec fēcit.

Paulō antequam abīvit jussa dedit.   Abitūrus jussa dedit.

Rēgem antequam proficīscī potuit   Rēgem profectūrum interfēcērunt.
interfecerunt.

Drilling at the chalkboard

Since teachers realize the necessity of having a variety of activities during a class period, they will wish, at least occasionally, to make use of the chalkboard in drilling the verb. Here are a few suggestions.

1 Send students to the board by rows. Then conduct any of the drills that were suggested in the preceding pages. Speed is not the object but accuracy is.

2 Send students to the board and then dictate a sentence but omit the verb. Allow students to complete the sentence with any meaningful verb. Adverbs and adverbial expressions can be used to force the students to use certain tenses.

3 After sending several students to the board dictate a main clause. Then give a conjunction and ask the students to complete the sentence. Others can then be sent to the board and another conjunction given with a request to complete the sentence. This is an easy way to provide a review for subordinate clauses too. Here is a sample of such a drill.

$$
\text{Equitēs in silvā pugnavērunt} \begin{cases} \text{quia} & \underline{\hspace{3cm}} \\ \text{ut} & \underline{\hspace{3cm}} \\ \text{dum} & \underline{\hspace{3cm}} \\ \text{quoad} & \underline{\hspace{3cm}} \\ \text{antequam} & \underline{\hspace{2cm}} \end{cases}
$$

4 If the students are studying a particular construction, the teacher sends several to the board and after giving a main clause he will ask them to complete the sentence. This allows freedom for the individual student to express himself in the Latin since he will naturally talk about the things he knows.

5 After sending several to the board the teacher tells them to write out the principal parts of a verb and then to use one of them in a sentence. Should the teacher note that one or other sentence that has been written by the students can easily be expressed in another way in Latin he can call on another student to go to the board and write out the alternate version, or at least write a version that expresses substantially the same thought as the first sentence does.

6 Send several to the board and then dictate a verb form and ask the students to build a meaningful sentence around it. Such an exercise is good for competition between groups. The difficulty of the exercise is increased if subjunctive forms are given; gerunds and gerundives possibly make the exercise very difficult until such time as students are very familiar with their use.

If the teacher has such forms written on flashcards, he can hold up a card and then ask for a complete sentence.

7 Class project work maintains interest at the chalkboard. Write a number of nouns, then some verbs. Call for volunteers. Allow them to go to the board to write out as many sentences as they can using only the words that are in the lists. Such an exercise can profitably be used for constructions too. For example, give prepositions, nouns, verbs and ask for as many sentences as the class can compose.

8 Allow the class to test the student's knowledge. Call for a volunteer. Then allow the students to give a verb form and ask the volunteer to construct a sentence using the form. This scheme is good for competition too. Allow a representative of each row to go to the board. Allow opposing rows to give the verb form around which a sentence must be built.

The teacher will note that pracitcally all the drills use only Latin. If the student can properly compose sentences, then the teacher can be assured that there is comprehension at least on the part of the one writing the sentence.

60

Written homework

It must be remembered that written homework takes up a disproportionate amount of time. For that reason studying pattern drills and reading are to be preferred to written work. However, teachers must be realistic and realize that students need some writing to help them get down to work. Written work then has a place but only a minor one in the student's study outside class time. Here are some suggestions for assignment.

1 Duplicate a reading with which the students are familiar but change it and omit the verb endings. Students are to supply these. Careful preparation will permit the teacher to drill only certain forms.

2 Choose a reading with which the students are familiar and ask them to rewrite it and to use subordinate clauses wherever possible. They should be warned not to change the sense of the reading radically.

3 Tell students to write out the reading but to change to a definite person. If the original was in the first person, then let them write it out in the third person and so forth.

4 If the familiar reading has two hundred words for example, tell them to write a twenty-five to fifty-word synopsis in Latin.

5 Ask the students to list the derivatives that are based on the Latin verbs. This is done first in Latin; for example, if the verb is «audiunt» they can give the related word «audītor». If the teacher wishes the English derivatives, then insist that the meaning of the English word be given and that it be used in an English sentence.

6 Give a list of special verb forms and ask the students to write a Latin sentence in which they use the form.

7 When studying a specific construction, for example, «postquam» and the pluperfect indicative, the teacher may ask the students to compose ten sentences in which they use this conjunction.

8 If the teacher insists on the students keeping a notebook, he can assign work in this. For example, he might ask them to write out a model conjugation.

9 Distribute a page that has partial sentences. Ask the students to tell what they know about the sentence and then to complete each one with a suitable verb.

10 Choose a particularly fine model sentence and ask students to compose five or more similar sentences.

11 Give several sets of sentences. Students are to mark those that have approximately the same meaning. Their mark can be an asterisk, underlining, or some other device of the teacher's choosing. For example, here is a set of such sentences.

Caesar cupit glōriam.	Caesar est cupidus glōriae.
Caesar est amāns patriae.	Caesar patriam dīligit.
Utinam mīles vīveret.	Utinam mīles vīvat.

12 The use of matching questions is good testing procedure; it can also provide good homework. List a number of sentences in the left column but omit the verb. Give verb forms in the right column. Students are to choose the verbs that are correct in form and at the same time express a thought correctly.

13 Multiple-choice questions can also be used for homework. Here is a sample that will determine if the student knows the grammar for purpose clauses — he cannot choose the correct form of the verb unless he knows the grammar.

Caesar mīlitēs mīsit.

1	quia vult hostēs vincere	3	quī hostēs vincerent
2	quod hostēs vīxērunt	4	quī hostēs vīcerint

It should be noted in passing that it is better policy always to use correct Latin in the choices. You wish to find out their knowledge of grammar, not how well they can proofread. Moreover, incorrect forms sometimes seem to be remembered only too well.

14 Give various structural outlines and ask the students to fill them out with meaningful sentences. This is particularly helpful if the teacher wishes to drill definite items and yet leave the students free to supply the lexical items. Here is an example.

(Hostēs)	(malōs)	(mīlitēs)	(in carcerem)	(dētrūdunt).
Object	adj.	subj.	prep. phrase	verb

Incidentally such an exercise could be used later when teaching elements of style. They can be thus taught to imitate a certain feature, for example, chiasmus.

15 It is a profitable bit of homework to have students write out drills that are similar to the ones they hear on the tapes. If these are done well, the teacher can use parts of them for oral drill in class or he can choose parts for examinations.

Form and usage

Just as in the case of nouns, so in the teaching of the verb forms, the teacher will realize that he is at the same time teaching the student the grammar of the language. And this is as it should be, for it is futile to learn the forms only. A student could know all the forms of the verb but if he does not have experience in their use then his knowledge will not help him understand what the Latin says.

A matter of emphasis

In the foregoing suggestions concerning the drilling of the verb the passive forms have been slighted. It is taken for granted that in the actual classroom situation the teacher will also drill the passive. But it is also taken for granted that the teacher will drill the active far more thoroughly than the passive, since students will meet the active forms so often in their reading. In all the years of your study of Latin and in all the reading that you have done, how often, for example, have you met the forms that and in «-minī»?

Chapter 4

The teaching of vocabulary

Modern textbooks abound in wonderful pictures and most of these have captions and even abundant explanation. However these explanations and captions are generally in English. If the explanations were in Latin and this Latin were graded to suit the level of the student's ability in reading Latin, the books would be more valuable. They would be teaching much Latin indirectly and without formal instruction. Teaching by pictures, especially in the beginning, is one of the best ways to give students a start in learning the vocabulary of a foreign language.

What's wrong with vocabulary lists?

Vocabulary lists are found in all textbooks and most of them put an English word as the equivalent of the Latin. Many teachers then use the simple and easy way out. They read the Latin word aloud and have the class repeat it if they find time for this in class; then they assign the memory lesson. Students definitely get the impression that there is a word-for-word equivalency between the languages. Soon the alert student has the idea that learning vocabulary is like learning an immutable physics formula or an equation in algebra. Such an equating of words may at times be true for physical objects such as «nauta» and «sailor» but more often than not there is no real equation between the words of different languages.

Word-for-word equivalency does not consider the fact that all languages have their own way of saying something. Here are some of the meanings of the Latin verb «dēdūcō».

dēdūcere aliquem dē rōstrīs

    to escort someone from the rostrum

dēdūcere rāmōs pondere nivis
    to weigh branches down with the weight of snow

dēdūcere pectine crīnēs
    to comb the hair down

dēdūcere aciem in plānum
    to lead a column of soldiers down into the plain

dēdūcere tōta carbasa mālō
    to spread the sails of a ship

dēdūcere nāvēs in aquam
    to launch ships

dēdūcere aliquem in carcerem
    to imprison someone

dēdūcere colōniam
    to found a new colony

dēdūcere aliquem ad jūdicium
    to hail someone into court

dēdūcere centum nummōs
    to subtract a hundred nummi (coins)

dēdūcere fīlum
    to spin (a thread)

It is true, of course, that there is a fundamental meaning running through all the various uses of «dēdūcō», but this fundamental meaning will not be apparent until we know at least several uses of the word in context. Then our minds seize upon that which is fundamental and we get a notion of what the word means.

This multiplicity of meanings that is apparent in the Latin verb «dēdūcō» is typical of what happens in language. For instance, here are some of the uses of the verb «pass» in English.

to pass a car	to pass in football
to pass the time	to pass an examiniation
to pass out	to pass away
to pass in cards	to pass with a wand (magician)

Actual consultation of an unabridged dictionary will reveal some twenty-four meanings for the English word "pass".

Earlier we mentioned that there may be a fair equivalence between words that name physical objects. Here are the meanings for dog in various languages.

66

The French word «chien» means dog, but in addition it can mean a villainous person, stuff or rubbish, the hammer in a gunlock, a star, a tailless bat.

The Greek word for dog («kiōn») besides meaning dog can also indicate audacity, rashness, sea dog, star, fetlock joint of a horse, a nickname for the Cynics at Athens, a sea fish, a kind of nail, the worst throw in dice, and it can be used as a word of reproach indicating shamelessness.

The Latin word for dog, «canis», can also mean a malicious spiteful person, an accuser, a parasite or hanger-on, a star, a kind of fetter, the worst throw in dice.

A large English dictionary will give some fifteen meanings for the word "dog" including these: a mean worthless fellow, shortened form for hot-dog, prairie dog, the hammer in a gunlock, a device for gripping things in order to hoist them.

The error of word-for-word equivalency between languages becomes more apparent when the student deals with Latin poetry such as the works of Vergil. How often have teachers of Vergil been forced to explain to students that none of the meanings given in the vocabulary list can be used in this particular situation. Or if the meanings are given, how is the teacher to explain to the student which meaning is to be chosen for a given context?

Suppose a student meets this line in Vergil: «rōboribus textīs caelōque ēdūcere jussit», how is he to determine the correct meaning from these that are given in a textbook: «rōbur», the oak tree, anything made of oak, timber, might? It would seem ridiculous to one who is proficient in Latin to try to use the meaning "might" for «rōbur» in this context, but how is the student to know that this metaphorical meaning does not apply in this situation?

Vocabulary lists then can give students a wrong impression about the meanings of words. It is only the actual use of a word in context that will give a definite meaning, hence it would seem that vocabulary must be taught in context and that students will or should learn their vocabulary from their reading. How then are teachers to teach vocabulary? In this chapter it is hoped that the teacher will find some of the answers.

Early stages of learning vocabulary

Since vocabulary lists are not the ideal way of teaching vocabulary the teacher might find one or other of the following suggestions helpful.

Memory of simple sentences

At first the teacher can be content with having the students memorize some typical sentences in Latin. At this stage the meaning is unimportant but the pronunciation, intonation, and phrasing are important. These are learned in direct imitation of the teacher. The sentences should have a rhythmic swing to aid the memory. Sentences such as these, while fairly lengthy, can be memorized rather easily.

Mīlibus in mīlle cantor fuit optimus ille. Pingere difficile est animum dēpingere corpus hoc facile est. Nōn es, dum in somnō es, dum nec tē vīvere sentis.[1]

Teachers should consider giving sentences whose meaning can be rather easily conveyed by acting them out. For example, «Petrus crīnēs pectine dēdūcit». In the early stages of language training the teacher should make abundant use of pantomime. Students need not know the meanings of the individual words. It is sufficient at this stage that they comprehend the meaning of the entire sentence. The study of individual words will come later.

After the students are familiar with the sentences, then the teacher can help them get the meaning by giving pictures that rather accurately portray what the sentences say. He can also give them a good English equivalent of the sentence. The idiomatic translation does not give a word-for-word equivalency impression.

Use of pictures

In the beginning students can acquire much vocabulary from pictures. The pictures can be secured commercially or they can be garnered over a period of time from the newspaper supplements and picture sections, books on travel, and the like. Label the items in Latin only. Use the pictures as a basis for work in class until the students are somewhat familiar with the language.

If the teacher has a set of pictures they can be used in several ways. They can be distributed at random through the class for study. The better way is to use an opaque projector. Flash them on the screen, then talk about them, and allow students to ask for the Latin of objects that might be suggested by the picture.

A word of caution is in order. Pictures must be chosen judiciously so that they do not scatter the attention of the student. Choose those that have only a few objects and these clearly delineated. Usually the picture

---

[1]These epigrams were composed by St. Thomas More.

will have its own unity. This again is important since the teacher will not wish to give too many words at one time. A few words at a time used quite often in the drill will help to fix the words in the memories of the students.

Stick men

If the teacher is good at sketching then he has an invaluable tool for the teaching of vocabulary and for helping students to comprehend the story they hear or read. Stick men or more conventional drawings will quickly illustrate the meanings of concrete objects such as man, table, dog: and with a bit of cleverness action too can be indicated, for example, one boy hitting another.

Teachers whose drawing abilities are limited need not deprive themselves and the class of this tool. With a bit of practice even the non-artist can do a sufficiently creditable job. It is good to do a bit of practicing before going into the classroom. For examples of what simple sketching can do, the teacher is referred to «Spanish Through Pictures» by I. A. Richards, Ruth C. Metcalf, Christine Gibson, Pocket Books, Inc., New York.

Giving directions in Latin

From the very beginning teachers find it profitable to give most of the ordinary classroom directions in Latin. At first the students find it difficult to understand but with help in the way of acting out the command students soon learn to respond in action. Forms of the verb and other expressions are used that are unfamiliar but repeated use makes them familiar. Then when they are studied formally the student feels that he already knows them and can use the familiar forms to help learn the new ones. Do not be dismayed at the laughter when first using the forms. This seems to be the student's way of reacting to something that sounds so strange.

For the teacher who feels somewhat diffident in the use of such terms the author recommends «Quomodo Dicitur» by Sister M. Emmanuel, O. S. U., Haefling Printig Company, Tiffin, Ohio, 1955. This is a small brochure of some sixty pages. The perusal of this booklet will give the teacher a start toward forming his own set of phrases and directions.

Using English derivatives

Teachers might start the teaching of Latin by using Latin phrases that are in use in English. There are many such, among them being «Magna Charta, Anno Domini, Alma Mater, Pater Noster, and habeas corpus».

After this initial acquaintance the teacher gives a listing of nouns whose Latin ancestors are rather evident. Or he can give Latin nouns whose English derivatives can be easily recognized. He might give a list such as this.

contrōversia	injūria	victōria	numerus
memoria	nātura	fēmina	populus
prōvidentia	poēta	fortūna	toga
prūdentia	prōvincia	causa	familia

After calling for the English word, the teacher proceeds to list a number of Latin verbs whose English derivative is apparent. They might include the following.

sonō	exstinguō	vexō	temptō
tonō	dīvidō	apprehendō	accūsō
condemnō	resistō	dēscendō	dēclārō
adhaereō	dēfendō	respondeō	violō

Once these two steps are completed the teacher gives the simple directions that in the sentences he composes the ending «-t» will indicate the verb, the ending «-m» will point out the object, and all other endings will be a signal for the subject. He is in a position then to draw up a number of sentences using the words he listed. He can be rather certain that the students will also comprehend what he is saying. If need be, he might occasionally ask them what was said. Note that he does not ask for a translation. He asks instead that the student give the thought.

Such a scheme of teaching Latin in the very beginning can be effective, but it is possible that the students will be using English to secure the meaning. Once they start with English as the reference point for meaning it is difficult to break the students of this habit.

Defining words in Latin

Once the students have a fair vocabulary the teacher should not give the meanings of the new Latin words in English if that can be avoided. If he is telling a story, he should rather rephrase the text in simpler Latin. He may wish to give definitions in Latin. For example, suppose the word «rūgītus» occurred in the story. He might help the students arrive at its meaning by telling them that it is «vōx quam leō ēmittit quandō vult alia animālia terrēre; Tarzan etiam hanc vōcem ēmittit». As a definition of «mūs» the teacher might give «parvum animal quod fēminae timent et elephantī». These definitions were actually used in a classroom and the students readily caught the meaning as was evidenced by the English equivalents that were given. The humor of «fēminae timent et elephhantī» is not to be eschewed since humor helps to fix the words in their minds.

Direct association

First-year texts should at the beginning make use of illustrations and pictures to convey the meaning of the Latin word. Students should learn as much vocabulary as possible without the intervention of the English words. If they make a direct association between the object and the Latin word, the students are on the high road toward achieving direct comprehension. They are in a position then to read Latin in a limited way — that is, within the sphere of their experience. In the years that follow the teacher should give directions in Latin, define words in Latin, and carry on the class as much as possible in Latin. Thus the students come to interpret the Latin and progress in their reading.

Time consuming

Teachers may feel that in the beginning they are making no progress if they use Latin as much as possible in the class. There must be much repetition before the students comprehend and valuable time is lost. It is lost now, it is true, but the training the students receive will more than adequately repay the time and effort involved. Progress later will be much more rapid because of this time-consuming labor now. Moreover, students find the work interesting and are inclined to make more of an effort to learn. An ability to express themselves even in a halting way and an ability to understand what is said in a foreign language gives them a thrill that they will never have from simply being able to decline «aqua» without a mistake. Teachers, too, will find the presentation of vocabulary much more interesting and will be thrilled with the students' growing power to comprehend the spoken and the written word.

An expanding vocabulary

Many texts that give vocabulary lists give individual words and never make an effort to associate the individual word with others. This seems a needless waste of effort for the student. Frequently while learning one word he can learn several. How this can be done needs fuller explanation and the author offers the following suggestions.

71

From the beginning of the study of Latin it is imperative that students be taught the formation of words. They need not know all the possible ways but the more common ways of forming words they should know. This does not mean that they must necessarily form all the possible words that can be derived from a root form, but it does mean that their familiarity with the principles permits them to recognize a new word at least in part. Knowing that «-tor» indicates the doer of an action, they may be able to arrive at an approximate meaning of the root from the context, or at least they can get sufficient meaning to permit them to understand the thought. Similarly, a knowledge of the modifications of meaning that prefixes induce can be a help toward understanding what is read. If the student knows that «per» indicates completion or a high deree of some quality, he will at least partially understand the meaning of the verb in «Cibōs percoxit».

Word families

From the beginning students should be made aware of the fact that there are certain roots and they should know their general meaning. Such can profitably include the following: «cept, dict, duct, fer, fert, gress, ject, pell, press, script, spect, tort, tract, cess, miss, vers, ten, and ora».

If the students meet «vocō» they can be given «vōx, vōcālis, vocātiō» and «vocātor». Suppose they met «tegō» in their reading, the following list will provide interest as well as expand their vocabulary:

tegō	tegillum (cowl, hood)
tēctum	tegmen (covering)
tēctor (plasterer)	tegimen (covering)
tēctē (cautiously)	tegumentum (covering)
tēgula (roof tile)	tēctōrium (plaster)
tēctōrius (relating to plaster)	

The first time the student meets the verb «ferō», for instance, is the time to give all the compounds. Very few texts do this. Generally texts list the words separately. Learning the compounds along with the simple verb does not put an extreme burden on the memory; moreover, after this has been done several times students begin to formulate their own ideas about the shades of meaning that are induced by the prefixes. Certainly «cōnferō, differō, īnferō» and «referō» will not prove to be difficult even for students in first year; similarly this listing: «mittō, āmittō, admittō, committō, dīmittō, ēmitto, intermittō, permittō, praemittō, remittō, submittō».

If students meet these words in separate listings they usually do not advert to the fact that there is a relation with a word they have seen before;

in their hurry to finish the work assigned they usually memorize it and do not take the further step of associating it with other words.

Typical endings

As typical endings are met in the reading they should be explained to the student. Suppose the teacher knows that the students will meet «ōrō» in their reading. He can explain what «-tor» indicates and then help the students form «ōrātor» ; he then gives the meaning for the «-tiō» ending and helps them form «ōrātiō», A short drill with other verbs such as «accūsō, dēfendō, explicō» and others will fix the meanings. Students thus can learn three words while learning the word «ōrō».

Once the students have learned the principal parts of the verb they can be shown that many nouns are formed from the fourth principal part. This helps them in their reading because they will recognize that the word might be a verb and it might be a noun. If the forms of «est» do not appear with the fourth principal part, then it is likely a noun. Here are a few examples of such nouns: «adveniō – adventus, ēgrediō – ēgressus, discēdō – discessus, inveniō – inventus».

Not all the typical endings need be taught, but here are some of the commoner ones that even freshmen can readly learn.

1   -tās   celer – celeritās   auctor – auctōritās
             crūdēlis – crūdēlitās   hūmānus – hūmānitās
             līber – lībertās   lēvis – lēvitās

2   -tia   audāx – audācia   prūdēns – prūdentia
             tristis – tristitia   puer – pueritia
             jūs – jūstitia   inimīcus – inimīcitia

3   -tūdō   fortis – fortitūdō   aeger – aegritūdō
             magnus – magnitūdō   sōlus – sōlitūdō
             lātus – lātitūdō   plēnus – plēnitūdō

As occasion warrants the teacher should explain endings such as the following, especially should this be done in the years following the first.

1   -ānus   indicating that someone pertains to something
             Trōjānus, Rōmānus, cotīdiānus, urbānus, pāgānus

2   -īvus   indicating a reference to something
             captīvus, aestīvus, fugitīvus

3   -ōsus   indicating a fullness of something
             ōtiōsus, cōpiōsus, labōriōsus, verbōsus

When the teacher shows how words are formed from verbs he must indicate the necessary vowel changes in order that students may recognize the partially hidden root. Such an explanation is particularly necessary in the case of prefixes where assimilation occurs. For examples, «teneō – attineō, portō – supportō, faciō – efficiō, capiō – incipiō».

Note that in the beginning students are not given a specific treatise on word building. Only that information is given which is helpful for recognizing words that they may meet in their reading. In the following years as the students progress in their study of Latin more details can be given.

Unit building in vocabulary

More helpful possibly than a knowledge of the formation of words is the process whereby words are learned in groups and for convenience we may call it "unit building of vocabulary". Rather than learn isolated words the student should be given the words that relate to one topic — the topic itself is the cohesive force that helps students associate words. Here are some examples of unit building.

Should it be that words which express certain features of the human head occur in their reading, students can be given a picture of the head together with a listing of the words for the various parts. Here is a partial list of such words: «caput, oculus, auris, lingua, dēns, comae, cervīx, collum, gena, barba, capillus, supercilium, nāsus, labium, mentum», and «rūga». Together with these some opposites can easily be taught. For example, «caecus, luscus, monoculus, surdus, surditās». And then there are a goodly number of verbs which can be taught at the same time: «flet, rīdet, videt, audit, lacrimat, mordet, dīcit, loquitur».

If the reading the student encounters talks about a ship, the teacher can help him learn many new words in this context. There would be the «nauta, nāvita, gubernātor» and then the host of related words such as «flūmen, unda, fluctus, mare, arēna, lītus, portus, ōra, pelagus». The verbs might be «nāvigō, nāvem cōnscendere» and many others.

There are many such topics around which the student can build his vocabulary: the sky, the home, the table and its foods, the soldier and his weapons, the man and his clothes, the woman and her clothes, travel — in fact any of the experiences that comes into the lives of the people or things about which the students is reading.

Unit building helps provide a number of associations that make it easier to learn vocabulary. It is for that reason more interesting and more satisfyng and provides a greater reward for the effort expended.

74

Using a dictionary

Here is an experiment that will readily reveal the necessity of teaching the students how to use the dictionary to expand their vocabulary. Call upon them to look up a certain word in a dictionary and then use it in a sentence. Then ask them to write the word that appeared before and the one that appeared after the word they looked up. Then ask them to tell all they can about the actual word they consulted. The results of such a test are quite revealing — students do not use the dictionary to advantage in building their vocabulary.

Teachers must frequently show students how to use the dictionary. When they consult the dictionary, they should take time to carefully study the word itself that they look up, noting all that is said about it; then they should look at the words in the vicinity. It is surprising how often related words will be found. And if related words are not there, students will find that they frequently learn a word rather permanently because it was so closely placed in the dictionary with the word they looked up.

Stimulating vocabulary study

The teaching of vocabulary in accordance with the suggestions given under "Expanding the vocabulary" will stimulate the student's interest in words. Once this interest is aroused, the teacher needs but stimulate it from time to time. This can be done in a number of ways.

Many texts now do not give English meanings in the comprehensive vocabulary at the back of the book. Rather they refer the student to the pages in the text where the word occurred. Looking at the page where the word first occurred is likely to recall the student's first impressions, and the actual place where the word occurred will stimulate his local memory; this means a deepening of impressions that were once made and this will help the student remember the word better. Moreover, the labor involved in looking up the word impresses upon the student's mind the necessity of trying to remember words that have been seen.

Interesting reading suited to the level of the student's ability to comprehend is in itself a stimulus for learning vocabulary. If he is reading a story that has intrinsic interest, he will wish to understand it and will be impatient with himself at the vocabulary barrier. Teachers who have used readers like «Civis Romanus» by J. M. Cobban and R. Colebourn (St. Martin's Press, New York) will attest to the truth of these remarks. Students who are quite proficient in Latin will enjoy books such as «Max et Moritz, puerorum facinora scurrilia septem fabellis quarum materiam repperit depinxitque Guilelmus Busch» (Monachii, in aedibus Braun and Schneider, Bibliopolarum, Munich, 1951).

The assignment of short original compositions based upon pictures that the students themselves choose will help to stimulate vocabulary study. Again, they will soon realize that the more vocabulary they know, the quicker they can do the assignment and the better the grade that they can get for it.

Variations can be worked with pictures. Allow them to choose their own picture and then to give the Latin names for all the objects that appear in it. If the teacher duplicates the picture and distributes the same picture to all and then asks them to identify as many objects as possible, he has a definite means of stimulating their vocabulary study. Especially is this true if he gives grades for such a procedure.

Vocabulary study as outlined in the preceding pages will necessarily involve some changes in the more obvious stimuli that teachers have been using through the years such as games, spell downs, and so forth.But this is no loss as the changes will give even greater stimulus to the study of vocabulary.

Flashcards can still be used effectively in the teaching of vocabulary. Instead of using the English word, use the Latin word. As soon as the card is shown, some time is given for all to think; then one student is called upon to use the word in a Latin sentence. If the sentence is correct, the student is given credit for knowing the word. Points can be given for each word in the sentence. This prevents the student using just the minimum number of words for he will want to increase his score. Should there be a mistake, the student who corrects it scores a point at the expense of the one who originally gave the sentence. Thus all are kept busy and interested.

Challenge games that younger students seem to like so much can be used effectively with but slight changes from what we have used in the past. Allow the student whose turn it is to give a Latin sentence that contains a new word. It is the task of the opponent to guess the meaning of the word from the context that is given. The teacher must, of course, be the arbiter when there is question of sufficient hints given for the meaning of the word. He might wish to expand the original sentence. Students will prepare well for such contests and do much work in vocabulary, especially if the rewards for the winners are commensurate with the labor involved in preparing for the challenge game.

The review of units of vocabulary (confer unit building of vocabulary on page 75) can be used for spell downs. Suppose the class is divided into two groups, then the topic is chosen by the teacher. A representative of each group is sent to the board. As each side gives a word, their representative writes it on the board. The side with the most words wins. A more difficult version would be the use of the word in a sentence as soon as it is given.

Football games and basketball games can still be played, but here too changes must be introduced. Suppose the teacher wishes to review a rather large body of vocabulary that students have seen. The teacher uses these words to draw up a paragraph or two that tells a story. These paragraphs are duplicated and passed out to the students. Be sure to number all the words. After captains are chosen, the teacher proceeds to allow each captain in turn to ask a question. The opponent chooses the one who is to respond. Questions can concern the meanings of individual words, the meaning of a sentence, the giving of synonyms and antonyms, English derivatives, related Latin words, the components of a compound and their meaning and other items connected with the paragraphs. The words are numbered to permit the students to readily find the word about which the opponents have a question. Scores are kept as formerly when playing such games — so many points for a touchdown or for a basket. Even penalties can be assessed for incorrect questions and other infringements of the rules that the class under the direction of the teacher has established for the conduct of the game.

For more detailed descriptions of such games and contests the teacher is referred to the Service Bureau of the American Classical League, Miami University, Oxford, Ohio, the Classical Journal for December, 1937 (football), January 1937 (baseball). Only slight modifications need be made to adapt these for use. The schemes suggested in «Practice», edited by R. J. Knoepfle, S. J., and published by Loyola University Press in Chicago, can also be used to stimulate the study of vocabulary and only slight changes need be made in what is given in that volume.

Interest in words

The use of external stimuli such as pictures and games is good for stimulating vocabulary study, but there is a better way and that is to create an interest in word study. The creation of such an interest in young students is not easy but teachers should attempt it even in the early stages of the student's study of Latin. Here are some suggestions that will no doubt stimulate the teacher's memory for other and better schemes.

Suppose we met this sentence in Latin.

Leō caput magnum habet in quō sunt crīnēs multī, et in cervīce sunt comae longae et flāvae.

After the students have comprehended the sentence, then they are given the following sentence.

In caelō paucae sunt stellae quae celeriter movent et hīs sunt crīnēs longī et igneī. Quae sunt?

With only a small amount of questioning, and perhaps with no questioning at all, the students will understand that the «crīnēs» in this case refer to the comet's tail. The teacher then gives this sentence from the second Aeneid (628–29).

Illa (ornus) tremefacta comam concussō vertice nūtat.

After some brief explanation of the setting in which the lines appear, the students will readily realize that «comam» refers to the foliage of the tree that is threatening to fall.

In the study of the contrasts between «coma» and «crīnēs» the derived meanings were fairly obvius, but there are other situations when the metaphorical usage is not so clear. Suppose we work with this example.

Give the following sentence to the students.

Cuneīs fissile rōbur ab agricolīs scinditur.

Once the students have comprehended this sentence, then give the following one.

Cuneō hostēs superātī sunt.

With some questioning the students will come to realize that «cuneō» refers to a wedge-shaped battle formation. We might use the term «cuneus» for the "flyling wedge" that was at one time allowed in football for the return of a punt. After the students have comprehended this sentence, then give the following.

In amphitheātrō sunt cuneī multī.

Herī sēdimus in cuneō sextō.

If students know the general outline of a Roman theatre or the Circus Maximus and realize that the oval at the top is larger in circumference than the oval at the bottom, they will come readily enough to understand that a section of seats can be called a «cuneus»; they can then be told that Latin authors occasionally use the word for an individual seat or bench in the section.

If the teacher from time to time prepares items such as the above to help the students remember words, he will without doubt stimulate their interest.

Needless to say, preparing examples such as the above requires much time but the ensuing knowledge that is imparted to the student is well worth the effort.

The teacher cannot hope to have such interesting items for every word that students meet, but such studies should be done occasionally. The teacher's best source is the unabridged Latin dictionary.

After the teacher has presented a few such studies, he can assign such for the students to work out. He must of course have previously checked the large dictionary to find out what can be found there by the student.

If the Latin teacher is so fortunate as to have a good acquaintance with several languages, he will find it profitable from time to time to trace an individual word through many languages, for example, the word "victory" as it appears in French, Spanish, Italian, and other languages.

Intelligent guessing

Ordinarily when reading for comprehension we must know nine out of ten words in a passage. The meaning of the tenth can usually be determined from the context. Students though must be given abundant help if they are to learn how to get the meaning from context. They must be taught how to do some intelligent guessing at the meaning of words.

First of all students must be instructed not to go at once to the vocabulary for a word whose meaning they do not know. They should rather reread the sentence several times while trying to determine the meaning of the word from the context. They should then write what they think it means — the writing forces them to become specific. Only after writing what they think it means should they go to a dictionary for the meaning. Most of the time the students will come reasonably close to the meaning of the word.

Psychologically this process helps fix the word in the memory since the student approaches it as a problem that is to be solved and works on it for some time. If he were to look it up rapidly in a dictionary, then he will forget it just as rapidly. If the student spends time on it now, he can be sure that he will get a clear impression of the word, one of the requisites for remembering it. The fact that he came reasonably close to the meaning inspires confidence in his ability to read.

Let us suppose that a student is reading a passage of Latin aloud in class. Either from the way it is read or from questioning we find that the student does not know the meaning of a certain word, or he asks the teacher what the word means. Here are some procedures to be followed.

1 Tell the student to look up from the printed page. This is important

because we do not want him to continue to see the word and so fail to concentrate on the general context in order to arrive at the meaning.

2 Then give some Latin synonyms or antonyms or give some other explanation in Latin, including a definition in Latin. Let us suppose that the student still does not comprehend; then we proceed to the next step.

3 Give in English the thoughts that precede and the thoughts that follow and ask the student to complete the thought in English. Usually the correct meaning becomes apparent. It should be remarked that even the intonation of the teacher can help their comprehension.

Here is an example of what should be done. The sentence is taken from Cicero's «Prō Archiā».

> Quodsī ipsī haec neque attingere neque sēnsū nostrō gustāre possēmus...

If the student does not get the meaning of «gustāre» after working through the two steps we outlined above, then we proceed to the third as follows.

Give the English meaning: But if we were unable to reach these heights and... them with our senses...

Then we remind the student that we are talking about an appreciation of literature and we rephrase the English sentence thus: But if we are unable to produce literary masterpieces and... them...

At this point the student will probably supply the English word "appreciate" and that is the translation. Of course the teacher returns to the original sentence to help students see how the concrete "taste with our senses" conveys the same meaning as our abstract "to appreciate".

Here is another example taken from Caesar.

Cum Caesar bellum contrā Haeduōs intulisset...

Suppose the student does not know the meaning of «intulisset». Have him look up at the teacher while the instructor gives the following in English, "When Caesar... war against the Haedui". What will complete the thought in English? Usually the student will give an English expression that will be reasonably close to "had conducted" or he might even give the literal meaning "had brought".

Teachers may object that intelligent guessing fosters inaccurate thinking or so-called "fuzzy" thinking. This would be true if the student always followed this procedure in determining the meanings of words, but it is supposed that such a procedure will be used somewhat sparingly and only as a last resort to get at the meaning. If done intelligently, the guessing of the meaning of a word can foster the student's ability to correlate things and draw a proper conclusion — the process whereby we have come to much of our knowledge of the physical world and its laws.

Contrast teaching

There are in Latin, just as in English, some words that look very much alike in form, but are entirely different in meaning. It is the task of the teacher to make use of such contrasts in order to impress on the mind of the student the meanings of the words. There is no need for the teacher to duplicate for the students a long list of such contrasting words and then to require that such be memorized. If this is done, the student will likely remember them as isolated bits of knowledge. But if the words are presented as the occasion warrants, and if students are encouraged to enter them in a special section of their Latin notebook, it is likely that the words and their use will become functional. Here are some rather common contrasting words.

compellō, 1, address	compellō, 3, force
dēligō, 1, tie, bind	dēligō, 3, choose
ēducō, 1, educate	ēdūcō, 3, lead forth
fundō, 1, establish	fundō, 3, pour out
lēgō, 1, send	legō, 3, read
praedicō, 1, proclaim	praedīcō, 3, foretell
volō, 1, fly	volō, velle, wish
occidō, 3, fall	occīdō, 3, kill
fugō, 1, put to flight	fugiō, 3, flee
moror, 1, delay	morior, 3, die ·
jaceō, 2, lie down	jaciō, 3, throw
dēligō, 3, choose	dīlīgo, 3, love
dēligō, 1, fasten	
vincō, 3, conquer	vinciō, 4, bind
cadō, 3, fall	caedō, 3, cut
crescō, 3, grow	cernō, 3, separate, sift

Nouns and other parts of speech frequently have forms that are very much alike. To contrast them clearly is the best way to make certain that students use them correctly or interpret them correctly in their reading. Here are some such.

concilium – cōnsilium	voluntās – voluptās
līmen – lūmen	latus, -eris – lātus, -a, -um

ob – ab	flūmen – fulmen
mundus, -ī – mundus, -a, -um	nōmen – nūmen
medicus – mendicus	os, ossis – ōs, ōris
āra – ōra	flūmen – flāmen
calor – color	aetās – aestās

Here are forms that look alike until we realize that the quantity of the vowel helps to distinguish them.

ōrā (imperative)	ōra, shore
aquā (ablative)	aqua (nominative)
loca, places	locā (imperative)
regeris (present)	regēris (future)

And here are some forms that could be two different things.

corōnā (ablative)	corōnā (imperative)
ōra, shore	ōra, mouths
lūdō (ablative)	lūdō (verb)
vītā (ablative)	vītā (imperative)
laudēs (nominative, accusative)	laudēs (present subjunctive)

Another feature of contrast teaching concerns itself with the teaching of synonyms and antonyms. These should not be neglected for they can help to fix the words in the minds of the students. Students will not normally on their own look for the synonyms or antonyms — teachers must motivate their doing so.

Contrast teaching can be intriguing

Just to give students a listing of words such as are given above will not stimulate their study of words. However, if the teacher gives a sentence that has a number of words in contrast, then he can hope to elicit at least some interest. Here are some examples that will no doubt suggest others.

«Mea mater in silvam tuum filium lupus est» will cause trouble unless it is written «Meā, māter, in silvam, tuum filium lupus ēst». "Run, mother, into the forest, the wolf is eating your son". It usually takes much time before students arrive at the correct meaning since words like «meā» and «ēst (ēdō)» are used in a way that is not immediately apparent to most students.

«Mālō malō in mālō quam vīvere malō» when written on the board will invariably bring some laughter but students soon try to determine the meaning when they are told that it is a meaningful Latin sentence. It is usually some time before they arrive at the meaning: "I prefer to live on a mast with a bad apple than to live with a bad man".

Here are two good examples taken from «The Factotum»: Some Varieties of the Latin Hexameter by Harry C. Schnur, «The Classical World», February 1960, Vol. 53, #5, p. 157.

Pāreō praeceptīs, pariō prōlem, parō mēnsam.

Clāva ferit, clāvus firmat, clāvisque reclūdit.

Difficulties in the learning of vocabulary

To read Latin with understanding one must know vocabulary, usually nine out of ten words. Since a knowledge of vocabulary is so necessary it is good to look at some of the difficulties students encounter in the learning of it.

1 The failure to get a clear impression of a word the first time it is seen is due to carelessness, a failure to take the proper amount of time to fix it in the mind and establish asssociations, or to a lack of interest and a will to remember. It cannot be impressed sufficiently upon the minds of students how important this first impression is. Writing the word and pronouncing it aloud helps the student to secure an accurate first impression.

2 Besides failing to get a good first impression of the word the student frequently fails to set up associations that will help his memory (synonyms, antonyms, related words). To help combat this lack of association it is good to remind students frequently that they must also look at the words that are in the vicinity of the one they are consulting.

3 A poor visual memory will handicap some in the learning of vocabulary. Most such have good aural imaginations and they should exploit them by doing much of their study aloud, particularly the reading of the Latin passages that they have mastered.

4 For many students a failure to syllabify and then to pronunce accurately is a stumbling block in the learning of vocabulary. We meet it frequently in English and it is also met in Latin.

5 Poor reading habits can be a hindrance for some. There are those who fail to distinguish between «cum» and «con», «per» and «pre», «pro» and «prae», and this failure carries over into words such as «lūmen» and «līmen», «lātus» and «lōtus».

6 A failure to recognize how words are built is a stumbling block for others in the learning of vocabulary. They do not recognize that «attineō» is nothing else than «ad-teneō». Teachers can help obviate this difficulty by constantly teaching how verbs and words in general are built.

7 Poor remote recall explains a lack of vocabulary knowledge for some students. It will be remembered that, to secure automatic response in the matter of words, a student must normally see the word about a hundred times, or he must hear it about twenty-five times and see it five times. Students who have poor remote racall must be trained to review often and systematically.

8 Poor eyesight has been a cause of difficulty for some students and their learning of vocabulary. Teachers should be on the alert for the student who constantly frowns when he reads, or who must bend down over the book to see, or who squints and tilts his head when he tries to read things that have been written on the chalkboard. Such students probably should use glasses or if they wear them the strength should be changed.

Poor hearing, too, must be accounted as an obstacle in the learning of vocabulary. Students whose hearing is impaired should be put toward the front of the room in order that they may hear the teacher better.

Students with speech defects occasionally have difficulty in the learning of vocabulary. Listening attentively to recordings and making recordings of their own for comparison purposes is good remedial work for these.

Fortunately at the present time the health programs in most schools help to minimize these physical difficulties, yet the teacher must be alerted to them as a possible source of difficulty in learning.

9 The time and circumstances under which students study outside of class time sometimes interferes with their learning the vocabulary as they should. Studying when they are too tired, competing with the program that the family is watching on the television, studying immediately after meals, and a host of such things make it difficult for students to study and learn.

Hints for studying vocabulary

Once the teacher knows that a student has difficulty in learning vocabulary, he should give direction and help. Students appreciate this and teachers will be gratified by the progress that the willing student makes. Here are some suggestions.

1 Read the text more carefully and oftener.

2 Underline the words whose meaning cannot be remembered. Then read these sentences oftener than the rest of the story.

3 Write the word several times along with synonyms and antonyms.

4 Pronounce the word aloud while the eyes are closed and the imagination is busy trying to picture the object or the action in a definite way.

5 Write the word in syllables and pronounce it that way several times.

6 Work on vocabulary many times rather than for one period of great length. Three five-minute sessions are better than one fifteen-minute study period.

7 Work on vocabulary when the mind is fresh such as in the morning before the day's work, or at the beginning of the study period.

8 Read the passage in which the word occurs first thing in the morning and the last thing at night.

9 Systematically review the Latin passages. For example, on Monday read again the passages studied the previous Monday and the one before that. On Tuesday review those studied or read on the two previous Tuesdays.

Review and self testing

Review and self testing encountered no great problems when students had lengthy vocabulary lists in their texts. Many procedures were suggested to them but most of these helped to train the memory but did nothing to help train the student to read the language with comprehension.

How then is a student to review vocabulary and test himself to find out if he knows it?

There is really only one answer. He must read and reread. Up to the present most students were content to prepare a small portion of text for class, to take careful notes during class, to review the material that night and then not to bother with it until a short time before the examinations.

Students should be taught to constanly reread the materials they have seen while consciously making an effort to understand it as they read. The rereading is their vocabulary review.

If the student has difficulty with some words he should underline them. Then the next time he studies he should reread these sentences. If he remembered the meaning of the word, then he can remove the underlining. If he did not he might consider composing a few sentences that use the word. He should also discuss the word with his friends. This constant attention to it will help fix it in his memory. Nor should the student fail to read the sentences aloud.

The student can test himself in several ways. When he has reread a passage and discovered words whose meaning escapes him, he should list these. Then he composes sentences in which the words are used. These he puts aside. Two days later he rereads them and if he remembers the meaning then he destroys the page — it is no longer serviceable for him. To assure correctness he might submit the sentences to his teacher.

The student may wish to go through a familiar reading and write down the meanings of all the nouns he meets, or adjectives, or verbs. He is testing himself in context and the English is a convenient way of determining his comprehension.

A test of vocabulary is had if the student has someone read the passage to him to see if he understands it. Tapes that have the text should be availabe to the student for such review, and testing of himself.

During review periods the teacher can be of help if he gives the students a new story that uses substantially the same vocabulary with which they should be familiar. If students can read it readily, then they are assured that they know their vocabulary.

The teacher can also help by suggesting that the students go through the readings they have seen and make a listing of all the words that would be serviceable for writing a composition on a certain topic. He might then suggest that the student write the composition on the topic and submit it for correction.

Let us suppose that none of the schemes suggested in this chapter work for the student. The teacher might then encourage him to write the word and its meaning together with a sentence that uses the word in a small notebook. This the student carries with him and as occasion offers he opens the notebook and reviews the word. After two weeks or so the student should be able to cross the word off the list as one that he will remember, provided, of course, that he looked at it several times a day during that period of two weeks.

Assignments for home study of vocabulary

The best assignment for home study in vocabulary is again the rereading of familiar selections in Latin. Students should during the reading consciously strive to understand as they read.

In order to be rather certain that the students are doing the reading of familiar selections, it is advisable for the teacher to assign specific selections in a systematic way, for example, each night review the Latin that was read two weeks ago. Test the students the following day on the selection assigned.

86

But do not use the exact wording of the selection, make a digest of it and at times change the point of the story in order to check the comprehension of the students. At still other times the teacher may bring in an entirely new story that uses only the words that appeared in the selection assigned.

There are other possible assignments for home study of vocabulary but they are second in importance to that of rereading. Here are some suggestions.

1 Ask the students to list the English derivatives that are suggested by specific words in the selections, such as nouns or verbs. Tell them to use the English word in an English sentence, and then to use the Latin word in a Latin sentence.

2 Ask for synonyms and antonyms for a specified number of words in the selection, or for as many as the student can give without referring to the English dictionary.

3 Assign certain words in the selection for special work such as that of giving the related words. For example, if «maculō» appears, the students would be expected to give words like «macula» and «maculōsus». Again these should be used in sentences.

4 Ask students to do a short original theme that uses only the vocabulary found in the selection. This can be quite difficult unless the selection is a fairly lengthy one.

5 Pictures can be used in assigning home study. Draw them on a ditto master, duplicate, and give to the students. Ask them to identify the objects, then write a short paragraph about the picture. Variations can be had if the teacher himself puts down several partial sentences and asks the students to complete them in view of what they see in the picture.

6 The study of Pattern practices or Drill masters can be a study of vocabulary if the students make a conscious effort at understanding each of the sentences. Teachers can occasionally check this type of study by asking for the English equivalent of some of the sentences that appeared in the drills.

Work at the chalkboard

Many teachers like to have students work at the chalkboard in order to help secure variety in the class procedure. Even though teachers are not working with isolated lists of words there are many things that can profitably be done at the chalkboard. Some of these might be used for assignments in home study also.

1   If students have read or heard a selection and know it quite well, it is not out of order for the teacher to send several to the chalkboard and ask them to write as many of the new Latin words from the passage as they can remember: nouns, verbs, adverbs, adjectives, and so forth.

2   This procedure can be varied by having the students close their books following the reading. Then send one student to the board; he writes the words that are suggested by the class. If the words were listed in categories (nouns, verbs, and so forth), the teacher can then ask for modifiers for the nouns and verbs.

3   Again synonyms and antonyms can be used effectively as well as related words. Send a student to the board, allow him to choose a word from the selection, then call on the class to supply a synonym or antonym or related word. If such are not known, then the class can help the student formulate a definition in Latin or at least a description.

4   The chalkboard affords excellent opportunities for drilling the related words and the compounds of verbs. Give a simple verb form such as «teneō». Allow the student himself to write the compounds he knows, then ask the class to complete the list. A variation can be had by asking the student to write the root of the word, for example, «ten-» and then asking for help in constructing words and giving their meaning.

Testing vocabulary

This will be treated in a later chapter. Vocabulary is an important part of language amd the teacher must be constantly on the alert for helpful devices in teaching it; but it should be taught as much as possible in context and not in isolated lists. If the student has a geniuine interest in words, and if he wishes to make progress in his reading, he will himself not only see the necessity of knowing vocabulary but will devise many schemes of his own for studying and remembering it.

The teacher who has been used to assigning lists of vocabulary for students to learn will find it difficult at first not to continue such a practice for he will continue to feel that students are not working on the building of vocabulary. But after a time he will see that the students have been learning vocabulary because they will be constantly making progress in understanding what he reads to them and what they read in the text. And this is the best test of vocabulary.

Chapter 5

Teaching the text

The goal that many Latin teachers have set for themselves is a realistic one, for they wish to teach their students to read the Latin as Latin. This means that they wish to use Latin as a vehicle of giving their students a real language experience. Consequently they do not wish to teach their students how to analyze a language, break it into its component parts, and then reduce them all to neat grammatical categories.

Giving students a language experience consists essentially in teaching them how to work with a new means of communication. This implies among other things a new approach to ideas with the consequent broadening of their vision which in turn will result in an appreciation of both their native language and the new language as well as the cultures for which the languages are a vehicle of expression.

Language then is a communication and it is primarily oral. We might perhaps define language as a system of arbitrary vocal sounds by which intelligent beings communicate with one another.

It is a succession of vocal sounds and by this is understood the sounds that are made with the speech organs and therefore such things as signs, gestures, grunts, coughs, and the like, are excluded; even writing is not language since it gets its meaning only from the spoken words which human beings use to communicate with one another.

The sounds of language are arbitrary, for there is no necessary connection between the physical object and the identifying word that is attached to it. The Latins call a certain animal a «canis» while the Germans refer to that same animal as a «hund».

In the definition of language the words "intelligent beings" are very important since this will help distinguish real language from the various imitations that can be made, for example, by parrots.

Communication refers to the conjuring up of an idea in the mind of the person addressed. When a person uses the word «run» the auditor will have in his mind quite a similar thought.

The words "with one another" stress the social aspects of language and the possibility men have of cooperating with one another because of language. All are familiar with the story about the confusion which resulted when men wished to build the tower of Babel but could no longer communicate with one another — cooperation was impossible without a common medium of communication.

Unfortunately the teaching of Latin has for a long time neglected the elements of the definition of language, and in particular they neglected the oral-aural phases of teaching. There was an almost exclusive reliance upon the eye and the native language was at all times used as a point of reference. Fortunately the newer methods stress the oral-aural approach which brings Latin back to its rightful place — a real means of communicaton.

Actually the newer approaches are going back to what was originally done it the teaching of Latin. One needs but a superficial acquaintance with the «Ratio Studiorum»[1] that was published by the Society of Jesus to realize that this method (the oral-aural approach) stressed the teaching of Latin as a means of communication. Here is one of the suggestions found in the «Ratio Studiorum», "Let him (the master) read the whole passage without interruption, unless in rhetoric and the humanities, it would seem to be too long." This is a clear reference to the oral-aural approach.

The oral-aural approach has definite implications for teaching the text. Here are some suggestions that will help to restore Latin to its rightful position of language and remove it from the category of "dead languages" to which so much of our teaching had relegated it.

Here are the steps a teacher might follow in teaching the Latin text.

Read the text interpretatively TO the students

The first step in the presentation of the text is that of reading it TO the students. Note the preposition "to". It is significant. Students should first become acquainted with the text by means of the ear, not the eye. No printed page can preserve the multiplicity of signals that help toward comprehension — signals that most teachers have for many years neglected when teaching

---

[1]The reader is referred to «St. Ignatius and the Ratio Studiorum» edited by Edward A. Fitzpatrick, McGraw-Hill Book Company, 1933.

the text, and because they have neglected them Latin teaching has indeed concerned itself with something that was dead.

Interpretative reading by the teacher signals meaning in a variety of ways. Noting these signals for the ear and for the eye helps to make a communication come alive. The activity of the listener is elicited and when this is united to the activity of the speaker there arises a genuine language situation in which the auditor's comprehension is helped by devices that all too frequently are neglected by Latin teachers. Interpretative reading will certainly include

> varied intonations and facial expressions,
> proper pauses and grouping of words,
> suitable gestures (including a moderate use of mimicry),
> and rapid or slow articulation as demanded by the thought.

The written page can convey but few of these signals of meaning. Some are indicated on the page but they have no life.

Here is an experiment that will prove the need of an oral presentation. Let the teacher take the first oration of Cicero against Catiline and read it aloud. Surely it will make quite an impact because Cicero was a great speaker. Now listen to a recording of that speech such as that which can be secured from EMC Recording Company, 806 East Seventh Street, St. Paul 6, Minnesota. The teacher cannot listen to the full rich tones and the charm of the language without his feelings being deeply stirred — something Cicero wanted in the souls of the senators who were listening to him, including the mind and spirit of Catiline himself. The recording can be played for students after they are acquainted with the speech. To play it before would not be advisable since understanding is a requisite for inspiration.

Read the text aloud a second or even a third time

One interpretative reading of the text is not enough. It should be read to the students at least a second time, preferably a third time or even a fourth time and that for a variety of reasons.

Students learn by imitation and the teacher is the best model for the students in this matter of reading. He uses certain intonations, groupings of words, pauses and the like, that students can profitably imitate when they come to reading aloud.

Phrases and words that seemed strange the first time they are heard become more familiar when the text is read aloud several times. Second and third readings frequently stir up associations that were missed earlier. If certain associations were made the first time, then these are strengthened and deepened in the subsequent oral presentations.

New words become familiar sounds at least and if the reading is properly graded the student can in the second or third reading tentatively fix the meaning from the context.

Several readings too are required for the student to correlate the various parts of the story. Few can do this satisfactorily when hearing a thing once only.

Perhaps most important of all this oral reading by the teacher is one of the finest ways of achieving the goal — comprehending Latin as Latin. The attentive listening of the student to what the master reader (the teacher) wishes to communicate becomes a daily exercise in comprehending the Latin in the Latin word order — there is no looking back, nor is there any looking forward for subjects, modifiers, verbs, and so forth. The student must follow as the story unfolds through the words of the teacher — he is being trained to comprehend in the natural flow of speech something that is of inestimable value when he comes to reading the printed page.

This oral reading by the teacher affords yet further training that will benefit the student in his reading. We refer to what might be termed "expectancy". If the teacher should suddenly stop in the midst of a Latin sentence, the student who has been comprehending should know in general what to expect in the remainder of the sentence. This is an important element in learning to read Latin because when the student hears an accusative ending he quite naturally should expect a reason for it in the subsequent parts of the sentence that will follow.

«Repetītiō est māter studiōrum» and that is nowhere truer than in the learning to read Latin as Latin.

Give a synopsis of the story in Latin

After reading the story several times the teacher will give the students a synopsis of the story in simpler Latin. He will use words and phrases and constructions with which the students are very familiar and his purpose in so doing is to assure the comprehension of the student. Comprehension is in fact the yardstick that both teacher and student use to check progress from day to day.

This telling of the story in simpler Latin is perhaps more important than the readings. Telling the story is the ideal situation for communication. The teacher watches the faces of his listeners and their comprehension (as evidenced on their faces) and this is a spur to him to make the story come alive. There is genuine satisfaction too for the students as they get the thrill of understanding what the teacher wishes to communicate. Both students and teacher forget the medium of communication and are intent upon the thought.

Students soon realize the importance of the summary that the teacher gives as they see how it helps their comprehension. This realization of the student spurs him on to greater efforts in comprehending as the story unfolds itself, again a daily lesson in reading or in comprehending Latin as Latin.

Read the story again

When the teacher is satisfied that the students are acquainted with the content of the story, he reads the original text again with as much interpretation as he can command.

In the course of this reading he may stop from time to time in order to explain new words. He does this in Latin not in English. He can give synonyms or lengthier explanations. For example, suppose the story was a fable that included the actions of a «vulpēs». The teacher might indicate that the «vulpēs est animal ferum quod astūtiā praeditum est. Dīcitur semper astūtē agere et per astūtiam saepe sē salvat.»

New constructions are also explained. For these the teacher may wish to use English in order to make certain that students get a good clear first impression of the new usage. For example, suppose that «nāviget» occurred in the passage. The teacher would recall for the students the previous passage in Vergil in which Jupiter called Mercury and told him that he was to convey a command to Aeneas. Jupiter's word would have been, if he talked directly to Aeneas, «nāvigā». Now Mercury is conveying the command in «nāviget», and this usage indicates that the command is not his but someone else's. Note that there is no tagging of this as a jussive subjunctive. Such tagging can wait until later, perhaps the third year even of the study of Latin when students can be expected to be somewhat familiar with grammar. Meantime the student is well served so far as comprehension is concerned by having a functional knowledge of the grammatical usage.

It need hardly be remarked that during this reading-explanation part of the presentation the teacher should answer as expeditiously as possible any questions that the students may have concerning the text or the story.

Explanations of new items may not be enough to assure comprehension. Items that have been met before may need recall, especially those that do not occur frequently, for example, the tone that is set when the author uses a word like «scīlicet».

During the course of this reading-explanation the teacher should supply other items that are needed for fuller comprehension such as an explanation of the mythology involved, how the Romans used names, social customs, political implications, and the like.

A final reading

When the foregoing readings have been completed the teacher gives a final reading of the passage in order that students may get a fuller understanding since by this time most difficulties have been eliminated.

The teacher then assigns the story for study outside of class time. The students are encouraged to read it many times and to strive to comprehend it as they read. They are to be encouraged to recall the explanations given by the teacher. Their reading should include oral reading during which they strive to imitate the teacher as closely as possible.

A word of warning

A word of warning on general methodology is in order. The reading-explanation part of the presentation must not degenerate into a lecture. Much of the explanation, and especially the recall, and even the mythological references and other explanations, should be elicited from the students. Students must actively participate in this part of the presentation in order to feel that they have a part in the learning process.

During the readings the students should listen, not follow with the eye in the text. Obviously all writing is prohibited during this time since it would seriously interfere with the communication between the teacher and the student. There is too much danger that students will think, if they are allowed to write, that they can study the material later — hence their concentration is on getting down on paper as much as possible of what the teacher says rather than on concentrating on understanding what is said with a definite will to remember since they know its importance for their study of the text.

If the teacher feels that some of the material is very important and that it should be written down, he should take the time for such work after the final reading, or better still he will at that point distribute a page that contains the material he wishes them to have. It is not distributed before the final reading since students would be tempted to read that explanation rather than to pay attention to what the class is doing.

94

There are other reasons why students should not follow the presentation of the text with books open. Suppose a difficulty occurs; if the text is closed, the teacher can bring the students to think for themselves and to strive to solve it. Actually modern texts often do the student a disservice when they fully explain all difficulties. The solution for many of the difficulties would better be relegated to the teachers' manual. The teacher can then present the solution after the students are aware of the problem and have striven to solve it themselves.

If the story that the teacher has been using does not appear in the text that the students have, the teacher should distribute copies of the text to the students. While doing this he might profitably have one of the students read the story aloud for all to follow once more.

If the teacher follows the presentation as envisaged here, he can be certain that he has fully equipped his students for studyng the text on their own. Moreover, his presentation was an object lesson in the correct study of a text as well as a lesson in how to read with comprehension.

Home study of the text

What type of assignments can the teacher make in order to make certain that the students study the Latin text? Here are a few suggestions.

1 Read the story through five or six times or more. Strive to comprehend it as you read. Do not go back to read individual sentences but read the story as a unit.

2 Diagram one or other sentence, particularly if there happens to be a long and involved one in the text. Such work will assist the student when he reads the sentence and tries to comprehend it as it unfolds itself.

3 Give a Latin synopsis of the story.

4 Be prepared tomorrow to tell the story to the class in Latin, or to write out a synopsis of it during the test period. This is perhaps one of the best ways of making certain that the students do the requisite reading. They have a compelling motive for remembering.

5 Rewrite the story but change the time. If it is told in the present, change it to the past and vice versa.

95

6 Rewrite the story and subordinate clauses where possible, or change clauses into ablative absolutes where possible, or express the ideas of causality in a way other than that which appears in the text.

7 Give a list of English words and ask the students to give the Latin words from which these are derived.

8 Give a set of circumstances very similar to those that appear in the story and ask the students to tell the story in Latin.

9 Translate one or other sentence into good English. This type of exercise should be used sparingly in the first two years. Only one sentence is to be translated because it will then be easy for the teacher to check the student's work the followig day. He can check this work by calling upon students for their translation. After several have read their translations the teacher asks if anyone thinks he has a better one — if so, allow it to be read with appropriate comments. Or the teacher can check it by assigning some work to the students during which time he goes from desk to desk to read the translations and corrections in private.

10 Distribute a sheet that contains questions in Latin on the text and tell the students to write out the answers in complete Latin sentences. This exercise prepares the student for the teacher's questions the following day. The teacher might wish to make up a page of incomplete sentences about the story. Students are then required to complete them in the light of the events in the story.

11 Assign the composing of comprehension questions on the text they have read. Let these be used the next day during the recitation. Students usually are quite serious in their efforts if they know that some of the questions they draw up will appear in subsequent tests.

12 Occasionally the Latin teacher may wish to give an assigment in common with the history teacher. This can be done when there is question of the historical background for a particular text or author.

13 Occasionally the Latin teacher may wish to work in close cooperation with the English teacher by giving assignments that will be corrected by both teachers. Tell the students to write out the story in good English. The Latin teacher grades it for accuracy of content as judged by the elements appearing in the Latin story; the English teacher grades it for correctness of expression and other items that he stresses in his

teaching. If the story is lengthy, several days might be allowed for the preparation of the assignment.

14 At other times part of the home study for the students may consist in choosing a good title for the story and then listing the reasons for their title. Sometimes it is good to have students write a topic sentence for each of the paragraphs in the story.

Advantages of proposed presentation of the text

The presentation of the text as I have outlined it is far superior to merely reading and translating, or worse; just translating.

There is real contact between the teacher and the student. The teacher is at all times fully aware of the attention of the students or the lack of it in the daydreamer. But the most significant part of this rapport between teacher and student is the ease with which the teacher can become aware of the light of comprehension that dawns in one student after the other during the presentation. This is a concrete reward for the teacher and his hard work, and it acts as a real stimulus and gives genuine satisfaction.

By way of contrast there is nothing so dull as the extreme situation in which the teacher keeps his eye glued to the page, remains seated at his desk, and allows the students to drone on and on with translation with only an occasional break by parsing a word or two. Such a situation makes communication impossible and there is little if any teaching.

The presentation of the text as it was outlined demands real attention and concentration on the part of the student to everything the teacher says and does. Note the word "does" — actually at the end of the period the teacher will feel exhausted. Moreover, the student must get the class matter quickly and just as it is presented; there is no looking forward and very little time for a backward glance. He is constantly involved in what is going on in the present.

When the printed page is in front of the student, what assurance has a teacher that the student is working right along with him? The method proposed above prevents students from becoming interested in footnotes, looking at attractive pictures, or reading ahead in order to try to anticipate the next question of the teacher. In other words, all twenty-eight students work at the same task at the same time, and the teacher can elicit the full play of every student's intellectual powers without hindrance from the text and its embellishments.

Using stories is far superior to running through a number of disconnected sentences. The continuity of the story is in itself a help to comprehension, and students have a natural desire to know how the story ended. Such a desire is a strong stimulus for comprehension. Moreover, students soon become aware of the fact that their neighbor seems to have gotten the meaning of the story. If they themselves have not comprehended, then they wonder why and for what reason and will probably pay better attention in the future. Stories, too, come to an end and the student has the satisfaction of having completed a task; sentences on the other hand supposedly could go on forever.

Students love the air of challenge that is created when the teacher reads a story to them. They love to excel in being the first to comprehend. And I might add that they are constantly competing with themselves — they strive to better their own comprehension from day to day. They fully realize that good comprehension during class makes for easier work outside of class time.

The oral presentation of the text also gives the student the thrill of discovery. Nothing so elates us as having the sudden realization that we have solved a problem or have arrived at a new conclusion, and that through our own efforts even though we may have worked under someone's direction — we feel it is our own. This thrill of discovery and realization is the basis for a very real and ever mounting interest on the part of the student in the language he is studying. Such an interest is far superior to that which stems from external stimuli such as ornate books, slides, pictures, and so forth.

The frequent rereading that is called for in the presentation as it was outlined above will help fix the words and phrases and clauses in the minds of the students. Many of the more facile students will probably be able to give the entire story from memory and this is good too. Soon entire phrases and clauses will come spontaneously to mind when the student comes into contact with situations that are akin to those which he has studied. Such a student is on the high road to reading with comprehension and even to a facile production of the language.

In order to make the presentation of the text successful there is need for much strictly graded reading material. Because there is only a small quantity of such available, teachers should not hesitate to rewrite and simplify the readings of the masters in order to temper them to the abilities of the reader or listener. Later on when students can read with facility they can enjoy reading the masters. In English we certainly do not start the reading of the classics until such time as the students are very familiar with their native language. Even students who are fair scholars find the plays of Shakespeare more intelligible if beforehand they have the opportunity of reading a digest such as those which are found in Lamb's «Tales from Shakespeare».

Much preparation is needed

The teacher who wishes to read the text to his students interpretatively and to present it as something very much alive must of necessity spend much time in preparation. He must himself frequently read the passage aloud — far better, of course, is it if he has memorized it by the time he goes into the classroom.

Questions on the text must be prepared in advance. He may not use these during the class period, but the preparation of them gives him facility in formulating them when needed during class.

Quite obviously, too, the teacher must determine what elements need clarification and how he will explain them. Background material must also be prepared, such as the mythology that is possibly involved in a text.

Until such time as the teacher has achieved some facility in expressing himself in Latin, he will find it profitable to write out the digest of the story that he intends to give to the students. He will not use this in class, but the fact that he has written it will help his expression during the class period.

The teacher must be convinced that without adequate preparation he cannot hope to conduct a class that will be stimulating for the students. If he has not determined upon specific questions, his questioning will be sporadic and usually of little help to the student's comprehension.

The presentation of the material is the most important part of the class. A good presentation will secure interest on the part of the student and this interest in turn will result in a willingness to expend the labor entailed in mastering what the teacher presents. Hence the next day's recitation will be good or poor in direct proportion to the teacher's presentation.

The recitation of the text

If the preceding pages that concern themselves with the presentation of the text have been read rapidly, the reader is likely to wonder how the teacher can conduct a profitable recitation the next day since so much of the work has already been done.

Much work has been done, it is true, but it was merely a presentation. The student still was faced with the necessity of making his own what was presented to him. This he is supposed to do in his home study. The teacher

99

gave the example of how to study the text and what to study in it but the student himself had still to master the material.

How then can the teacher conduct a profitable recitation the next day? It will be supposed that the student did the requisite work that was assigned. It should be noted, too, that the suggested order of the items in the recitation may be changed at the discretion of the teacher.

1 Call for an interpretative reading of the text

This interpretative reading will immediately reveal whether the student did the work that was assigned, unless, of course, the student has some reading disability that is independent of Latin, such as stuttering.

It is not necessary that one student read the entire passage. The teacher can and should call on several. If a sentence has not been read well, the teacher should call upon another student and ask him to try to improve upon the reading just heard.

During this reading by the students the teacher should have nothing in his hands and should depend entirely upon the reading of the students for his own comprehension. As soon as he loses the thought he should ask the student to repeat, telling him that he could not understand what was read. This, of course, is an indirect rebuke to the student for his poor reading.

The teacher can be rather certain that interpretative reading is a good indication of comprehension on the part of the student. Should he doubt this, he needs but perform an experiment such as this. Hand a fairly difficult paragraph or fairly lengthy sentence to a student and ask him to read it aloud. You may even allow him to do it several times. Then go over it with him to make sure that he understands the entire sentence or paragraph. Then call for a reading. The difference between the first attempts and this last reading will be tremendous.

2 Ask questions about what was read

Following the interpretative reading by the students, the teacher asks questions about the passage in Latin and expects the answers in Latin. The teacher will, of course, not ask exactly the same questions that he asked the day before. At this time he is intent upon making certain that the students have comprehended the passage. He can ask questions that reveal the student's knowledge of structure but should go beyond that to determine their comprehension.

Let us suppose that the student read «Inter Rōmānōs Augustus rēgnābat». Merely asking «Quis inter Rōmānōs rēgnābat» will not clearly establish the student's comprehension if he answers correctly. But if the question is phrased thus «Quis fuit rēx Rōmānōrum» and the student responds correctly, the teacher has fair assurance that the student has comprehended the original sentence. If the student can answer the following questions about the sentence correctly, then the teacher is definitely assured that the student has comprehended what was said. Here are the questions: «Quis imperium apud Rōmānōs tenēbat? Quis potestātem apud Rōmānōs exercēbat? Cūjus in manū fuērunt fascēs apud Rōmānōs?»

Beginning teachers will find it handy to use this scheme. It will permit them to draw up the questions during their preparation for class and will make it possible to use these very same questions. As he prepares the questions, he writes them out on cards (3 × 6 cards cut in half are handy). When he comes into the classroom and the students have read the text, he shuffles the cards and then hands them out one at a time to the various students upon whom he wishes to call. (Do not hand them out to all at once — students will then prepare their question and pay no attention to what the others are doing.) The student reads the question on the card and attempts to answer it. If he fails, the teacher calls upon another to supply the correct answer. This set of cards can be your test question for the student and your scribe can keep the score for you. Be sure not to skip the scribe in your questioning, and it is advisable to have different students act as scribe on successive days.

This card system works well, too, in contests. If a student answers correctly, he keeps the card. If he fails and a student on the opposing side answers correctly, the card must be surrendered to him. The side having the most cards at the end of a given time is the winner.

3 A written test is not out of order. More will be said about this in a later chapter.

4 Call for a synopsis of the passage in Latin. In the beginning the students should be allowed to use the text; later this should be done without the help of the text.

This synopsis in Latin will be quite halting at first, especially when it is given orally, but soon the students will acquire confidence and facility in expressing the ideas in simple Latin. When a student cannot go on, others can be asked to help him out of his difficulty. This keeps all attentive. Such oral presentations impress upon the students the necessity of careful and frequent reading of the Latin together with comprehension.

101

5 If the class is working with the text of the masters such as Cicero and Vergil, then it is not out of order to question them about rhetorical devices, use of words for effective expression, and other elements that contribute to style, even though these may not have been discussed during the presentation period.

6 Part of the recitation will consist in answering difficulties the students encountered in their home study as they prepared the text.

The teacher can easily prompt such questions by asking whether there were parts that they did not understand or forms with which they had difficulty.

7 Synonyms, antonyms, related Latin words, derivatives and the like that were discussed during the presentation period, can with profit be repeated during the recitation.

Such repetition is not to be eschewed at any time, for it is precisely the repetition of material in passages that have been understood that helps the student fix the items in his mind.

8 Call upon the students for the translation of one or other of the sentences with the emphasis being on idiomatic translation.

Note that this translation is for a sentence or two. Translating is an art quite distinct from comprehension and comprehension in the early stages of learning a language achieves the goal, that of reading Latin as Latin.

9 Occasionally the teacher should call for group reading, either by the entire class or by the students within a single row.

This is advantageous for the slow reader because it helps him move along faster when the group reads faster than he does. Also, as he reads aloud he becomes aware of how his intonations fit with the rest or do not fit. If his interpretation does not fit, he is acutely aware of it without embarrassment and will be urged to improve.

Home study of the text after recitation

After the teacher has taken the text in the recitation period, he may wish to assign homework in order to assure himself that the students will again review it that night. This assignment should be in the nature of a review. The teacher should be certain that fulfilling the assignment will not take long since the students must also prepare the text that was presented today. He might make some assignment such as the following.

1 Assign one or other item from the suggestions of the previous section.

2   Assign the composition of two or three or more sentences in direct imitation of one or other in the text that was studied. Such imitations should certainly concern themselves with the word order, though the thought content may be different.

The time required for presentation and recitation

If the students and teacher follow carefully the presentation and recitation as outlined in this chapter, there will be plenty of time for both in an ordinary period.

The teacher should be able to take the students through the recitation in approximately ten to fifteen minutes. This he can do if the students have done the proper amount of preparation outside of class. If the work is completed in fifteen minutes, the teacher has approximately two thirds of the class time left for presentation of new material.

If the teacher starts the period with a ten-minute quiz, he could allow ten or fifteen minutes for the recitation, and still have twenty minutes left if the period is forty-five minutes in length. If the periods are fifty-minutes in length, he would have half the period left for presentation.

Teachers, however, should not be governed by the clock. If during the recitation the students are learning, then there is no need to necessarily complete it within the time suggested above. Home-study assignments can easily be adjusted in such a situation.

The recitation should not be just a repetition

If from day to day the recitation consists merely of a repetition of points that were covered in the presentation, then soon the students will tire of the recitation and it will become dull and drab. Interest on the part of the students will lag and the teacher himself will soon shorten this important learning device.

To guard against such undesirable features of the recitation, the teacher should be certain that he is saving some of the material he has prepared in order to bring it in during the recitation. The news items he introduces during the recitation might include such things as the aptness of the use of words, interesting word studies, highlights of Roman customs, alternate versions, and even the explanations of difficulties that the students themselves did not discover in the text. Occasionally, too, when the students are dealing with the masters, the teacher may bring in several translations and allow the

103

students to evaluate them in the light of what they themselves have seen in the passage.

Oral testing as opposed to written tests can help change the pattern of the recitation period.

When studying the masters in third and fourth years, the teacher can occasionally assign an oral report on some topic for the recitation period. Suppose the class is preparing to read Vergil's description of the funeral of Misenus, or for that matter even after they have read about it, the teacher will find it profitable to have some one of the students give a five-minute report on Roman funerals and funeral rites. Such a report helps to break the monotony of a recitation.

Class work and home study

Here is a schematic view of the procedures that are followed each day except for those occasions when full period tests are given.

	M	Tu	W	Th	F	M
Class						
Reading and explanation of new text	1	2	3	4	5	6
Recitation		1	2	3	4	5
Translations and other written assignments			1	2	3	4
Home						
Study of assignment	1	2	3	4	5	6
Translations, reading, and other assignments		1	2	3	4	5

The arabic numerals refer to the number of the story that is the text. Note that students work on story one on three successive nights, and on story two for three nights, and so forth.

The scheme should be varied a bit if the teacher is working with students in their third and fourth years of the study of Latin, and if these students have achieved much facility in the reading of Latin. It is therefore supposed that they are students of more than average ability and good study habits.

	M	Tu	W	Th	F	M	T
Class							
Assignment for preliminary private study	1	2	3	4	5	6	7
Thorough class study — the presentation		1	2	3	4	5	6
Recitation			1	2	3	4	5
Review and correction of written assignments				1	2	3	4
Home							
Preliminary study	1	2	3	4	5	6	7
Thorough study		1	2	3	4	5	6
Review			1	2	3	4	5
Written assignments				1	2	3	4

Better students can get much on their own before the presentation in the class. If they have prepared the text, the period of presentation is lively as all contribute and it is finished in a shorter time. This permits more text to be seen in the course of a week or month.

Moreover, students know where the difficulties are and are anxious for a solution. Note how often the students work with the text in the above schemes and that within a relatively short space of time, thus securing excellent review.

The above schemes apply to the study of texts such as the speeches of Cicero, the «Aeneid» and other more difficult Latin writings, therefore to the third and fourth years of Latin and even presentations in college classes. These schemes must be adopted if the students are doing what is called extensive reading.

Extensive reading

Once the students have completed two years of the study of Latin, the teacher should at least periodically take what is conveniently called "extensive reading". By this we mean reading more or less at the level of difficulty that is suited to the student's power in comprehending. Such readings are taken to bolster the confidence of the student in reading. Comprehension only is the purpose and only this is tested.

Extensive reading may be taken from the Scriptures, one or other of the readers on the market such as «Balbus» by G. M. Lyne (Edward Arnold Publishers, Ltd., London), «The Story of the Kings of Rome» by G. M. Edwards (Cambridge University Press), «Julia and Camilla» by Maud Reed

Teach the Latin, I pray you

(The Macmillan Company), «A First Latin Reader, A Second Latin Reader» by C. J. Vincent (Oxford University Press).

It is suggested that the teacher assign one or other story for reading that night. The next day in class he asks questions about it either orally or in a test. The answers, of course, are expected in Latin. Following this there is a general questioning about the story. Then it is assigned for reading that night in order that students may profit by the class discussion. The teacher answers any difficulties the students may have had. The text itself ordinarily is not translated in class.

Some helps for teaching difficult texts

Since classes vary in abilities and since there is variation in ability within the same class, the teacher must be prepared to explain the text in a variety of ways in order to help the student achieve comprehension. We have mentioned some of these in passing, but it is good to bring them together and to add other schemes that the teacher may use.

1 The most obvious way of treating a text whose comprehension was missed is to reread it several times while trying consciously to note the various relationships suggested by the conjunctions and other signal words. This will be treated more in detail in the next chapter.

2 When taking the text for the first time in class, it is expected that the teacher will give a digest of the story in Latin that is much simpler than the text; consequently it should be an aid to the student in comprehending the original.

3 If the digest does not help, then the teacher can give detailed help in the sections which the student found difficult. Such help would consist in defining the words, explaining the constructions, indicating agreement, and the like.

4 Diagramming can be used to help students see how the various parts of the sentences are related. Let us take an example from Caesar.

> ...sē obsidēs datūrōs quaeque imperāvisset factūrōs esse pollicitī sunt.

The teacher might thus diagram it for the student:

106

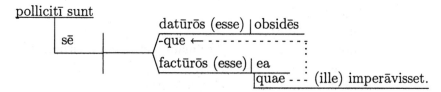

Here is another somewhat difficult sentence that might be diagrammed thus:

Hunc illī ē nāvī ēgressum, cum ad eōs Caesaris mandāta dēferret, cēperant atque in vincula conjēcerant...

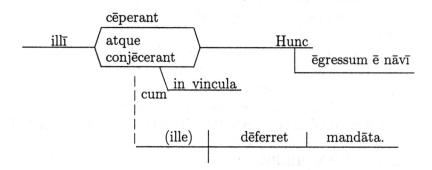

It should be noted that diagramming such as the above is not intended to teach the students to look for the subject, then the object, or any such scheme. It is used to give the student a visual picture of how the components of the sentence fit together. After the diagram has been mastered, it is essential that the student go back and reread the sentence several times until the meaning unfolds itself for him in the Latin word order.

Note that in this second diagram the text is not preserved exactly. This is good training for the student as he must make the necessary changes when he goes back to the original.

5 A very effective way of helping students to comprehend the text is to set it in sense lines. It is not necessary that the teacher know all the fine points of colometry, for it is sufficient that he put the sentence into thought units.

By way of example let us take the lengthy sentence from the second chapter of Cicero's «Pro Archia», which can cause difficulty for even the best students of Latin. Note how various parts of the text are indented in order to try to highlight the subordination.

> SED NĒ CUI VESTRUM MĪRUM ESSE VIDĒATUR
> MĒ in quaestiōne lēgitimā et

in jūdiciō pūblicō
 cum rēs agātur
  apud praetōrem populī Rōmānī, lēctissimum virum, et
  apud sevērissimōs jūdicēs,
 tantō conventū hominum ac frequentiā,
HŌC ŪTĪ GENERE DĪCENDĪ
 quod nōn modo ā cōnsuētūdine jūdiciōrum
 vērum etiam ā forēnsī sermōne abhorreat.
QUAESŌ Ā VŌBĪS
 UT IN HĀC CAUSĀ MIHI DĒTIS HANC VENIAM,
  accommodātam huic reō,
  vōbīs, quemadmodum spērō, nōn molestam
UT MĒ
 prō summō poētā atque ērudītissimō homine dīcentem
  hōc concursū hominum litterātissimōrum,
  hāc vestrā hūmānitāte,
  hōc dēnique praetōre exercente jūdicium,
PATIĀMINĪ DĒ STUDIĪS HŪMĀNITĀTIS AC LITTERĀRUM
PAULŌ LOQUĪ LĪBERIUS,
ET IN ĒJUSMODĪ PERSŌNĀ
 quae propter ōtium ac studium
 minimē in jūdiciīs perīculīsque trāctāta est,
ŪTĪ PROPE NOVŌ QUŌDAM ET INŪSITĀTŌ GENERE
DĪCENDĪ.

Once the text has been arranged as above, the teacher reads only the parts that are capitalized and makes certain through pertinent explanations that the student comprehends that much of the sentence.

Next the teacher reads the sentence and includes some of the other parts such as «in quaesitīone lēgitimā et in jūdiciō pūblicō», the «quod» clause following «veniam», then «prō summō poētā» and the part that follows. After making certain that these things are comprehended, the teacher proceeds to read the entire sentence. As the teacher reads the sentence, he can help bring out the meaning by the various intonations that he uses.

The gradual expansion of the sentence will make it easy for the student to build up the comprehension so that he can finally comprehend the entire sentence as it unfolds itself in the Latin.

After the student has comprehended the sentence, the teacher will show the balance and the interrelation of the various parts. This is done to help the student appreciate the Latin periodic structure.

The example we have chosen is a difficult one but it was used to help the teacher see that even in the fourth and fifth and sixth years of the study of Latin the sense line presentation can be of help for the comprehension of a periodic structure.

6 This scheme is taken from «Practice», edited by R. J. Knoepfle, S. J. (Loyola University Press) and is entitled "Ciceronic Algebra". It is given somewhat in detail as it is such an excellent scheme for helping students understand difficult texts.

The teacher writes on the chalkboard some algebraic nightmare like this,

$$(a - b)\}[(c - d)[e - f(gh - h)\}$$

There will be consternation on the part of the better students. Then the teacher calls upon one of them to go to the board and to correct the algebra.

The teacher then writes the following sentence on the board («Pro Archia», chapter x, «ad initium»). He then puts in the algebraic symbols as they appear here.

Quāre,   sī rēs eae   (quās gessimus) orbis terrae
regiōnibus dēfīniuntur,   cupere dēbēmus...

After asking the students what has been done, the teacher can give the following rules:

(a) Before an introductory word (like «quāre, sī, quās») put one of the algebraic signs.

(b) If you meet another introductory word BEFORE you meet a finite verb, then put another sign before it as was done before «sī» in the above sentence.

(c) The first finite verb you meet will always go with the most recent sign you made. The next verb you meet will go with the second last sign you made.

In other words the innermost subordinate clause is closed first, and you work out from there. Algebraically you close your parentheses before you close your braces.

It needs hardly be noted that this scheme does not supplant frequent reading of the sentence. But once the sentence has been analyzed, the subsequent readings will more readily convey the thought to the student.

Instead of using algebraic symbols, some teachers prefer to underline the various parts of the sentence in different colors.

Still other teachers prefer to use a solid underlining for the main clause, a wavy line for subordinate clauses, a broken line for adverbial expressions, and so forth.

7 Duplicating text explanations can be a help to the student in his home study provided that it is used judiciously.

Following the final reading of the text, the teacher distributes pages which contain in large part the explanations that were given. When a large body of text is covered in the presentation period, it is advisable to give such helps. This saves time for the teacher in class. Were he to dictate the helps, much time would be wasted that can more profitably be spent on drill and other learning procedures.

Here is something of a sample of what a teacher might give to the class after the final reading.

Vocables

ob: prep. w. acc., on account of
cōnstituī: from cōnstituō, to ground, that is, a ship
manibus: manus, manus, f.

Explanations

quod (because) followed by three reasons
1 nāvēs...cōnstituī nōn poterant
2 mīlitibus dēsiliendum et cōnsistendum erat
3 illī audācter tēla conjicerent et incitārent.

Idiom and phrases

nisi in altō: except in deep water
obtestātus deōs: praying the gods, praying to the gods

8 Distributing a rather full presentation of the explanations given during the period is good, but it can be objected that this does not sufficiently involve the student to make it an effective teaching help. That may well be true. For that reason very many teachers prefer to distribute an outline of what they will say. They permit the students to fill it in during the course of the presentation. Here is how the outline would look for the material that appeared in the previous division.

Vocables

ob _____
cōnstituī_____ manibus

Explanations

quod _____
1) _____
2) _____
3) _____

110

Idioms

nisi in altō _____

obtestātus deōs _____

Such an outline is not too distracting for the students. Moreover, it permits them to write down notes on material that appeals to them and which the teacher might not have thought worthy of notice.

The outline is also excellent for helping the beginning teacher make certain that he covers in class the materials he prepared. It is also something of a deterrent to the one or other student who might wish to ask questions just to make the time go with the avowed hidden purpose of not having so much to study that night. He knows that if he asks too many questions the teacher might not finish the work and then the student would himself that night need to complete the outline.

9 Translation into English is to be the last method that the teacher uses in order to help students grasp the message of a certain text. Ordinarily he will give the student an idiomatic translation because more than likely this is sufficient to clear up the difficulty. Should the failure to comprehend persist after the idiomatic translation, then a more literal one may be given in order to show how the idea is expressed in Latin. The teacher should invariably point out the contrast (if there is one) between the way the Latins view a thing and the way those who speak English see it.

Use of translations by the students

As long as the standard authors are used for reading in the Latin class, teachers must face the problem of the use of translations by the students. The paperbacks have but added to the difficulty since these can be purchased so cheaply.

In the early stages of learning Latin it would seem that translations of the connected discourse should not be in the hands of the students. It will seriously interfere with the efforts that the student will make to comprehend what he is reading. Having read the English translation will also destroy the effectiveness of exercises in oral comprehension.

It is important, therefore, that the first-year teacher use materials for which translations are not available. Teachers should be aware of the translations that are handed down to other students. Hence, if at all possible, the alert teacher makes certain that he never uses the same material two years in succession.

111

In second year and thereafter translations will do harm so far as training in comprehension is concerend but the harm can be minimized if students know how to properly use translations. The teacher must then from time to time indicate how to use translations with profit.

If students are working, for example, with a speech of Cicero, they might read the entire speech in English. Then as the class progresses through the speech, they should, prior to their study, read the entire section of the speech, for example, the «cōnfirmātiō» or «argūmentātiō». Students should then put the translation aside and read the Latin carefully and try to get the thoughts as they are given in the Latin. Students should be warned not to consult the translation if they miss the thought but should rather reread several times. If after five or six readings students do not comprehend the thought, then they might again consult the English. In no case should they work with both English and Latin at the same time.

The use of interlinears will effectively prevent the student from ever learning to comprehend the Latin as Latin. The best way to prevent their use is to make certain that students are not reading beyond their abilities. But since this is not always possible, the teacher can prevent the need for interlinears by giving adequate explanation and help during the presentation. All too often teachers have forced students to use these methods by giving reading that was far too difficult. Remove the student's feeling of need for such devious helps and he will not invest in them.

If the text is taught properly, there will no longer be the problem of translations made by the students and handed down to those who follow them. Since translation is no longer the order of the day, students will not be able to make them. And this is desirable, for the translations by students frequently helped to perpetuate errors.

The use of outlines

If the class is reading a long work such as an oration of Cicero, then it is quite essential that students frequently consult the outline. This is necessary if they are to see how the various parts fit together. Even in the teaching of Vergil it is necessary that the teacher frequently show the students where they are in the the story. Giving a brief digest each day of what preceded, or asking for this from the students, will make certain that students build up a continuous story rather than a mere series of episodes.

Should it be that the text the teacher is using does not give an outline, then it is up to the teacher to make one, duplicate it, and give it to the students. The various divisions should indicate the lines that are covered in the text. This small help is a big help for the students.

When studying Vergil's «Aeneid» students should be encouraged to read Church's «Aeneid for Boys and Girls». Such a simplified version helps them to understand the poem.

A plea

Since teachers have developed a fine appreciation for the uniform grammatical usage of Caesar, the superb rhetoric of Cicero, and the humanity of Vergil, they are desirous of sharing this with their students. And this is as it should be. But have they not in their enthusiasm been trying to induce this appreciation in the students before they are ready for it?

Give the students, therefore, Latin that they can understand even if it means that such Latin is definitely on the simple side so far as the teacher is concerned. In the early grades English students are not expected to be able to read and appreciate Webster's superb orations. So why should we feel that such a scheme will work in Latin? Give the students, therefore, simpler Latin. Then we can hope that eventually we can bring the student to the point where he can read the masters and enjoy them because he can comprehend them.

Perhaps teachers and authors of texts have forced the students into what has been jeeringly called "the hunt and peck" reading of the masters because they too soon gave reading that was of interest to and could be comprehended by the teacher only.

Chapter 6

Teaching the reading of Latin

Reading Latin as Latin is a highly complex skill and this skill is acquired only after considerable practice. To make a list of all the skills that constitute reading Latin as Latin is probably impossible if we consider the persons and their backgrounds, their interest or lack of it, their memories and general understanding, and even their physical abilites, such as correct eye movements. However, there are certain fundamentals that can be acquired, and it is our purpose to consider some of these fundamentals in this chapter. These fundamentals will concern themselves with methods of trying to help students achieve the goal — reading Latin as Latin.

In order to read Latin as Latin we must know two things, the structure of the language and the lexical items.

The structural elements

The structure will concern itself with

1 declinable elements such as the nouns, pronouns, adjectives, cases, gender, and number

2 inflectional elements such as the verbs with their mood, voice, tense, person, and number

3 indeclinable elements such as adverbs, prepositions, cojunctions, and interjections.

In the declinable and inflectional elements we will find smaller elements that will signal meaning such as the «-ba» for the imperfect tense and the «-a» for the present subjunctive. These signal meaning but they never appear alone but only as part of the entire form. Besides the small elements that form part of the word, we will also find combinations of words whose constituant parts can be used independently. For example, «locūtus erat» is a specialized form of the verb but both «locūtus» and «erat» can appear alone in a sentence and convey meaning.

    4 the way all these elements are combined to make meaningful expressions. This we normally call the grammar of the language. In this grammar part we will find the five linguistic functions into which all the declinable, indeclinable, and inflectional elements fit.

"The nominal element"[1] will concern itself with all words, phrases, and clauses which fulfill the subjective, objective, or appositional functions, that is,

1) nouns and substantives in the nominative, vocative, or accusative cases (with reservations in this latter case)

2) pronouns in the same cases

3) infinitives

4) gerunds

5) supines

6) indirect statements

7) noun clauses — indirect questions, quod (the fact that), quōminus, quīn, ut, nē

    The adnominal (adjectival) functional class includes all words, phrases, and clauses which modify, define, or limit units in the nominal class, such as

1) adjectives

2) gerundives

3) nouns in the genitive case

4) adjectival prepositional phrases

---

[1]This analysis is taken from «Handbook for Latin Teachers», pages 16–18, a private document for the New York Province of the Society of Jesus, 1959.

5) relative clauses — simple, purpose, result, characteristic, causal

The verbal function includes all those words whose function it is to indicate

1) action

2) occurrence

3) mode of being

The adverbial function includes all words, phrases, and clauses which modify, define, or limit verbs, such as

1) adverbs

2) adverbial prepositional phrases

3) nouns in the ablative and dative cases

4) adverbial clauses — conditional, concessive, causal, purpose, result, temporal

The directional function contains the connectives used to indicate relations in a sentence. Such are «cum, dum, quōminus», and the like. These words especially should be taught as functionally directing the subordination of thought and not as sources of syntactical debate, for example, not "a cum-causal clause" but "a clause which gives the reason for the main occurrence."

The lexical elements

In order for a student to be able satisfactorily to read the Latin as Latin it will be supposed that in addition to the structure of the language he also knows the meaning of at least eight or nine out of every ten words that he meets in the text.

If the student knows at least the above proportion of words, then he should be able ordinarily to conclude to the meaning of the tenth word unless perhaps it is some very technical or abstract word. Students do this rather satisfactorily in English and it should also be able to be done in Latin.

Just as our vocabulary in English grows for the most part through reading and usage, so in Latin will the vocabulary grow. Just as in English we need occasionally to use the dictionary to get the exact meaning of a word, so in Latin, too, there must be an occasional reference to the dictionary.

Simultaneity in learning

The student may know the morphology of a language, he may know its structure, and he may know the lexical items and yet he may fail to have the skill of reading Latin as Latin. Why? Because these things were learned in a disparate way, that is, he learned first the morphology by paradigm, then the grammar by set rules (to express purpose use «ut» and the subjunctive), and finally the vocabulary.

If he learned these elements and never learned their interrelation, the student will not be able to read Latin. And it does seem that this depart-mentalized type of instruction has been used all too frequently in classrooms.

Young children do not learn their native language in such a disparate way. They learn all the elements at the same time: morphology, grammar, and lexicon. Neither do they memorize rules of any kind. They simply hear, comprehend, and imitate. The seeing does not ordinarily come until they go to school where they learn the alphabet and how these small elements are put together to form words that in turn combine into sentences.

Since the students who wish to learn Latin are much older, they need not learn as young children. The process can be speeded up. After much hearing and valiant attempts to compherend and after difficult and halting imitation, the student is in a position to organize what he has seen and heard. Then he needs but reduce this knowledge to an automatic reaction. Once this automatic reaction has been established and the students have noted the similarities in the expressions, they can venture on their own to produce the language.

This production of the language will be slow and halting and full of errors but this should not worry the teacher. He should give the corrections but give them as we give them to a smaller child. Small children soon recognize that the past is signalled by «-ed» in English, for they hear it so often. Then upon occasion they will venture to produce this on their own. The results will be something like "I broked the train". Structurally the child was correct, but parents will tell the child to use "I broke the train." This is one of the many usages that do not follow the rule. So it is with Latin students. If they have ventured into the production of the language and have followed correct structural principles, then they should be praised for this; then the teacher should give the correct usage, not by way of rebuke but by way of information.

Rather young children have mastered most of the elements of structure in their native language, but even as old people they will continue to progress in the learning of vocabulary. Therefore it would seem that, since we are dealing with older children who can readily recognize common elements, the structure of Latin should be able to be mastered certainly in two years of study.

Elements of training to read

To train students to read Latin involves much hearing, valiant attempts at comprehension of what they hear, the organization of what they hear into meaningful patterns, and finally imitation which is the production of the language. Once these steps have been taken, the student is in a position to begin to read Latin as Latin.

The first element then is that of much hearing. Even from the earliest stages in the learning of Latin there must be constant emphasis on oral work. That is why the teacher should read TO the students. And that is why it is good practice to have the students listen to tapes both those that drill the structure and those that simply relate the study. The use of as much Latin as possible in the ordinary classroom situations provides auditional practice in hearing and in comprehending.

The second element, that of attempts at comprehension of what they hear, is very important. A young child knows after a short time that if he wishes a drink he must say at least "water." The thirst is the stimulus that makes the youngster remember and express the word. Students who wish to learn Latin have this desire as the stimulus to fix in their memories the forms and the meaning which will permit them to understand what is said. This desire to comprehend, coupled with an abundant hearing as outlined in the first step, promotes a familiarity with the language that should have comprehension as the immediate goal and imitation as the final goal.

The third element, that of organizing what they hear into patterns, can readily enough be done by older students under the expert direction of the teacher. Once the students have met a construction and seen it in use, the teacher can elicit from the students the conditions under which the usage operates; these conditions can be organized into rules based on observation. For example, after seeing the frequent use of an accusative and a dative after the verb «dō», they can readily conclude that the person to whom something is given is put into the dative case. Then when they see a sentence such as «Caesar lībertātem populō largītus est» they can see that it is a construction similar to that which follows the verb «dō».

The fourth element, imitation, concerns itself first of all with imitating the sounds of the language. They hear the teacher pronounce the word, and then they attempt to do so. They hear him phrase words in a certain way and read with a certain intonation and they attempt to do likewise.

The imitation will progress to the point where they will attempt to produce the language on their own. This will be halting and it will lag considerably behind their power to comprehend, but that is as it should be because imitation means ultimately production of the language — a production that is based on automatic responses to stimuli. This automatic respone will not be achieved until the student has heard and comprehended and imitated to the point of over learning.

Imitation and production are fostered by hearing and comprehending. The student, for instance, hears a sentence on the tape and comprehends it. He then changes the sentence in accord with the directions given. At first the changing is done slowy and deliberately but as more practice is had, the changes tend to become automatic and the comprehension is generally assured at the same time.

If the work is being done in class, the student hears a question about the passage put to him by the teacher. He comprehends the question. In the early stages of learning the language, the student will slowly make the changes that are requried in the answer, but later after much practice the student will do the changing without thinking, since he will be intent upon the thought.

Once the students can effect changes in the language automatically they are in a position to read and comprehend the Latin directly and the only stumbling block that might remain will be the lack of lexical information.

Reading is a matter of interpreting signals

If one wishes to understand a language he must be acquainted with the signals. That is why at the very beginning of the study of Latin the student is told that a word ending in «-t» will be the verb and a word ending in «-m» will be the object. This is the student's first introduction to the use of signals in the Latin. Such signals can be drilled without the benefit of meaning.

Knowledge of the signals, though, is not sufficient. This knowledge must be reduced to practice and for that reason the student must do much reading that will involve the signals. The reading will fix the signals and secure an automatic reaction.

Since any language contains a multiplicity of signals, it would be utter folly to give all the signals at one time. The student must be introduced to only a very few signals at any one time. Nor should other signals be introduced until the earlier ones have been mastered to a high degree. The signals are mastered through reading and through pattern or drill practices.

In the teaching of Latin, teachers should do their best to group the signals, and this is not difficult since Latin is a multiple-signal language. By that we mean that Latin uses more than one signal, for example, in the plural. «Nautae bonī maria omnia nāvigant» contains three signals for the plural, «-ae, -ī, and -nt». Hence the plurals of nouns, adjectives, and verbs fit together into something of a unit that can be taught simultaneously.

Signals should be contrasted, too, in order to secure accurate knowledge. The "a" of the subjunctive and the "e" of the future are good examples of contrast in signals.

To teach the students how to read Latin as Latin resolves itself into a proper interpretation of the signals. In the beginning the signals must be relatively simple, but as progress is made, their complexity can be increased until all the signals are learned and automatic responses are acquired. It is at this point that the student has learned to read Latin as Latin.

In the following pages we propose to look at some of the methods that teachers may use to help students interpret the signals correctly in order to arrive at an automatic response. This treatment will necessarily not be exhaustive since learning situations are so peculiarly individual in aspect. Since reading involves the interpretation of signals and these were studied in previous chapters, there will be some repetition in this chapter, but it will be pointed toward the teaching of reading.

Contrast in signals

Native speakers of English have learned a definite set of signals that convey meaning. Now when they approach the study of Latin, some of these signals will have little if any meaning in the new language. The new language then can contrast with the native. Where these contrasts occur, the students must not only be aware of the fact but they must strive to put aside their inclination to interpret the new in the light of the old. Let's list the contrasts to which the native speaker of English who is learning Latin is subject.

Position versus inflection

English signals meaning by position whereas Latin indicates meaning by the endings of the word. "The boy hit the man" is radically changed in meaning if we change the word order to "The man hit the boy." «Puer epistolam scrīpsit» can be written in a variety of ways so far as word order is concerned but the meaning will always be the same.

Noun inflection

English has only a vestige of anything like a case system. "Boy" can be used as subject or object of a sentence without change in form. "Boys" is plural, and "boy's" and "boys'" indicate possession. Latin, though, has several cases and each is clearly distinguished by a modification of the ending of the noun.

Because of this lack of signals in English and the large number of signals relatively speaking in Latin, the student must strive to acquire a functional knowledge of what each modification of the noun signals.

Verb inflection

In English there is only a vestige of inflection for the verb. "Walk" is present, and "walked" is past; and in the conjugation of the present only the third singular changes form by adding "s," he walks. For the future tense we make use of auxiliaries. But Latin contrasts heavily with the English since both the pronoun and the auxiliary are indicated by modifications of the ending of the verb. «Amābat» has the modifications "t" and "ba" to indicate the person and the time.

In English, when we form the plural of a noun, we modify the ending in a number of ways: boy and boys, knife and knives, lady and ladies.

Students then are prepared for changes in Latin for the plural of nouns. But they are hardly prepared for the way Latin builds the verb. English starts with the particular such as I, then gives the time element, for example, was, and then the verb. Latin does the reverse for they give the verb stem and then modify it for time, person, and voice as in the form «amā-bi-t-ur».

Contrast in mood

Were it not that our English grammar reflects much Latin grammar we probably would not have thought of the idea of mood in English. Because English really does not have a subjunctive mood, the student who tries to learn Latin must learn a whole new category for expression. Teachers can be of assistance by giving a general notion of what the mood does for Latin, how it affects the idea, and what the possibilities are for expression. Thus if the student sees the form «nāviget» he should know that it can express several ideas, a wish, a softened command, or it may be a verb in a dependent clause such as purpose.

Contrast in number of signals

Latin has a far greater number of signals for the same item than has English and consequently it should be easier to read Latin, whereas conversely it should be more difficult to produce Latin than English. Teachers therefore will be patient with the student who misses an agreement or two when writing Latin.

As an example let us study the number of signals for number in these sentences.

Puerī bonī quī litterās discunt sapientēs fīunt.

Good boys who study literature become wise.

The Latin has six distinct signals for the plural: the «-ī» ending of «puerī, bonī, quī», the «-ēs» ending of «sapientēs», and the «-nt» endings of «discunt» and «fīunt».

The English has only one signal for the plural, «boys». «Good» and «wise» can be used with boy or boys, «who» is the same form whether referring to singular or plural, «study» and «become» change only if they are used in the third singular and consequently these two forms do not necessarily indicate plurality.

Using these same two sentences, we can contrast the number of signals for case. If we include the predicate adjective «sapientēs» the Latin sentence signals the nominative case four times. The English on the other hand signals the subjective case only twice, and if we consider form only, it signals the subjective case only once. «Boys» can be subjective or objective case depending upon its position in the sentence. «Who» can be subjective only since the objective form is whom.

What the teacher can do

When two languages contrast in the ways we just indicated, how can the teacher help the student toward a reading of the new language? First of all he can present the contrast clearly to the student. This will prevent needless searching on the part of the student for the reasons for things and forestalls confusion.

After the teacher has presented the contrast, he must make certain that the student is thoroughly drilled in the new signal for meaning. For this reason modern texts present oral drill that is designed to secure an automatic reaction to the signal in a much shorter time than can be secured from writing.

Drills are likely to be artificial and for that reason the teacher introduces connected discourse as soon as possible. This reading material must be suited to the level of the student, that is, it must not make use of other signals than the ones with which he is familiar.

But in the reading the teacher must insist upon frequent rereading. Since he has used English as little as possible in the presentation the student usually does not have his native language to rely upon for meaning. In such circumstances the frequent rereading strengthens the comprehension of the signals, and if the text is memorized because of the frequent reading, then it is hoped that the signals too will be memorized.

New signals should be introduced against the pattern of those which the student already knows. This makes for a constant blending and a constant strengthening of the old while learning the new.

The five classes of nouns

If during the first class the teacher would tell the students that there are five classes of nouns and that each class has six forms for the singular and six for the plural, there can be no doubt that the student would despair of ever being able to remember and interpret such a large number of signals.

If on the other hand the teacher during the first few weeks of instruction has given the simple instruction that «-m» signals the direct object, «-t» the verb, and all other words are subjects, he can use nouns indiscriminately and the student can master the structure and with a little help can comprehend also.

Once the student has learned these signals well, the teacher can begin to classify the nouns according to declensions. If he takes the classification step by step and drills as he progresses through the signals, he will enable the student to keep building his ability to read Latin as Latin. As he progresses through the declensions, the emphasis should be on the similarity of endings rather than on the dissimilarities, for example, the similarity of endings for the dative and ablative plural.

The five classes of verbs

If we count the «-iō» verbs there can be said to be five classes of verbs. Just as in the case of nouns, the teacher can through the initial stages of the teaching of Latin use any verb provided that he has given simple signals such as «-t» for the third singular, and «-nt» for the third plural. He can even make use of the imperfect tense since it has the «-ba» signal. And the future can also be taught with but a few more signals.

Once the students has learned to react to these signals in his reading, the teacher can proceed to complete the various tenses by giving the signals for the various persons in the active, and then later those for the passive.

After the students have learned to interpret these signals in their reading, the teacher can bring order into the verbs by showing the students how to classify them.

If the teacher presented only a few signals at a time and then drilled them in pattern practices or drill masters, or/and in reading, there is no reason why the student, if he works conscientiously, should not continue to interpret the signals correctly as he proceeds. He will then be building his ability to read. Throughout there must be emphasis on the oral drill by forcing students to comprehend what the teacher says or reads to them.

Assignment to genders

For native speakers of English the arbitrary assignment to gender classifications can be a stumbling block not so much in the reading as in the production of the language. This classification is presented when there is question of teaching the adjective.

If at first the teacher presents the adjectives of the first and second declensions, then drills with all types of nouns until the student readily recognizes the agreement, then he will have given invauable aid to the student in his efforts at understanding the Latin as Latin.

Third declension adjectives can be learned along with third declension nouns or immediately after learning the nouns. If again the presentation moves forward slowly and with abundant drill, the reading habits of the student will be strengthened.

Simple rules for determining gender in the third declension should be given in order to assure students and to help them learn rapidly.

Prepositions

The native speaker of English is likely to be surprised when he meets Latin prepositions and finds that they are followed by nouns in special cases. Ideally the student should meet them in his reading before studying them formally.

As in the case of assignment to gender for nouns, so the prepositions with their special cases will not provide a problem for the reading since the author will use the correct case after the preposition. However, it would seem that reading ability can be increased if the students know in general what cases a preposition takes because they will not be surprised at the modification of the noun that follows the preposition.

It has been found helpful for teachers to give a listing of the prepositions that take the ablative. He can then tell them that all other prepositions take the accusative. Students then seem to feel that prepositions are no longer a mystery and this feeling of confidence is a help in their reading. Teachers might wish to give a ditty such as this:

> Put the ablative with dē,[2]
> cum and cōram, ab and ē (ex),
> sine, tenus, prō, and prae.
> In and sub with the ablative case
> Tell about a resting place.

Adverbs and pronouns

Once the student has learned the formation of adverbs, he will have no difficulty with them in his reading as they follow the English usage rather closely in that they precede the verb. The only problem will be a lexical one.

Pronouns too will be understood rather easily in the reading provided that the student knows the various forms for the various cases.

Teachers need, therefore, not spend much time with these when instructing the students in the reading of Latin.

Multiple meanings

Acquaintance, classification, drill, reading — these four steps can be followed in the teaching of reading when there is question of signals that have but one meaning, such as the «-iter» ending of the adverb.

There are in Latin, however, many signals whose meaning is multiple and the precise meaning for an individual context must be determined from the circumstances in which the signal appears. For example, the conjuction «ut» may have several meanings depending upon the way it is used. These words of multiple meaning cause confusion for the beginner in the reading of Latin and he must be given help in learning to interpret, for example, the meaning of «cum» when he meets it in his reading. In order to teach him what to do in a given circumstance the teacher will acquaint the student with the principle of expectancy.

---

[2]The teacher is referred to «The Gateway to Latin Composition», page 31, by E. A. Sonnenschein, C. S. Wilkinson, and W. A. Odell Oxford at the Clarendon Press, 1931.

126

Expectancy

Because Latin is a language of multiple signals, we can at any point in a sentence more easily know what to expect in the remainder of the sentence. For that reason the reading of Latin should be easier than the reading of English. Let us work for a bit with these two sentences.

Puerī bonī quī litterās discunt sapientēs fīunt.

Good boys who study literature become wise.

Suppose we consider the first word in the Latin sentence. We have three possibilities according to the signal at the end of the word: nominative plural, vocative, and genitive singular; but since we know that the nominative is used far more frequently than the genitive or the vocative combined, the teacher would indicate to the student that he should think of such a dubious form as being the nominative. Because he judges that it is the nominative, he will expect a verb that ends in «-nt». Occasionally such a prejudgment will not be verified in the sentence and in that case he must simply change his reaction.

The second word of the Latin sentence, «bonī», tells the alert reader that the «bonī» is either nominative plural or genitive singular. But since there is no noun in the vicinity that a genitive could modify, the prejudgment that the form «puerī» is nominative is verified. The student then knows for certain that the verb will end in «-nt».

The first word of the English sentence tells the reader nothing with regard to number except that if it were singular it should normally be preceded by the article «a» but this need not necessarily be so since we have sentences such as these, "Good sailing can help us weather the storm. Good hunting is sometimes a matter of luck."

Neither does this first word in the English sentence tell the reader definitely whether he is dealing with a noun or an adjectives since there are sentences such as this in English, "Good as he is, his talents will never be recognized by his peers."

As for the case of the word "good" which begins the English sentence, the reader cannot be sure that it might not be the case of address or the beginning of an expletive such as is had in "Good fighting, men!"

If in the teaching of reading Latin our consideration is restricted to the agreement of nouns, adjectives, and verbs, then Latin should be easier to read than English since Latin has many more signals that show agreement. Hence students readily enough learn how to predict what will follow in a Latin sentence, that is, they know what to expect in the verb when the subject is plural.

127

Expectancy and subordinating conjuctions

If we further consider the idea of expectancy and apply it to Latin and English, we find that in the matter of conjuctions, especially the subordinating ones, Latin offers the reader a great deal more trouble than does English. And this contrast between the languages stems not so much from the difference in mood as from the varied usages that Latin has for one and the same conjuction. Let us consider some typical subordinating conjuctions in the two languages.

If we look up a standard Latin grammar, we will find these usages for the conjuction «ut».

1 Purpose

Pugnat ut vincat.

> He fights in order to conquer.
> He fights to conquer.
> He's fighting with a view to conquering.
> He's fighting in order that he may conquer.

2 Result

Sīc vītam ēgit ut omnēs eum laudārent.

> He so lived that men would praise him.
> His life was such that men praised it.
> His life was so exemplary that all men praised him.
> His exemplary life merited the praise of all.
> Such was his life that it won the praise of all.
> (Note that in Latin there is usually a signal such as «sīc» indicating that a result clause will follow.)

3 Time

Ut hoc vīdit equitātum praemīsit.

> When he saw this he sent the cavalry on ahead.
> After seeing this he sent the cavalry on ahead.
> Seeing this he sent the cavalry on ahead.

4 Concession

Ut bonus sit, sapiēns nōn est.

> Granted that he's good, still he's not wise.
> We can concede that he's good; yet he's not a philosopher.
> Oh, he's good all right, but he's not wise.
> Despite his goodness, he's no philosopher.
> Even though we grant you that he's wise, yet we cannot admit that

he is a philosopher.

5 Conditional clause of comparison

Mihi loqueris ut sī fūr essem.

> You speak as if I were a thief.
> Your speaking thus makes me out a thief.
> Your speech would convict me of thievery.
> Your speech takes for granted that I'm a thief.

6 Comparison

Sīc est ut dīxī.

> It's as I said.
> It's as I said it was.
> In this instance my opinion is borne out.
> I was right all along.
> (Note that the «sīc» can be used with clauses of comparison.
> This usage though is rather rare.)

7 Noun clause of result

Effēcit ut pōns fieret.

> He saw to it that the bridge was built.
> His action brought about the building of the bridge.
> His action resulted in the building of a bridge.

8 Noun clause of purpose

Persuāsit ut dē fīnibus exīrent.

> He persuaded them to leave their territory.
> His persuasion effected their departure.
> He persuaded them to depart.
> His influence was such that they left their country.
> He influenced their departure.

9 After verbs of fearing

Timeō ut veniat.

> I'm afraid he won't come.
> I fear he's not going to come.
> I'm afraid his coming is too much to expect.

A student who is familiar with English only would hardly expect that the great variety of English sentences that we have just seen could ever be expressed in another language in such a way that they would all have a common subordinating conjunction.

The varied uses of «ut » in Latin will definitely cause a student great difficulty in reading because this conjuction can be used with the indicative or with the subjunctive and in the subjunctive there are both noun and adverbial clauses. However, there are some helps that the teacher can give the student which enable him to interpret the signal.

Environment

Besides the context there are certain environmental conditions that indicate to the alert reader what kind of construction will come in the remainder of the sentence. These the student must be aware of if he wishes to anticipate the meaning of «ut».

1 Adverbial result clauses will usually have a signal in the main clause such as «sīc, tantus» and so forth.

2 Noun clauses of result will usually follow expressions such as «accidit, sequitur, ita fit, fīerī potest» and so forth.

3 Noun clauses of purpose will usually appear in the environment of verbs like «postulō, dēcernō, persuādeō, optō, imperō» and so forth.

Some teachers give their students this mnemonic scheme:

With ask, command, advise, and strive,
By «ut» translate the infinitive;
But never be this rule forgot
Place «nē» for «ut» when there's a not [in English.]
Exceptīs: volō, nōlō, mālō, cupiō et sinō et prohibeō.

This scheme is more suited for the writing of Latin, but it also provides the student with a knowledge of what to expect after such verbs when he is reading.

4 Verbs of fearing will be followed by «ut» when the subordinate clause contains a hidden wish.

It is true that Latin word order is not rigid and so in some instances the clause introduced by «ut» may precede the signals indicated above, but this is rather rare.

Mood

Once the student sees the mood of the verb that is used with «ut», he can at once eliminate some of the meanings of this conjunction, namely, the temporal and comparison usages. This usually is not too much help though for the interpretation of «ut» since the verb comes so close to the end of the clause. If it is a short clause, then this might be a help in the reading.

Frequency of occurrence

The use of frequency tables is always fraught with danger since unwarranted conclusions might be drawn. In the interpretation of «ut» it would seem that we should make use of a frequency tabulation in order to make something of a prejudgment when an «ut» occurs in our reading. The following figures are based on the selections from Caesar, Cicero, and Vergil that are customarily read in high school, as well as the «Pro Archia» and «De Lege Manilia». This, it might be remarked, is a sizeable portion of Latin literature though it must be admitted that not all types of writing are represented. For example, the letters of Cicero might affect our findings but not to such an extent that we cannot help students to learn to interpret the correct usage of «ut».

Here are some rather reliable figures for the frequency of the various uses of «ut».[3]

	Caesar	Cicero	Vergil	Total	
Noun clauses of purpose	82	34	36	152	235[4]
Adverbial clauses of purpose	57	31	30	118	
Noun clauses of result	29	34	1	64	182[5]
Adverbial clauses of result	53	65	0	118	

---

[3] «The Syntax of High School Latin», pp. 9 sq., edited by Lee Byrne. University of Chicago Press, 1909.

[4] The total is given as 235 since under purpose, without distinction of kind, the «ne» is shown as being used 14–11–10 times («The Syntax of High School Latin», p. 17)

[5] There was no separate tabulation for «ut nōn».

131

Comprasion (all conjunctions)	1		16	18
Temporal	1	1	14	16
Fearing (no distinction between «ut» and «nē»)	5	5	2	12
Concession	1	17	5	23

The figures on the use of «ut» are such that we can formulate some rather definite conclusions which should be a help to one who is reading Latin.

When reading we shall generally interpret «ut» as involving purpose, because the only other usage that is rather common is result; but result usually has a signal in the main clause such as «sīc, tantus» and so forth. Verbs of fearing usually precede the «ut».

For reading purpose there is no need to distinguish between noun clauses and adverbial clauses of purpose. Even if we were to translate there would be no need for distinction since both use the infinitive in English, "He did this to save himself. He ordered them to come."

Purpose and result account for 85 per cent of the usages of «ut». Of those that remain, comparison with its 18 instances includes all conjunctions so that the «ut» will not occur too frequently; the temporal usage of «ut» occurs but 16 times and since both of these usages involve the indicative mood, the reader can readily enough interpret their usage, at least when he arrives at the end of the clause.

There remain the 23 instances of concession, but even here the figures do not list «ut» separately from «quamquam» and similar conjunctions. So the use of «ut» in concession is definitely rare.

The 12 occurrences after verbs of fearing do not distinguish between the positive and negative conjunctions; hence we cannot know how often «ut» is used, but it is not likely to be much more than six times.

How to interpret «ut»

When reading Latin we interpret «ut» to mean purpose except when there is a clear signal for result in the main clause. Vaguely in the back of our minds we keep the possibility that «ut» may take the indicative and express time; and rarely will it express the idea of concession. Cicero occasionally uses «ut» meaning "how" to introduce an indirect question. Students will rarely meet «ut» in comparisons.

Acquiring facility in interpreting «ut»

In order to acquire facility in determining which usage of «ut» is involved in a Latin sentence there is need of much reading. Of course, in our reading we normally do not stop at the «ut» in order to formally try to determine what usage to expect. In normal reading the eye goes along rapidly, so much so that generally there is no doubt at all about the usage of «ut» as in conditional comparison where the «sī» normally follows immediately after the «ut». If the meaning of «ut» is not thus easily signaled, then the reader makes a tentative judgment as to its meaning (purpose) — a judgment, it is true, that may sometimes have to be revised when we get to the end of the clause or the sentence.

When teaching students how to read Latin, the teacher needs occasionally to formally go through the process with the students in order to make them aware of the kind of thinking which will help them in the comprehension of the text. When reading a text to the class, the teacher should occasionally stop when he comes to an «ut» and ask the student to indicate what can be expected in the remainder of the sentence as well as what usage of «ut» is involved.

Pedagogically it would be unsound for the teacher to present all the uses of «ut» at one time. These should be presented at different times in order to give the student an opportunity in his reading to become familiar with the meanings of this conjunction that he already knows. When he has mastered one usage, then more meanings can be given to him until at last he has mastered all of them. Once he is familiar with all the usages, the teacher should, of course, give a summary presentation in order that the student may be able to organize his knowledge.

Once the student knows all the usages of «ut», his continued reading will be the best practice for achieving mastery in the interpretation of this conjunction.

Most Latin grammars, it may be remarked, are of little help to a student when he wishes to learn to read Latin. When the student meets a conjunction like «ut» in his reading and consults a grammar, he will find it listed in many places and under different types of clauses. If grammars would list all the usages of «ut» in one place, the student would find it easier to determine which usage is involved when he consults the grammar.

The conjunction «cum»

Another very familiar word in the reading of Latin is «cum». It has many usages and students must be taught what to do when they meet this conjunction or preposition in their reading. To help give the student this information we shall rely on a study of the uses of «cum» that appeared many years ago.[6]

«Cum» as preposition

The use of «cum» as a preposition will usually be rather evident to a student when he reads because immediately following it there will be an adjective and noun, or at least a noun, and if macrons are used in the printing of the text the student can recognize the ablative form of the noun without difficulty. It is possible of course to have sentences such as these, «Cum mīlitibus occīsīs Caesar abiisset, hostēs gāvīsī sunt; Cum aquā submersus est, omnēs luxērunt, » in which the ablative immediately following the «cum» has no connection with the «cum» but such situations are very rare.

«Cum» as a conjunction

Before we draw any conclusions as to the relative importance of the usages of «cum» and what usage we should keep in the forefront when reading, let us look at some figures. The following statistics are drawn from Caesar, Cicero, and Vergil. The table shows the number of times each is used.

	Caesar	Cicero	Vergil	Total
Temporal	137	92	68	297
Causal	47	34	0	81
Concessive	12	28	1	41

The following tables indicate the tenses for each of the usages of «cum».

---

[6] «The Syntax of High School Latin», pp. 12, 13, and 17.

«Cum» and the indicative (temporal)

Present	3	7	24	34
Imperfect	1	11	2	14
Future	0	5	4	9
Perfect	3	15	21	39
Pluperfect	4	2	2	8
Future perfect	0	0	3	3
				107

«Cum» and the subjunctive

Temporal

Present	0	1	0	1
Imperfect	73	25	12	110
Perfect	0	1	0	1
Pluperfect	53	25	0	78
				190

Causal

Present	2	25	0	27
Imperfect	37	4	0	41
Perfect	1	5	0	6
Pluperfect	7	0	0	7
				81

Concessive

Present	1	6	0	7
Imperfect	7	11	1	19
Perfect	1	6	0	7
Pluperfect	3	5	0	8
				41

«Cum» with the indicative occurs 107 times (35 per cent), while it occurs 312 times with the subjunctive (65 per cent).

Conclusions from the above tables

1 «Cum» and the subjunctive will occur three times as often as «cum» the indicative.

2 «Cum» temporal and the indicative will use the present or perfect tense 68 per cent of the time.

3 «Cum» temporal and the subjunctive will use the imperfect or plu-perfect tense 99 per cent of the time.

4 «Cum» causal will be followed by the present or imperfect tenses of the subjunctive 84 per cent of the time.

5 «Cum» concessive will more frequently be followed by the imperfect tense of the subjunctive, but other tenses also are used.

Interpreting «cum» when reading

The student can be told that when he is reading Latin he can make use of the following for the interpretation of «cum» as a conjunction.

1 When you meet a «cum» in your reading, your first reaction should be that of time (when). «Cum» meaning "when" occurs twice as often as "cause" and "concession" combined; and "cause" occurs twice as often as "concession". Interpret «cum» in this order: time, cause, concession.

2 When you meet a «cum» in your reading your first reaction should be not only that of the indication of time, but also that this time will involve the subjunctive mood. The subjunctive occurs three times as often as the indicative.

3 When you meet a «cum» in your reading and it is followed by the subjunctive mood, your first reaction is still that of "time" since this usage occurs about 60 per cent of the time; "cause" will occur about 26 per cent of the time, while "concession" will be met but 13 per cent of the time.

By way of summary the student can be told that when he meets a «cum» in his reading and knows that it is a conjunction (no noun in the vicinty the ablative case), he should interpret it as meaning "after" or "when" and expect the verb in the subjunctive mood. Should such an interpretation not fit the context, then he should interpret it as expressing "cause" or possibly "concession."

Relative clauses

When the student meets a word that introduces a relative clause, what can he expect? If we can rely upon the frequency counts,[7] he can be told that relative clauses in their adjectival usage will occur at the rate of four times with the indicative for every occurrence with the subjunctive (1223–268).

---

[7] «The Syntax of High School Latin», p. 12.

Relative clauses with the subjunctive will more often be characteristic clauses (152). The other usages are: purpose (67), cause (32), result (17).

«Dum»

The conjunction «dum»[8] is followed four times as often by the indicative as by the subjunctive. In the indicative the present tense is used twice as often as all other tenses combined.

Students should then react to «dum» as indicating an action going on at the same time as another, and they should expect that a present tense of the indicative will appear at the end of the clause.

«Quod» meaning "because"

«Quod» meaning "because"[9] will appear twice as often with the indicative as with the subjunctive. This conjunction will also appear more often than «quia, quoniam», and «quandō».

So far as reading is concerned students should be aware of the relative and causal usages of «quod». If no neuter antecedent has appeared, then interpret «quod» as giving the reason for some other action.

Expectancy in the use of cases

As students read the Latin text they are constantly meeting words in the various cases, and it is essential that they should be able to interpret the usage properly if the are to understand what they read. Rather than leave students haphazardly guess the usage, the teacher can give helps for interpreting the usages of the various cases that will speed the student's ability to understand the Latin as he reads it. It is presupposed that the student is sufficiently familiar with the declensions that he can recognize the various cases. Let us take the cases in order. The intrpretation of the usages will rely largely on the frequency count that have been made. Hence in any particular author the conclusions that are drawn may need modification.

The nominative case

Whenever a student meets the nominative case of a noun in his reading, he can expect that it is the subject of the sentence. The use of apposition is rare, and besides modern texts usually set the apposition word in commas.

---

[8] «The Syntax of High School Latin», p. 17.
[9] «The Syntax of High School Latin», p. 17.

The accusative case

When the student meets a noun that ends in «-m» or one that ends in «-s» preceded by the characteristic vowel of the declension, the odds are two to one that the noun is used as the direct object. Here is the breakdown for the occurrences of the accusative.[10]

Object	5900	Object of a preposition	982
Limit of motion	1223	Other usages	395
Subject of infinitive	1147	Total	9647

If the students know the cases that follow the prepositions, they will find little difficulty with the accusative since in prose the noun follows the preposition. Hence the odds are even higher that the accusative will express the receiver of the action.

The ablative case

When a student meets a noun in the ablative case, he should think of these three possibilities and in the order given here: means, place, and separation. The ablative absolute is usually easily recognized and so should cause no problems. There are several other usages that occur and some of them quite frequently, but it would be almost impossible for a student to keep them all in mind.

In order to help the student simplify his reaction to an ablative usage we should tell him that the ablative has an almost equal usage in telling something about place (in answer to the question, where?) and manner (how?), with a very minor use of time (when?) and cause (why?), and still less for quality (what kind?) and comparison.

The ablative absolute will be readily apparent from the punctuation, and the ablative following prepositions will be easily enough recognized by the students, except possibly where the adjective precedes the preposition. In this last instance, though, the eye will usually take in the entire phrase, and the macrons will help to interpret the usage correctly.

Here is a statistical analysis of the occurrences of the ablative as found in Caesar, Cicero, and Vergil.[11]

How? (manner)

---

[10] «The Syntax of High School Latin», pp. 9–10.
[11] «The Syntax of High School Latin», p. 10.

Means	1478	
Manner	432	
Specification	292	
Accompaniment	281	
Agent	218	
Utor, etc.	84	
Difference	76	
Price	6	
Penalty	4	2871

Where? (place)

Place	1258	
Separation	1161	
Source	84	2503
When? (time)		229

Why? (cause) | | 238

What kind? (quality)

Quality	94	
Comparision	22	116
Ablative absolute		729

Ablative with prepositions | 155

Here is a slightly different analysis of the use of the ablative (non-prepositional usages):[12]

Proportions of 100	Caesar	Cicero	Vergil	Total
Means	25	37	54	40
Absolute	41	14	10	20
Manner	5	15	14	12
Respect	6	11	8	8
Cause	9	7	5	7
Separation	8	8	5	7
Description	2	5	2	3
With verbs	4	3	2	3

If we omit the absolute construction which is readily recognized by students, we find that more than one-half of the usages of the ablative are accounted for by means or manner.

---

[12] «Reading and Translating of Latin», p. 27, by Hugh P. O'Neill and William R. Hennes. Loyola University Press, 1929.

Teach the Latin, I pray you

Summary

The student's reaction to the ablative can be indicated by a reaction to these questions and in this order: How? Where? When? Why? What kind? with the first two taking care of most of the occurrences of the ablative.

Illustrating the uses of the ablative

Should a teacher wish to combine a number of the uses of the ablative into a useful picture for the imagination, he can describe a harbor and port. The description would include statements indicating where the ships are, how far removed from land they are, by what means they are propelled, and in what kind of sea they ride; it would also include the fact that ships are beig unloaded, that the market place is busy with buying and selling, that the gang-plank is being lowered, and that people accompany those who disembark, and so forth.

The dative case

If the student remembers that most verbs compounded of prepositions take the dative case, his reading will be simplified so far as the dative case is concerned. But since the dative will usually precede the verb, the student must keep this fact tentatively in mind until he comes to the verb.

If he also remembers that the ideas of advantage and disadvantage will be expressed by the dative, then he has a satisfactory explanation for the dative that follows such verbs as «parcō» and «noceō».

Putting aside the dative that expresses the object after certain verbs, there are only two other dative usages that are important for the student in his reading, that of the indirect object and reference. The indirect object will usually have some kind of a verb of giving in the environment, while the dative of reference is used in such a way that there seems to be no connection with the rest of the sentence. Both of these situations are readily recognized by students.

In reading, then, the student will tentatively fix the dative which he meets as being in one of these four categories and that in the order in which they are given here: indirect object, after compounds, reference, special verbs.

Here are the statistics for the uses of the dative.[13]

---

[13] «The Syntax of High School Latin», p. 9.

Indirect object	436
Compounds	333
Reference	279
Special verbs	159
With adjectives	115
Possessor	105
Agent	100
Others	145
	1672

Environment plays a big part in the student's correct interpretation of the dative. Some kind of a verb of giving will result in an indirect object, a compound verb will explain others, as will special verbs. A few adjectives will be followed by the dative; possession will always have a form of the verb «sum» near it; agent will have a gerundive near it, and in poetry agent may appear with the compound form of a verb.

The genitive case

If in his reading the student meets a form that is clearly the genitive case, he can rest assured that this genitive will express possession, since this usage occurs twice as often as all the other uses of the genitive combined.

Here are the tabulations for the genitive.[14]

Possessive	2294
Objective	349
Partitive	269
Others	390
	3302

Under others we find material (191 occurrences), quality and adjectives with 77 occurrences each. The only other usages that need be mentioned are the genitive with «interest» and verbs of remembering which have 14 occurrences each. These last two usages can readily enough be recognized from the environment.

The order of the cases

Since the nominative, accusative, and ablative account for more than eighty per cent of the occurrences of cases, and since the accusative singular, the

---

[14] «The Syntax of High School Latin», p. 9.

nominative (with the exception of the first and second declensions) and accusative plural can be formed so easily from the ablative, some authors use a new alignment of cases and give the ablative when classifying nouns. Here is the frequency count as made under the direction of Lee Byrne.

Nominative	6088	Dative	1672
Accusative	9647	Genitive	3302
Ablative	6841	Vocative	369
	22.576	Locative	38
			5.381

In the new alignment of cases the dative follows the ablative because the forms are identical in the plural.

Prepositions ′

Prepositions usually take the accusative or the ablative case. When a student meets a preposition he can anticipate that it will govern the accusative, since the accusative will be used four times oftener than the ablative. Such anticipation though should be gradually eliminated by the sure knowledge of the case that follows each preposition. Earlier we gave a mnemonic scheme that students should know in order to know definitely the case that follows each preposition.

Statistically the prepositions using the accusative occur 982 times in the readings covered by the study we quoted, whereas the ablative occurs only 155 times. One must remember though that there are many prepositions which govern the accusative, whereas there are but few whose object is in the ablative case.

Voice

When a student meets a noun that is in the nominative case he can expect that the verb will be active rather than passive, and that by a proportion of about 7 to 1. The active voice occurs about 88 per cent of the time, while the passive voice will occur only about 12 per cent of the time.

Person

The third person will be found in the verb rather than the first or second by a proportion of about 5 to 1, since the third person occurs 85 per cent of the time, the second 6 per cent, and the first 9 per cent.

Voice and person

When teaching students how to read they should know something about the relative frequency of the use of the voice and person but they should also be warned that not all types of writing are covered by such statistical analyses. Hence they can expect from time to time to meet reading that will have a higher proportion of first and second persons, as well as a more frequent occurrence of passive forms.

Tenses

When a student meets a noun in the nominative case he can be rather sure that it will be the subject of the sentence. Moreover, the tense of the verb will be present or perfect rather than any of the other tenses by a proportion of about 3 to 1. And he can expect that the present tense will occur a slight bit oftener than the perfect. Here are the statistics.[15]

Present	40 per cent
Perfect	32
Imperfect	13
Pluperfect	7
Future	4
Future perfect	1

The infinitive

Before making any statements about the use of the infinitive and how to interpret it, let us study some statistics. The figures are based on the number of occurrences in the writings of Caesar, Cicero, and Vergil.[16]

Indirect discourse	1174
Complementary	816
Object	259
Subject	212
Others	103
	2564

Analyzing the uses of the infinitive in indirect discourse reveals the verbs that are most commonly used.[17]

---

[15] «Classical Journal», Vol. 33, p. 18.
[16] «The Syntax of High School Latin», p. 13.
[17] «The Syntax of High School Latin», pp. 19–20.

videō and videor	200
dīcō and dīcor	136
putō	63
existimō	45
arbitror	43
intellegō	42
respondeō	33
praedicō (-āre)	32
loquor	28
sentiō	26
sciō	20

The common verbs followed by a complementary infinitive and the number of times they are used are:[18]

possum	347
volō	65
cupiō	9
nōlō	4

The objective infinitive classification reveals the following verbs and the number of times they are used:[19]

jubeō	112
volō	36
cupiō	5
nōlō	4
mālō	4

The infinitive and reading

The teacher can tell students that when they meet an infinitive in their reading

1 it will more likely be the verb in indirect discourse rather than a complementary usage. The complementary usage will usually be quite evident because of the verb, and the indirect discourse will also be evident, unless the verb of saying or thinking is implied or comes at the very end of the sentence.

---

[18] «The Syntax of High School Latin», p. 19.
[19] «The Syntax of High School Latin», p. 19.

2 if the infinitve is not the main verb in indirect discourse then it will be complementary more often than all other uses combined. Actually the infinitive as the verb in indirect discourse and the complementary usage account for 80 per cent of the uses of the infinitive.

3 omitting the verbs that are followed by indirect discourse, the infinitive will probably be dependent upon «possum, jubeō» or «volō» in the vast majority of the cases in which the infinitive is used.

The participles

The perfect passive participle

An analysis of the figures that are available for the occurrence of the perfect passive participle highlight some differences between the reading of prose and poetry in Latin. The figure in parentheses indicates the number of times that the case appears in the «Aeneid».[20]

nominative	847	(515)
accusative	514	(326)
ablative	91	(57)
dative	39	(29)
genitive	37	(29)
vocative	35	(25)

Even a cursory glance will reveal that the perfect passive participle in its various cases (excepting the ablative absolute) will occur on the average twice as often in Vergil as in the prose authors.

Contrariwise the perfect passive participle in the ablative absolute will occur almost 3 to 1 in prose as compared with poetry. Here is the listing by authors.

Caesar	384
Cicero	58
Vergil	126

If we concern ourselves with the number of times that the perfect passive participle is used in the three authors, we find these figures.

---

[20] The Syntax of High School Latin», pp. 13 and 20.

Caesar	797
Cicero	330
Vergil	1260
	2387

Here is the distribution of the various cases of the perfect participle for deponent verbs. The number in parentheses indicates the occurrences in Vergil.

nominative	214	(119)
accusative	15	(8)
ablative	2	(1)
dative	0	(3)
genitive	0	(1)
vocative	0	(6)
middle nominative	0	(16)

Again the predominant occurrence is to be found in Vergil.

The present participle

The present participle shows this distribution in Caesar, Cicero, and Vergil. The number in parentheses indicates the occurrences in Vergil.

nominative	288	(270)
accusative	270	(223)
ablative	23	(20)
dative	38	(28)
genitive	29	(23)
ablative absolute	45	(27)

The present participle occurs five times oftener in Vergil than it does in Cicero and Caesar.

The future participle

If we exclude the active periphrastic (which has this distribution among the three authors: 4–10–1, indicative 7, subjunctive 8), the future participle occurs only in Vergil and shows this distribution:

nominative	14
accusative	9
ablative	1
dative	4
genitive	2

The participles and reading

Participles occur more frequently in Vergil than in Caesar and Cicero combined except for the perfect passive participle in the ablative absolute. The future participle is used exclusively in Vergil if we disregard the active periphrastic.

For prose reading, therefore, the perfect passive participle is the only participle that need be known thoroughly, and that more particularly when reading Caesar where it is important in the ablative absolutes.

Before introducing Vergil, the teacher should alert the students to the fact that the participles will be used frequently and in all cases.

The gerundive

The gerundive including the periphrastic uses has this distribution among the three authors we have been considering: 130–190–43. Here is the distribution by cases. The number in parentheses indicates the occurrences in Vergil.[21]

nominative		16	(7)
accusative		30	(16)
cūrō	3 (0)		
ad	75 (0)		
ablative		34	(1)
dative		3	(1)
genitive		27	(0)
with causā		19	(0)
vocative		0	(1)

The passive periphrastic has this distribution among the three authors: 50–88–17. The distribution according to moods is as follows:

indicative	65	(12)
subjunctive	12	(0)
infinitive	78	(5)

[21]The Syntax of High School Latin», pp. 13 and 21.

147

When preparing students for the reading of Latin teachers should be aware of the fact that the gerundive is far more important for prose than for poetry. This construction occurs about 9 times in prose for every occurrence in poetry.

The gerund

The gerund has this distribution among the three authors: 52–49–27. The occurrences for the individual cases are as follows:

ablative	35	(16)
accusative	0	(0)
ad and accusative	19	(0)
dative	0	(0)
genitive	62	(11)
with causā	11	(0)

The gerund then, so far as reading is concerned, is important in the reading of prose but not in poetry since it is used four times in prose for every use in poetry.

The supine

The supine has this distribution among the three authors:

-um	6	0	2	8
-ū	3	2	11	16

There is about an equal distribution in prose and in poetry.

Teaching emphasis

Perhaps prospective teachers have been wearied by this lengthy presentation of statistics, but it is important for all teachers of Latin to know in general how often the individual forms are likely to occur in the text that the student will be called upon to read.

Knowing the relative frequency of occurrence enables the teacher to determine the emphasis he must give in the teaching of morphology. Forms that occur frequently must be thoroughly known if the student is to comprehend what he reads. Other forms such as the supine which occur less frequently need, of course, to be known if the student is to fully comprehend what he reads in Latin. However, in the beginning stages of learning how to read, the teacher can give abundant help when the less frequently occurring forms appear in the text.

The statistics we have studied emphasize the need of graded reading materials. If in the first year the student would have at his disposal an abundance of reading material that uses only the more common Latin constructions, he could be given confidence in his ability to read and understand as he reads. Once his knowledge of an experience with the commoner constructions is brought to the point of mastery, the teacher can introduce the less frequently used constructions without harming the student's confidence in his ability to read.

Word order

After students have become acquainted with the order of words in a Latin sentence, the teacher can help improve their comprehension by explaining both the normal and the emphatic word order. It is possible for a student to comprehend the thought of a sentence such as this, «Exīre ex urbe jubet cōnsul hostem», but unless he knows that the normal word order is not observed he may readily miss the emphasis that is achieved by the position of the verb and the object. In like manner students should know the types of subordinate clauses that ordinarily precede the main clause, as well as those that normally follow.

Usage

Even in the earlier stages of learning to read Latin, students should know something about the ordinary usages which they are likely to meet. They should know, for example, that the Romans tend to put negatives in the conjunction or in the verb; that pronouns are generally juxtaposed at or near the beginning of a sentence; that the subject of two clauses frequently appears outside the first clause; that adjectives of quantity generally appear before the noun while those of quality come after it; that «quī» at the beginning of a sentence can be equivalent to «et is, nam is, is autem, is igitur, is tamen».

Such usages should be pointed out to them as they occur in the reading. Nor is it sufficient to call their attention to it once. Whenever such usages occur, the teacher should ask questions about it until such time as he is rather certain that students know the usage and understand it as they read.

149

Stylistic ornamentation

Once the students have acquired facility in the reading of Latin and have progressed to the point where they can read the masters such as Cicero and Vergil, the teacher should acquaint them with the stylistic devices that the Roman used — figures of speech, rhetoric, and syntax. These the student should not only recognize but, what is more important, he should acquire a "feeling" for their effect upon the reader. Once the student has made such progress in his reading, he will read for the delight that full comprehension alone can bring. Then it can be hoped that the reading of Latin will no longer be looked upon as something of a chore but rather as something that gives the same delight as the reading of English classics. And we can confidently expect that the skill of reading will be exercised all through the student's subsequent life — something to which he will turn in his leisure moments for that thrill which comes from true mastery.

Improving reading

Students who wish to improve their reading ability should be comvinced that the rereading of passages with which they are familiar is helpful provided that during the reading they make a conscious effort to comprehend the thought as they read.

The rereading of these passages should not be done too slowly but more or less at the student's normal speed of reading. Neither should the student stop when the meaning of a sentence or word is not clear. He should read the entire passage as a unit several times. What was obscure at first will frequently be clarified in subsequent readings because of the general context.

Students can also improve their abilities to comprehend by reading material with whose content they are familiar, for example, the Gospels or the Old Testament, particularly the narrative parts. This type of reading poses problems for the teacher so we shall consider it more in detail. We might refer to this type of reading as "extensive" as opposed to the "intensive" such as is customarily done when studying the speeches of Cicero where each phrase and clause is frequently studied in detail in order to arrive at a heightened appreciation of how the thought was expressed. Extensive reading is primarily concerned with getting the thought rather than with how it is expressed.

Extensive reading

The purpose of extensive reading of materials with whose content the student is familiar can only be the strengthening of the student's ability to comprehend what the Latin states without the intermediation of the English. Since the general story is known, the student can concentrate on the skills that help comprehension.

The student's activities

Students who wish to improve their reading must have a real desire to improve. The very desire helps them discover ways and means to improve their understanding of what they read. Unless the student has this desire, no amount of coaching or help that a teacher gives will help him improve.

Besides desiring to improve, the student must be ambitious enough to spend the time that is required for reading the selection many times. The frequent reading of the passage helps to fix words and phrases in his memory — items that will help him understand more readily what he subsequently reads.

As the student reads, he must force himself to follow the thought as it is revealed by the Latin. Teachers can be of help here by giving a text that is set in sense lines. As the student reads, he keeps the text covered except for the line he is reading. Frequently during the reading he follows these steps:

1 he thinks of what he has read thus far

2 considers what he can expect in the remainder of the sentence

3 and then proceeds to the reading of the next line.

If the text is not set in sense lines, the student can follow the above procedure by taking the text a clause or sentence at a time.

Teachers can also help if they type the text for the students and put the main clauses in capital letters. They should also give the student the helps we indicated earlier when discussing the handling of the periodic structure in Latin.

Students should be encouraged to analyze the conjunctions that appear in their reading, especially the subordinating ones since these reveal how the thoughts are connected.

Reflection upon what he has read with comprehension will also help the student. After reading a paragraph several times, he should attempt to give in his own words the thought of the paragraph. So much the better if this is done in Latin, but doing it in English will also be satisfactory. At other times he might draw up a comprehension question or two in order to try to fix the thoughts in his memory and to force himself to actively use words and phrases that he has just read.

The student should also be encouraged to at least periodically do some exercise such as this after he is quite certain he has fully comprehended the paragraph. Close the text and then write out in Latin as fully as he can what he has read in Latin. When this version is completed, open the text and compare the two for thought and even expressions that occurred in the original. Such comparisons can reveal his observance of how words are spelled, how thoughts are expressed by this author, as well as what errors in agreement and so forth he has made.

The teacher's activities

The teacher's activities in helping students to read for comprehension will find their full scope during the recitation period. Presupposing that the student has rather thoroughly prepared the reading outside of the class time, the teacher can profitably conduct the recitation and be of help to the student in many ways such as the following.

The most obvious thing for the teacher to do is to read the text to the class and then ask questions about the structure as well as about the student's comprehension of what he has heard. At times the teacher should ask the students to do the reading, but he should insist upon interpretative reading.

Occasionally the teacher will call for a class summary of what has been read. Ideally this summary should be written on the chalkboard as it is given by the students, but since this is slow, the teacher can content himself with calling upon one student to start the summary, then call upon another to continue, then upon another, until the entire story has been told.

At other times the teacher may wish to use the comprehension questions that have been composed by the students the night before. Each student composes one question. In class the teacher collects these, shuffles them, and then asks them of the class, either calling for volunteers for the answering or singling out individuals to give the answers.

Teachers may wish to use a grading system in order to make certain that students endeavor to draw up good comprehension questions. Suppose he picks a student's question. This question is asked of the class. If the class answers it satisfactorily, the author of the question gets a grade of 70. If the class cannot answer it, then the author gets a grade of 100 provided that he himself can answer the question to the satisfaction of the class and the teacher.

These same comprehension questions can be used in competition, one row against another, or one-half of the class against the other, with the winning row or side getting a suitable reward such as a perfect grade for a class quiz.

It might be remarked that the students' questions can help the teacher achieve quite a stockpile of comprehension questions that are useful for examination purposes.

Part of each recitation period will be taken up in the answering of difficulties that the students encountered in the reading. If the students do not have such, the teacher can easily propose some.

A concrete lesson in how to improve reading can be conducted from time to time. The teacher reads the passage a phrase, or clause, or sentence at a time. Each time he stops he asks the students to give the thought thus far and to tell what can be expected in the remainder of the sentence. Occasionally he stops after an initial word in a sentence, for example, «Animī», and asks the students what to expect; he then takes the next word, for example «magnitūdinem», and so on until the sentence is completed.

In order to more definitely train the students to follow the thought as revealed in the Latin word order, the teacher will take material that was not studied the night before, for example, the next paragraphs that follow the previous night's assignment.

By changing the expression of the thoughts the teacher can exercise the abilities of the students to comprehend in the Latin word order. For example, suppose the reading concerned itself with the capture of the conspirators in the Third Catilinarian. The teacher would do well to put the narration into the first person by having the informer come to Cicero and give an account of what went on. Then allow Cicero to give the orders for the arrest and so forth. This lends variety to the story, yet exercises the student's ability to comprehend as he hears. The thoughts are familiar but the expression is not.

If the story the students read has conversation in it, then it is good to assign character roles to various students and read the story aloud in class. Such a reading can help the story come alive for the students. Commercial tapes are a help at times in giving the story. If such are not available, the teacher can without too much difficulty record such himself for use in the class.

153

Memory work and declamation

Judicious memorizing of selected passages and then their declamation can help improve reading. Once the passage is fully comprehended and then committed to memory and declamed the student will have a rather permanent possession that can help him understand other passages that have similar expressions. Such declamations, it might be remarked, might will be given on a contest basis in meetings of the Latin Club.

Checking on students' work

It is quite necessary that teachers check constantly on the work of the students, for many of them do not have motives that are proof against the many things that conspire to lure students from their studies. Here are some suggestions which teachers may use to check on the progress of their students.

At the beginning of the class period the teacher gives the students some minutes in which to review what they have read the night before. Then with books closed he asks them to write in Latin a précis of the story.

At other times the teacher distributes pages that contain a paragraph or two from the story with some of the words omitted. Students are then to supply these. Reasonable synonyms are of course to be admitted as correct. At times the teacher may omit the verbs, or the nouns, or the adverbs, or a combination of these. He must be careful though not to omit so many words that it becomes almost impossible to establish a context.

The teacher may wish to distribute pages which contain a paragraph or two of the story written in simple sentences. The students are then asked to rewrite the story using subordination wherever possible.

At other times the check on the students' work may consist of answering in writing the comprehension questions that the students themselves prepared the night before. Each student prepares one question. These are collected by the teacher and he chooses those he wishes the students to answer.

Teachers can check on the students' comprehension by distributing pages that contain a paragraph or two of the story. Certain parts are underlined and students are asked to give an alternate version for these parts being careful not to alter the meaning. For example, they could substitute a «cum» and the subjunctive for a causal clause introduced by «quod».

Rewriting some of the paragraphs of the story permits the teacher to check the student's comprehension. In the rewrite the teacher uses a number of constructions that are different from the original; he also uses a different vocabulary to express some of the thoughts. After such paragraphs are given to the students, they are allowed a few minutes for reading. Then the teacher asks questions about the structural elements in the story as well as the meaning.

If the students have written a précis the night before, the teacher may read one or other to the class and ask for the items that were omitted. The teacher should, as he reads, correct any mistakes that the student may have made in agreement and so forth.

In order to check how well the students comprehend what they read, the teacher may distribute a page that contains ten incomplete Latin sentences that deal with the matter the students have read. He then asks them to complete these sentences in Latin.

Sometimes the teacher may be fortunate enough to possess an alternate version of a story. For example, if students have been reading Cicero's description of Catiline's character, he may bring in that done by Sallust. After reading Sallust's version, he checks on the comprehension of the students by suitable questions. Or if the students are reading a harmony of the Gospels, the teacher may read the version of the episode as written by one or other of the inspired authors.

Public recognition of work well done is always pleasing to the students. If the teacher has several students who can express themselves fairly well in Latin, he might consider this scheme. Ask two of them to go to the board and write out a précis of what was read the night before. While they are writing, the teacher proceeds with the recitation for the rest. When the summaries are complete, the class can be asked questions about them. For example, he might ask what points are treated in summary A that are not contained in summary B, or what points would they add to each of the summaries.

Conclusion

Teachers who try to help their students improve in reading are much like the coach who tries to help a youngster become a good pitcher. Once the coach has explained the correct stance and other such items, it is up to the student to practice constantly if he wishes some day to become a good pitcher. Once the teacher has explained the principles that help students become good readers, it is his function to give an adequate stimulus for continued practice.

Chapter 7

The use of tapes

A language laboratory with all its devices can be of immense help to the teacher of Latin if he uses it judiciously. Everyone recognizes the need of drill in order that students may learn the structural elements of a new language, but not all teachers have the skill that is needed for drilling, nor do they have the time in an ordinary class period to sufficiently drill each student. The use of tapes in a laboratory makes it possible for both the skillful and the not so skillful teacher to give every student the drill he needs to help him master the elements of a new language.

Purpose

The use of tapes is intended to help secure that automatic response to language stimuli and language situations that makes the difference between a halting and a facile reading and production of the language.

A student may be said to have an automatic response to a stimulus when he can react to the stimulus correctly and without thinking about the mechanics of language. He has a thought and he wishes to express it and he does so without consciously adverting to the grammar, morphology, or vocabulary.

The tapes seek to create a language situation to which the student must give a response. This is somewhat artificial, it is true, but if the student through such drill secures an automatic response, then he is ready to read Latin as Latin since his knowledge of the structure permits him to concentrate on the lexical items.

157

Format

The format of the material that appears on the tapes may vary somewhat but in general the material will follow this pattern.

First there is a set of directions and possibly an example or two of what is to be done by the student.

There follows the sentence or question. Then there is a period of silence during which the student is supposed to perform the operation called for in the directions. This student response may be done privately or it may be recorded, depending upon the equipment of the laboratory and the desires of the teacher.

Finally the tape gives the correct answer or correct change that the directions called for.

Content

The tapes usually drill significant language situations such as those involved when passing from the active to the passive, learning new constructions and the mastering of idiom.

The content of the tapes generally concerns itself with the contrasts between Latin and the native language. Where there is the greatest contrast, there the student must be thoroughly drilled. For example, the positional versus the inflectional ways of signaling meaning, the use of the subjunctive mood, the correct interpretation and use of such words as «ut» and «cum».

Tapes are handy for drilling the contrasts within the Latin language itself, for example, the learning of an instinctive reaction to the forms «audit, audiet» and «audiat».

During the first two years the tapes usually concentrate on the learning of morphology and grammar; in the remaining years of the study of Latin there should be progress into word order and idioms. Various studies and frequency counts can be a help to the teacher in determining what constructions to emphasize, for example, the ablative absolute in Caesar, and the varied use of participles in Vergil.

Tapes can also be used effectively in the teaching of text. Students are asked to listen to an entire speech of Cicero, or an entire book of Vergil. When hearing it for the first time they may miss much of the story, but by the time they have listened to it five or six times they usually have rather complete comprehension of the text. Even in the first year, teachers may prefer to tape the stories they wish to tell the class in order to allow the students to listen to it several times in order to strengthen their comprehension.

Taping the story permits the teacher to be his own critic when he plays it back, and it allows for corrections in interpretation which an oral telling in the class would not allow.

It should be remembered, however, that even if the tapes are of the best, they cannot and should not supplant the teacher. Tapes are mechanical and students want, at least occasionally, the dynamic presentation of the teacher and they react to it more vigorously.

Effective use of tapes by the student

In order that the use of tapes achieve the purposes that the teacher has in mind, there must be strong motivation on the part of the students — a motivation that will result in the willingness to give the best in the way of concentration and hard work. Unless the student works faithfully with the tapes he is not likely to profit much.

The student must also be willing to give an adequate amount of time outside of class in which to work with the tapes, and this should be a minimum of fifteen minutes a day.

And there must be regular attendance at the practice sessions. Presumably the tapes progress from one item to another through a regular series; thus if some items are missed through absence or carelessness, there will be the necessary lacunae in the student's knowledge.

The teacher and the effective use of tapes

On the part of the teacher there must be adequate checks on the student and his work. Even part of a class period, for example, the first fifteen minutes can be spent in the laboratory. This supposes that the laboratory is centrally located in order that not too much time be lost in going from the classroom to the laboratory.

If no other group is in the laboratory during the remainder of the period, the teacher can conduct the remainder of his class in the laboratory provided that the booths are such that he can see them all readily and that his platform is high enough to permit a full vision of the operations of the students. Many modern booths have glass in the front, or they have fronts that fold down, thus forming nearly regular classroom desks. Students could be permitted to keep the headphones on, and the teacher can use the system as an intercommunication one where everyone can hear what everyone else responds as well as hear what the teacher says.

159

If the laboratory booths have records, it is possible to record the student answers and then play them back later for checking. Such checking though is tedious unless the laboratory technician can record them on one tape for the teacher.

If the laboratory consists of simple listening posts that are connected to one recorder, the teacher might himself be present for the laboratory periods in order to check the work that the students are doing. In the early stages when the students are enamored of the newness, he need not do too much checking. Later, however, as the novelty wears off and the student realizes that much hard work must be done, it is essential that the teacher or someone deputed by him constantly check the work of the students. Here are some schemes he might wish to use.

It has been found effective if the teacher also listens to the tape and requires that the students in turn give the responses out loud in order that he may hear what each says. This can be done rather easily if the teacher keeps one of the headphones turned away from his ear. It is advisable that the teacher keep a record of the number of correct responses. Freshmen in high school are very much interested in how the record proceeds from day to day. Teachers might also wish to give a separate grade for the work done in the laboratory.

The author has found that it stimulates interest if he keeps a numerical record of each laboratory session for each student. Use the numbers 1 to 10 instead of 100, 90, and so forth. Students then can easily compute the average for any one session. They can also compare today's work with yesterday's. Such a scheme helps the teacher easily compute a grade for the week's work.

The presence of the teacher during the laboratory periods helps to keep the students working earnestly, and his listening to their responses keeps them interested, especially when they realize that such laboratory work can help their general grade.

As the year progresses and the better students achieve a facility in the laboratory work, teachers should adopt some system of rewards. The author has found that this scheme works well. If a student gives five correct responses in a row, he need not report for the next laboratory session. Five responses does not seem to be much, but suppose one is working with twenty students. By the time the individual student achieves five correct responses he has listened to approximately one hundred responses. For most students this should be enough to assure automatic response at least for the time being.

Content and the effective use of tapes

So far as content is concerned, the successful and effective use of tapes requires proper material that is well organized and progresses through an orderly presentation. For example, the tape will drill the first person, then the second, and then the third. As soon as it can be expected that such a presentation is mastered, the teacher proceeds to require answers in any order for the persons. Progress to what might be called the scrambled presentation is important since normal language situations will not proceed regularly through the three persons.

There should be an abundance of material for drilling any one point because otherwise it is possible for the student to memorize the answers after two or three sessions in the laboratory. If he memorizes an entire drill then that drill is useless since it will no longer drill him on the response to a language stimulus but will rather simply trigger his facile memory. If the drill in the text is too short, the teacher can easily lengthen it by varying the order of the questions.

Recording is not easy

From all that has been said about tapes teachers will not be surprised when they are told that the drawing up of material for tapes is a difficult task. Besides the actual composition of the examples there is the work of recording. There is one consolation, however, since, once the teacher has made the tape, he has it at hand for future use.

The work of recording should not be minimized. It is quite difficult to record for any length of time without making a mistake unless the teacher has been used to making recordings over a long period of time. Patience and constant effort on the part of the teacher will bring its rewards in the way of a recording that is good and can be used almost indefinitely. As experience with recording grows, the teacher too will make fewer mistakes.

As the teacher records there is the problem of keeping out extraneous noises unless he has a commercial recording booth at his disposal. But here again the teacher learns rapidly from his experience and soon he can make a tape that does not have too many distracting noises.

Further observations on recording

Earlier we stated that all tapes have a period of silence following the question in order to give the student time to orally do the operations as directed at the beginning of the tape. If too much time is given for the response (before

161

the correct response is given on the tape) then the student becomes lazy and really does not learn. On the other hand if too little time is given, then the student easily becomes discouraged. It is important then for the general rhythm of the drill that the proper amount of time be allowed for the student response.

Here is a practical norm for a teacher to follow when making the recording. If the teacher himself answers the question twice before giving the correct answer on the tape, he will find that he has usually given the student enough time to answer.

Experience has shown that tapes are more effective if several voices are used in the recordings. At least two should be used, one to give the question and another to give the answer. Subsequent recordings should occasionally bring in a third voice. This provides welcome relief for the student and helps to eliminate some of the dullness of routine.

Teachers should be warned of one thing. Quite frequently in class the teacher is overly careful in his pronunciation. This is a mistake. Ordinarily in class and in the making of tapes he should keep a normal pace of speaking. Students must accustom their ears to receiving the message at a normal pace, for this is the normal language situation.

When composing the practice drills the teacher should keep the sentences relatively short in order that there may be no undue burden on the memory. The concentration of the student should be directed to the changes that are to be made rather than to the content. Hence familiar material is always good when endeavoring to teach a new construction or usage. The sentences can express thoughts that appeared in recent readings and so eliminate the guessing of students at the meanings of words or phrases.

Tapes not a substitute for class

Ideally the listening to tapes in the laboratory should be part of the work that the student does outside of class time; it is part of his homework. Teachers whose students regularly attend the laboratory sessions should not make the mistake of thinking that they need not do any drill in class. The laboratory session can never supplant the teacher's work in the class. He must also conduct drills himself.

Drills conducted by the tapes are absolutely impersonal and for that reason they miss the interplay of mind and mind. Students need the stimulation that comes from hearing a living person give the question, for then it more nearly approximates the normal language situation. Should teachers omit all drill in class, they will soon find that students lose all interest in mastering the drills. Students, too, like to impress their teacher with their knowledge and one way in which they can do this is to correctly and rapidly respond to the drills that the teacher himself conducts.

Time and tapes

Since laboratory sessions can be very tiring because of the concentration required, the teacher should normally not conduct a laboratory session for longer than fifteen minutes, at least for freshmen in high school. If the teacher prolongs a session, he will find that he rapidly approaches the point of diminishing returns. If there is question of listening to a continuous text such as a book of Vergil, the student is able to concentrate for longer periods of time but hardly ever beyond a half hour. After this length of time the words are likely to become mere sounds and the listener is likely to become quite passive.

The effective use of tapes is also affected by the time of the day in which the students listen. The later it is in the course of the school day the less effective is the laboratory session, and this is understandable in view of the efforts expended by the students in their successive classes.

The author has experimented with the times of the day for the laboratory work. Students came in the morning, at noon, and after school. Records were kept for the same group on the same content, and these definitely indicated that more accurate work was done in the morning, less accurate work was done at noon, and very faulty work was done after school. These results occurred despite the fact that on successive days the same material was used in the laboratory. Ordinarily one would expect that better work should be done after the third time over the tape, but the work of the students was affected by fatigue from the day's work in the classroom.

The laboratory itself

So far as equipment is concerned, the requirements vary. For the teaching of modern languages there is need of much equipment since the student must learn to utter the sounds of the new language. Fortunately the uttering of sounds does not ordinarily pose too much of a problem for the student of Latin.

The minimum requirements for the Latin teacher are a recorder and a sufficient number of headphones. The earphones need not be of the expensive type since all they need to convey is the sound of the voice. The recorder itself might well be one that has four sound tracks, for this helps in saving

163

money and in conserving storage space. Seven or eight seven-inch reels will usually be sufficient for the recording for the freshman year.

It is advisable to have a separate room for the laboratory if this is at all possible; however, if such a room is not available, the teacher can readily adapt the classroom into a laboratory if the seats are movable. Instead of having "mixer boxes" to which six earphones can be attached, he will find it better to have a long strip attached to the wall on one side or two sides of the room into which the jacks of the earphones may be put. Then the students simply sit along the wall during the laboratory session. The total cost for such an installation should not exceed $350.00, including the tape recorder.

In order to permit the students to concentrate, the laboratory should be located in the quietest part of the building, yet it should be readily available to the language classes in order that teachers may not lose too much class time in taking the class from the classroom to the laboratory.

Ideally the laboratory will have individual booths for the students which are so constructed that the front can be lowered to permit all to see the teacher. The teacher himself should be on a platform which is about twenty to twenty-four inches above the level of the students. This permits all students to see him easily and permits the teacher to readily check on the activities of the students.

In the absence of booths the use of tables will prove rather satisfactory. If these are narrow then they might be put around the walls of the roof in order that students may look at the wall rather than across the table at another student. If the tables are wide, then students can sit on both sides of the table, but in this case some kind of a divider should be put in the middle of the table to prevent students from being distracted by those across from them. If wide tables are used, then two long ones are sufficient with a table for the teacher and the recorder — the entire arrangement forming a large "U". Even though there are dividers on the tables the teacher can readily see each of the students. There are no dividers between students but this is not absolutely necessary.

This type of listening post is rather inexpensive and most schools could afford such equipment.

More expensive laboratories permit the student to record his answers on tape. They also allow the teacher to have several tapes in use at the same time; thus he can adapt the work more readily to the level of each student. Where possible, of course, the teacher should have at his disposal a laboratory that consists of more than just listening posts, for it will increase

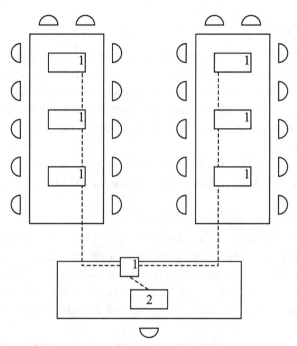

1 mixer boxes
2 recorder

the effectiveness of his teaching and speed the learning of the individual students. Where listening posts only are had the teacher must keep all on the same lesson, unless he wishes to take the students in small groups at different times. Such an arrangement it would seem demands too much of a sacrifice of the teacher's time.

The light in the laboratory should not be glaring but rather on the soft side and the colors such that they will soothe the eye. In actual practice many students keep their eyes closed for the most part during a laboratory session in order that they may concentrate better.

No school, however small or poor, should feel that it cannot provide at least listening posts for the students in Latin. All they need is a recorder, headphones, mixer-boxes, and cords to connect them. The work involved in arranging the room can frequently be done by the teacher himself with the help of one or other member of the staff such as the teacher of physics.

Teach the Latin, I pray you

Sources of tapes

Most modern texts that concentrate on the teaching of Latin as a language have arrangements whereby the teacher can borrow the master tapes and make his own from these; in some instances the publisher will make the recordings if tapes are sent, or they will even furnish the tapes and make the recordings for a nominal fee. Usually this fee is sufficient to cover the cost of the tapes only.

If a teacher is using a text for which tapes are not available, then he must make his own tapes. Elsewhere we discussed the making of the tapes and their content.

Besides the tapes that are adapted to specific texts, there are others that concern themselves with a broader view of Latin. For example, EMC Recording company of 806 East Seventh Street, St. Paul 6, Minnesota, has excellent tapes for Caesar and Cicero. These can be used once the student has finished the reading of a particular part of those authors. They act as a summary and a stimulus and bring out the forcefulness and beauty of the original.

As time goes on undoubtedly more and more tapes will be available for the teacher. He needs but watch for the advertisements that appear in the journals that concern the classics.

Advantages of using tapes

All teachers recognize the need for personal work and concentration when there is question of learning a language. The drills that are conducted in class can easily be escaped by a student, but there is no escaping the sound that is immediately in his ear when he has the headphones on.

Then there is the eternal problem of allotting enough time in the class periods for conducting drills. The tapes provide just such opportunities and that under conditions that are far more ideal than the ordinary homework of students. Teachers cannot expect that all their students have recorders in their homes.

Ordinarily when students do their homework there is a period of several to many hours between the work and its correction. Not so on the tapes. The tape gives the correct answer just as soon as the student has given his reply. If the reply was incorrect, the student hears the correction at once; and if the reply was correct, the correctness is immediately reinforced by the tape.

The tapes accomplish more in the time allotted for homework. If a

166

student were to write out ten sentences, he would use several minutes at least in completing the task, but ten sentences on the tape will probably not take more than two or at most three minutes. Tapes provide more repetition in a shorter period than does writing and this makes for a faster learning of the language. During the fifteen-minute laboratory session the students will be exposed to at least five times more drill than could possibly be had if writing were involved. We might say that he is being bombarded to the point of saturation.

Since the tapes are always using the Latin there is a constant teaching of the language. For example, the student hears a purpose idea that is expressed by «ut» and the subjunctive and he must turn it into a gerund or gerundive construction. He is working with the Latin without the interference of the English.

When presenting material in class or when conducting a drill, the teacher must rely on the interest of the student to attend to what is being done here and now in class, but all teachers know how prone students are to look ahead in the book during a class recitation. In other words the teacher seldom has a real assurance that all the members of the class are working with him here and now on a definite point. The use of tapes helps obviate this difficulty at least during the laboratory sessions. As the tape is being played, the student cannot work ahead, nor can he look back over other material. He must follow exactly what the teacher presents as it is presented and he must keep a steady pace of work. The student is constantly occupied by the forward moving "now".

Psychologically, too, there are advantages in the use of tapes. For one thing, the tape helps the student immeasurably to secure concentration and we can hope that this ability to concentrate will have some transfer value to other subjects. Fifteen minutes a day of trying to concentrate should result in the formation of a habit of concentration.

And during the building of these habits of concentration there is no need for stimuli from the teacher which in some cases at least results in a sort of resentment toward the teacher. The correct answer of the tape is always a silent rebuke to the student who has given an incorrect answer.

All teachers are familiar with the so-called slower student. He always seems to need a little more time than most to give an answer to any question. Despite their best efforts teachers frequently succumb to the weakness of the student, for they do not wish to be told constantly, "I knew the answer, but you did not give me time enough to reply." Moreover, all the teacher's counseling and efforts to get the student to try to think more quickly and respond more rapidly frequently results in resentment on the part of the student which is expressed by the statement, "He's not fair." But one never hears such a complaint about a tape. In other words the tape is relentless and the student who takes his time in replying will be daily given an object lesson in the need of speeding up his reply; moreover, he sees that others meet the demands of the tape, and this is an encouragement for him to continue trying.

Occasionally teachers have a student in their class who stammers. Frequently the stammering is due to an inability of the student to communicate quickly with persons, and since in the laboratory he is not dealing with a person but with a tape, he finds that much of his stammering ceases. The teacher can thus find out more readily what such a student knows about the language.

There are teachers who feel that there is too much competition between students. If such is the case, then, the use of tapes obviates the difficulty. If the laboratory sessions are handled correctly, the student feels only that he is in competition with himelf. No relative standings of students are published, but students do have access to their own record to see how they progress from day to day and from week to week. And experience has proved that interest in the language mounts as real progress is made in the use of the tapes.

Using the tapes

The content of the tapes should be printed or at least some kind of text should be available for the students to use in their study. There are several ways of combining the tapes and the text for rapid learning.

«See, hear.» In this scheme students study the material that they will hear on the tape. During the laboratory session they hear only. This procedure works quite well when students are learning the morphology of the language.

«Hear–see.» In this scheme the student first meets the material on the tape and studies it in the text later. Grammatical constructions such as purpose clauses can be effectively learned in this way.

For very difficult material it is good to use a combination of the methods. Allow the students to have the text of the tape in front of them as they listen to the tape. Besides learning the material on the tape, the student can improve his pronunciation. After this initial laboratory session, the student studies the material on the tape outside the laboratory session period. The following day he should be in a position to go through the work of the tape by ear only.

Ideally the student should be able to come to the laboratory whenever he is free. And the student should be permitted to ask for any of the tapes. Such an ideal arrangement would permit him to work at this own pace and drill himself in those areas in which he knows he is weak. But it is only the school with a full laboratory that can offer such advantages.

Most Latin teachers will have to settle for something less than the ideal. Usually they will need to drill the students as a group on a particular tape. If some do not master the material while working with the group, the teacher must provide other times for drill if that is feasible.

The number of times that a student must listen to the same tape varies in accord with the difficulty of the matter and the student's ability to learn. For freshmen in high school it has been found that ordinarily three fifteen-minute listening periods will give fair mastery, provided that there is adequate private study outside the times of the laboratory sessions. When the matter is relatively easy, as in the case of learning numbers, the students usually master it after two listening periods, provided that the teacher does not require an exhaustive knowledge of numbers but restricts the area of learning to those numbers that are used more frequently.

Teachers will find it helpful when they make their recordings or when they listen to commercial recordings to note on the footage counter the beginning number of successive drills. This notation makes it easy to find the exact drill that is wanted upon a particular occasion. If the tapes are stored in boxes, it is easy to type a directory and paste it in the cover of the box. The tape boxes themselves should be numbered consecutively. If a notation is also made in the text giving the number of the reel and the beginning footage of the exercise, the teacher can at any time readily find the tape.

Stimulating students in the use of tapes

Particularly when younger students first start to use the laboratory, the teacher needs give little encouragement to spend the time profitably. Unfortunately the novelty soon wears off and the students are then faced with the continuous effort to work diligently. It is at this point that the teacher must provide stimuli. Ideally, of course, the stimulus that comes from mastery should be sufficient for the student, but the ideal is seldom realized.

To give further incentives for mastering the material on the tapes, the teacher can occasionally set up a reward system such as this. As soon as the student has five successive correct replies, he is allowed to leave the laboratory. Suppose there are fifteen students in the laboratory; each must give a reply in turn. Hence to secure five correct replies the student has listened to some seventy odd sentences of the drill. Even though students leave only a few minutes before the end of the session, such a reward system stimulates their efforts. It is flattering to them to be able to leave before the others because of good work that has been done.

If the early dismissal of students creates problems of discipline in the school, the teacher can vary the reward system by exempting those with five correct replies from the next laboratory sesssion.

The alert teacher will find other ways of rewarding the student, such as the giving of a grade for a perfect recitation, or posting their names on a chart with a gold star after it. Such schemes work well for the younger students particularly.

Testing by means of tapes

Tapes can be used in a variety of ways to test the students. Actually the oral response when the teacher is present in the laboratory and is keeping a record is a sort of daily test for the students.

Essay questions can be given to the students by means of the tapes with but one disadvantage, the vast amount of tape that is used. However, using the tape for essay questions is likely to be better than dictating the questions since it requires greater concentration by the students. The students cannot ask for a repetition of the question and so the teacher is spared the possibility of seeming to be unreasonable in refusing a repetititon. The time allowed for the response forces the slower workers to work more rapidly.

But how is the teacher to gauge the amount of time that should be allowed for the answer? It has been found that this is a good procedure for determining the time allotted for the answer. The teacher asks the question on the tape. He then writes out the answer to the question without hurrying. He notes how much time this takes. He then allows this much more time for the students. In other words, double the amount of time that it takes for the teacher to write out the answer to the question.

Multiple-choice questions can also be given by means of the tape. There is no need for four or five choices. Three choices are enough since the student cannot use his eyes to go back but must remember what the choices were from simply hearing them. A standard multiple-choice answer sheet can be used for the replies, provided that enough time is allowed the student for thinking about the choices in order to determine the correct one. There is no handy rule for determining the amount of time to be allotted the student for giving the answer. In general, be generous in the allottment of time. It should be remarked, too, that the questions should not be long, nor should the choices given be unduly long. If they are long then there is an undue burden on the student's memory. True–false questions may also be asked on the tape but sufficient time should be given for the student to answer.

If the drills that appear in the text are on tape, these drills can be used for a test. The teacher will need to make a new recording, though, since the drills ordinarily give the correct answer. If he uses such drills, ask the students in turn down the row and record the quality of the response. This procedure is much like the checking the teacher does in the laboratory.

Tapes are very handy for giving tests in comprehension. The teacher records a story with as much interpretation as he can master. He then plays the recording for the class, and either gives the questions orally himself or gives them by means of the tape.

Teachers should remember that testing by means of tapes is likely to cause the student far more difficulty than he experiences in the more ordinary ways of testing. The student must rely entirely upon his ear to get the question. Because it is difficult for the student, the teacher will keep the questions relatively simple, especially in the multiple-choice types. In the later years of the study of Latin such testing by tape will be easier since students are more familiar with the language as well as the procedure itself. Teachers should remember when they correct such tests that the understanding of the question is in itself a sort of test of the student's knowledge of Latin and give credit for it accordingly.

Reviews

From time to time the teacher should make a tape that contains significant portions of drills that the students are supposed to have mastered. Each portion of the tape will then be a review of what students have seen before.

Using portions from previous drills will make a satisfactory tape, but at the end of each section the teacher should include a few drills of his own. These will follow the regular procedure but the thoughts will be new. Such unfamiliar sentences provide the teacher with a yardstick for measuring the true ability of the student to make the changes required by the drill, and they reveal to the student how much real mastery he has achieved in manipulating the language.

If the stories that the students have read are on tapes, these can be played and comprehension questions asked. If the teacher makes a new tape, he should change the story somewhat in order to keep the students alert and to prevent them from answering the questions from the memory they have of the story when it was first given to them.

Should the teacher wish to review a rather large quantity of vocabulary, he should draw up a new story which makes use of most of the words in the list he wishes to review. If the students comprehend the story without great difficulty then he can rest assured that they know the vocabulary quite well.

Contests

As a welcome change to the ordinary routine of class, the teacher will find that contests of various kinds will stimulate interest in the study of Latin. And tapes can be used effectively in the conducting of contests between rows or between the two halves of the classroom. Such contests work well in freshman and even in sophomore classes, but they are most effective when there is the possibility of conducting a sort of intramural competition between various divisions of the freshman year.

The contest material can be drawn from the pattern drills that are in the text, provided that these are on tapes. These tapes provide just a certain amount of time for the student's reply and, hence the teacher is freed of the possible charge of favoritism for either side.

Since tape recorders have the instantaneous stop mechanism, the teacher can conduct the traditional football, basketball, and track contests. Instead of having questions written on cards, they are recorded on tape. The teacher allows the students to hear the question and then stops the tape. The captain decides who is to answer the question and then time is "in". If the student beats the tape, his side scores.

The procedure may be varied slightly by the teacher indicating on the tape what the value of the following question will be. As soon as such information is given by the tape, he stops the tape and awaits the captain's choice. Only after the choice does he permit the tape to go on.

There is one disadvantage with recorded questions of this kind. Since the questions are recorded in a certain sequence, the captains are not free to call for a specific quality question.

The full possibilities of conducting contests with the help of tapes has by no means been fully explored by teachers, since the use of the recorder for teaching languages is only now becoming popular.

Conclusion

Teachers who have never used tapes in the classroom may feel a bit ill at ease at first, but they soon overcome this feeling and make use of the recorder as readily as they make use of the chalkboard and other standard helps in teaching. Students, too, at first are somewhat uncomfortable when the tapes are used, but they too soon adjust to new procedures.

It is hoped that the teachers will share their experiences in the use of the newer aids by writing articles for the various journals in order that the teaching of Latin may become increasingly more effective.

Chapter 8

Testing

Those of us who are older teachers frequently have a rather rude awakening when we look back over tests that we have made years ago. We usually find that they tested mostly the science of grammar and translation. All too often we were satisfied to ask for the "tag" for a grammatical usage. Seldom did we realize that, until the student translated, he could hardly "tag" the usage. Students often asked: "How do you remember whether this is a noun or an adverbial clause of purpose?" And about the only answer we gave them was that of suggesting a translation of the sentence and from this to determine the usage.

The tests of some years ago were largely concerned with translation. If the students translated well, then the teacher took for granted that the student knew the Latin, but most of us failed to see that there is no necessary connection between the two steps — the ability to translate a passage taken in class is no guarantee that the student knows Latin.

How often we have seen young children secure an amazing facility in putting together a jigsaw puzzle after they have worked it a few times! Often, when translating, our students did much the same thing. Repetition made it easy for them to puzzle out the subject, verb, and object and then to arrange these into a meaningful English sentence. Sometimes they did what was worse, they memorized the translation. Then one or two key words in a sentence readily brought to mind the entire thought which the student then proceeded to set down in a creditable English rendition.

In many examinations there is all too little in the way of interpretation because teachers were satisfied with translation, or they were content to have students master what they read in the notes.

All in all most examinations put a premium on good memory and gave the student very little in the way of language experience. Generally the questions were in English as were the replies. As a result the tests themselves were not a teaching device for the new language.

Let us make a brief list of what not to do in an examination, and I am sure that most teachers will be surprised at the elements such a category will contain. Here is the list of don'ts.

What to avoid in examinations

Examiners in Latin will do well to observe these prohibitions.

1 Do not ask for vocabulary in isolated forms or in lists.

2 Do not ask for the "tagging" of the grammar.

3 Do not ask for parsing of forms.

Incidentally, through the years teachers have been forcing the students to do unnecessary mental gymnastics. They usually asked for the third person singular of the imperfect indicative for example. Little did they realize that the student could not begin the formation of the word until he heard the last part of the teacher's direction (unless he had the facility to work backwards in forming words). Teachers should have asked for the form thus: indicative, imperfect, third person singular active. If the teacher had given the word before asking for such a scientific formation, the student could have been forming the word as the teacher was giving the directions and could have finished it at almost the same time that the teacher finished speaking.

4 Do not stress translation.

After reading the prohibitions, older teachers no doubt are wondering how they can test the students since the don'ts practically discard all the methods that were taught in courses of methodology for the giving of examinations. But everything is not lost. In fact, testing takes on new meaning and ever-widening possibilities if teachers make use of the newer methods in the teaching of Latin.

Here are some proposals for testing that try to keep in mind the goal of reading Latin as Latin. It should be noted that the tests themselves involve a learning situation since the students are being constantly forced to use the language to answer the questions.

176

Text tests

Sight comprehension

Ideally speaking, all examinations that teachers give on the text should be sight comprehension. Note that we said sight comprehension and sight translation. Comprehension is quite different from translation. It is quite possible that the student can understand the thought of the passage rather easily without being able to express it in adequate idiomatic English. Translation is an art that is more or less separated from comprehension as is evidenced by the immigrant who would tell us to make the door shut in imitation of his native language.

This sight-comprehension passage should approximate in difficulty the material with which the students have been working. It will therefore be necessary for the teacher to make a judgment about any text he uses and he should rather sin on the side of making the passage less difficult than the material with which the students are familiar.

The content of the sight comprehension passage should, as far as possible, restrict itself to the thoughts with which the students are familiar. This is necessary if we are not to involve the teacher in the neccessity of giving a large body of vocabulary in order to try to help the students comprehend the passage. For example, if students are reading about a Roman family, the sight comprehension passage should not concern itself with situations like army life or the courts of law.

Why should the test in text concern itself with a passage for sight comprehension? Because the teacher wishes to test the language skill of the students and not their memories. If the teacher gives a passage that students have studied and read, they can frequently answer the questions without reference to the text, particularly if the questions are of the comprehension type. Teachers should be intent on giving some kind of a communication in Latin and then phrasing the questions in such a way that they can easily determine whether or not the students have comprehended what was said or read.

The examination should be oral

The examination should be oral, at least in part, and this to emphasize the fact that Latin is a means of communication. Also in the examination teachers wish to give the students the benefit of all the signals for meaning that we discussed earlier — signals that are not had in an adequate way on the printed page, signals to which the student has a right when we test his comprehension.

Oral examinations may be given in a variety of ways. We list some of the more obvious schemes.

1 The text may be handed to the students in order that they may follow with the eye as the teacher reads it interpretatively. Students then proceed to the answering of the questions while retaining the text. The questions may be dictated, as in a short test during the recitation period, or the questions may be written on the page. This latter scheme permits the students to answer the questions more at leisure and in the order they wish. The questions, needless to say, should be in Latin and the answers expected in Latin.

2 The teacher may wish to read the passage several times as interpretatively as possible, and then distribute the text to the students and proceed as above.

3 This is a more difficult testing procedure. Give the text to the students, read it interpretatively for them once or twice, then allow time for the students themselves to read the text quietly. Collect the papers that contain the text and distribute the papers that contain the questions. This method is open to the objection that it puts an undue burden on the student's memory since the passage itself is a sight comprehension passage.

4 To find out who the students are that comprehend most rapidly, this type of testing may be used. Read the text interpretatively, distribute the text and allow the students to read it quietly. When the students feel they have comprehended the passage, they surrender the text and pick up the examination questions.

In order to keep students from translating the passage, the story should be relatively long and the time allotted for comprehension relatively short. Bonus points might be offered. For example, the first student to pick up the questions gets a bonus of twenty points, the second fifteen and so forth; the intervals between bonus points can be lessened in order to provide more incentive for more students. The teacher need not fear that the students will get a perfect paper, especially if he has worded the questions carefully.

5 If the comprehension passage is rather short, the teacher may wish to read it to them two or three times and then ask the questions without the students ever seeing the text. This procedure is handy for the shorter tests that are given during part of a recitatioin period.

6 Choose a lengthy passage. Allow five minutes for reading. Collect the text and distribute the questions. Those students who read only a small portion can answer only one or two questions; students who read rapidly

without translating can usually answer several questions. The student who has answered the most questions correctly gets a hundred, and the others are graded in relation to his paper. Such a scheme definitely penalizes those students who rely upon translation for comprehending the Latin.

Using Latin in the examination questions

The questions in the examination should be in Latin almost exclusively, and the answers should be given in Latin. This can be done even in first year and that after only a very short time in the classroom. Students come to realize very soon that «quis» asks for a personal noun in the nominative, while «quem» asks for the object of the verb. Questions on the structure of the language easily lend themselves to replies in Latin.

Latin is used in the questions and expected in the answers in order to force the student to constantly work in Latin and so eliminate English as the reference point for comprehension. The comprehension of the question is always considered part of the examination.

Preparing such examinations

The preparation of apt questions will undoubtedly be difficult in the beginning, but soon the teacher learns different ways of phrasing the questions in order to elicit the answers he wants. Experience in drawing up the questions, evaluation of these following the examination, and notations on how they can be improved in the future are steps that every teacher must willingly undertake if he is to draw up effective examinations.

Composing comprehension questions is a real challenge for the teacher in the beginning, but soon he learns techniques that make it easier for him to draw them up. Questions about forms and meaning are relatively easy. There are no easy rules to follow in composing the questions, but it has been found helpful for the teacher to ask a colleague to answer the questions on the text. If the colleague gives only one answer, then it may be safe to assume that the students too will give only one answer. In the beginning teachers should not be surprised that several answers are possible for the comprehension questions they ask.

Essay vs multiple-choice questions

From what has been said thus far it must be quite evident that the essay type question is the more apt for testing the student's comprehension. Such questions give no real clue to the correct answer and eliminate the element of guessing.

If essay questions are asked, the teacher has more assurance that the students know the Latin since they give the answer without the helps that are given in multiple-choice questions (which always give a correct answer). Moreover, the very composition of the answer indicates the student's knowledge of the language, for it is presupposed that he would be expected to answer in complete sentences.

It would seem, too, that the essay question is more in accord with ordinary language experience. Ordinarily we do not answer questions put to us by marking a pad; we use the language itself to indicate our thoughts.

Types of questions

Let us now make something of a list of the types of questions that teachers can ask in an examination. The questions deal with the essay type and are applicable to both the sight comprehension passage and the text that might have been studied in class.

1 Signal questions

Signal questions concern themselves almost exclusively with the structure of the language and need not embrace the student's comprehension. Usually he can answer such questions correctly if he knows what the signals mean. Signal questions make use of such words as «quālis, quantus, quōmodo, cūr, quō auxiliō, quem ad fīnem, quid patitur» and so forth. Here are some examples and the teacher will note how they resemble questions that are found in the drills.

Quālis vir est?	Bonus vir est.
Quantus vir est?	Magnus vir est.
Quōmodo hoc fecit?	Celeriter hoc fēcit.
Cūr hoc fēcit?	Ut sibi dīvitiās acquireret fēcit.
Quid patitur?	Amātur ille.

Such questions give the teacher no assurance about the student's comprehension of the passage. Hence the teacher must proceed to further questioning if he wishes assurance that the student has also comprehended the passage.

2 Transformation questions

Transformation questions involve some kind of change in the Latin that is given to the student. For example, a change from the active to the passive, from singular to plural, from present to past, involves a transformation.

Fēmina amat puerum.	Puer ā fēminā amātur.
Puer in agrō lūdit.	Puerī in agrō lūdunt.
Nauta natat.	Nauta natābat.

Besides the simple changes indicated above, the questions might involve a change in phrases or clauses.

Mīles vēnit et Caesarem salūtāvit.	Mīles postquam vēnit, Caesarem salūtāvit.
Postquam hostēs superātī sunt Caesar abīvit.	Hostibus superātīs, Caesar abīvit.

Even entire sentences can be changed.

Servus dominō servit.	Utinam servus dominō servīret.

Transformation questions readily enough reveal the student's knowledge of grammatical changes. But such a transformation can be done without a full comprehension of a sentence. Therefore further questions must be asked if the teacher wishes to test the comprehension of the student.

To assure himself that transformations can be effected without comprehension, the teacher himself might try this question.

Transform the active statement to passive. «Crābrō» and «olor» are nouns; «āles» and «cicur» are adjectives.

Āles crābrō pungit olōrem cicurem.[1]

Since it is not too likely that most Latin teachers will know the meanings of the words, the only point about which they might doubt when making the transformation to the passive is the use or non-use of the preposition, «ab».

3 Substitution

This type of question can concern itself with individual words.

In the sentence, «Nauta dīves est sed nōn est fēlīx», what conjunction can be substituted for «sed» that will retain the idea of contrast even though it may intensify the contrast?

---

[1]The answer is: Olor cicur pungitur ab ālite crābrōne. Āles, ālitis, winged; crābrō, crābrōnis, hornet; pungō, pungere, pupugī, punctum, 3, prick, annoy, sting; olor, olōris, m., swan; cicur, cicuris, tame.

The student should give this answer: «Nauta dīves est at nōn est fēlīx.»

Substitution type questions can involve entire clauses.

In the following sentence substitute another construction for the subordinate clause without changing the meaning: «Si tū dux noster es, nōn timēbimus.»

The answer might be something like this: «Tē duce, nōn timēbimus.»

Phrases, too, change in accordance with substitution.

In the following sentence substitute another construction for the underlined phrase but be careful not to change the meaning: «<u>Propter victōriam</u> gaudet.»

The answer will be: «Victōriā gaudet.»

Substitution questions come closer to revealing the student's comprehension of a sentence, though it may be objected that they come dangerously close to the "tag" type of question that was discussed earlier. Since substitution usually involves a change in the structure of the sentence, it is possible that the student could make the change without fully understanding the thought, though this is rather unlikely as can be seen from the examples given above.

4 Completion

If completion questions are worded properly they will show clearly whether or not a student comprehends a given sentence or passage, especially so if the question changes the construction from what it was in the original.

Mātrona et Sēquana Gallōs ā Belgīs dīvidunt.

Inter Gallōs et Belgās fuērunt flūmina _____.

Completion questions are handy for testing morphology.

Puer___ bon___ et puell___ sapient___ Deum lauda___.

They are also handy for testing grammatical usages.

Decem mīlia mīlitum mīsit___ facilius urbem caperet.

Lēgātōs_____ dē pāce agerent mīsit.

Vēnit_____ cum eō loquerētur.

Multōs explōrātōrēs mīsit_____ explōrandum.

Multōs explōrātōrēs explōrandī___ mīsit.

Vocabulary too can be tested by completion questions. If the students are quite familiar with a passage, the teacher can give the passage but omit significant nouns, verbs, pronouns, or other parts of speech and expect that the students will be able to fill in the proper words. Teacher must, of course, allow synonyms or expressions that make reasonable sense. This type of testing, it may be objected, puts a high premium on memorizing the text.

> Castra _(1)_ in Ītaliā contrā _(2)_ Rōmānum,
> in Etrūriae faucibus _(3)_ .
> crēscit in diēs singulōs hostium _(4)_ . (Cat. I)
> (1) sunt, erant, fuerunt
> (2) populum, exercitum
> (3) collocata, posita
> (4) numerus, manus

5 Matching

Take items from the passage and even change them somewhat. Put these in one column. Put phrases or clauses about the items in the other column and ask the students to match them. If students are allowed to have the text in front of them, there will not be such a burden on the memory and it will more clearly indicate their knowledge of the content of the passage.

> Senātum frequentem celeriter, ut vīdistis, coēgī. Atque intereā
> statim admonitū Allobrogum Gājum Sulpicium praetōrem, fortem
> virum, mīsī quī ex aedibus Cethēgī, sī quid tēlōrum esset, efferret;
> ex quibus ille maximum sīcārum numerum et gladiōrum extulit.
> (Cat. III.)

1 Senātus	1 convēnit
2 Praetor	2 admonuērunt
3 Allobrogēs	3 missus est
	4 sīcās numerāvit
	5 gladiōs extulērunt

The difficulty of such questions can be increased if there are several items in the right-hand column. Students should be told about this and should be expected to give all the references that are applicable to any one item in the left-hand column.

6 True–false

Statements about a certain passage can be given and students asked to indicate whether the statement is true or false. If the students do not guess then such questions will clearly indicate whether or not they have understood the passage. For example, the following statements might be given (based on the passage in the previous section):

   1 Paucī tantum senātōrēs adfuērunt.

   2 Domī Cethēgī fuērunt multī gladiī.

   3 Cicerō scīvit gladiōs domī Cethēgī fuisse.

7 Comparison

This type of question will clearly reveal the comprehension of the student or the lack of it.

Give two versions of a story and then ask the students to list the discrepancies in the thought but not those in the grammatical constructions. When writing the second version, teachers should be careful not to introduce mere negatives from time to time, but they should strive to change significant parts of the story.

Stygia Prōserpina,	Stygia Prōserpina, uxor
soror Dītis, pecudēs	Dītis, palūdem jūxtā
nigrās in nemore o-	Avernī rīpam in nemore
pācō regit.	lūcidō nūmine torquet.

8 Summary

Ask for a written summary of what the students have read or heard, preferably in Latin. Teachers should remember that if students have the text in front of them they may be able to write a fair summary without fully understanding the story. Hence it is better to read the passage to them and then ask them to write the summary.

If the teacher wishes to allow them to use the text to make the summary, he might then ask for the summary in English.

9 Relationships

Give a paragraph but omit all the conjunctions. Leave a space where they should occur. Ask the students to supply them in accord with the meaning. Reasonable synonyms should always be allowed.

The passage that is used should be a text that the students have not seen before in order to prevent mere memory from aiding them in answering the question.

    Nōn es dīves [sed] es beātus [quia] scīs Deum tē semper dīligere.

    Fierī nōn potest quīn sīs beātus [sī] Deō tōtō corde serviās.

This type of question can be varied by giving the students a paragraph in which there are many individual sentences, some of which are connected by coordinating conjunctions. Then ask the students to rewrite the paragraph using subordinating conjunctions where possible. Such rewriting cannot be done unless the student comprehends what he reads.

10 Translation

Translation can and should be asked in examinations. If part of a passage is to be translated, the teacher should make sure that the students are given adequate time for such work. Students should be encouraged to make a rough copy first, and then during the rewrite they should strive to express the thoughts idiomatically in English.

Translation should not constitute the major portion of the examination except perhaps in fourth year since it must be remembered that translation is a skill over and beyond comprehension. In the earlier years teachers should be content with the translation of only a few sentences in any one examination.

11 Appreciation

Questions involving appreciation are certainly apt when the teacher is testing the student about his knowledge of the masters, Cicero, Caesar, Vergil, and others.

There is a wide range of possibility for this type of question involving such things as aptness of expression, clarity of presentation, use of rhetorical devices and their effectiveness, contrast between the expression of the thought as given by later authors including those of other languages, the contrast between the poetic and the prose presentation of the same thought.

If such questions are given, teachers should indicate to the students that it is not satisfactory to merely parrot what the teacher may have given in class; the emphasis is to be on the student's own observations.

For example, suppose the teacher has been explaining how the ancients used their imaginations to conjure up an image such as the chimera (description of a volcano). In an examination he might ask what the ancients might have had in mind when they spoke of Medusa the Gorgon whose look turned the beholder to stone. He should not be surprised if he gets an answer such as was given the author a few years ago, that of a decomposing corpse.

185

12 Reference

This type of question will concern itself mostly with background material that gives full meaning to the text. For example, the «saevā Gorgone» used of Minerva's shield. Who were the Gorgons? Who killed Medusa? How did he kill her? These and the like questions help to find out what the student knows by way of background that should enhance the thought which the author wished to express.

A variation of this type might be something like this. If «Cernēs urbem et prōmissa Lāvīnī moenia» were in Vergil's second book of the «Aeneid» to whom would it refer? The student should answer, Creusa, since it is she who foretells the future to Aeneas in order to console him, just as Jupiter in Book I foretold the future to Venus in order to console her.

> So spake th' Eternal Father, and fulfil'd
> All justice: nor delayed the winged saint
> After his charge received.
> Milton, Paradise Lost, V, [246–48]

If these words were in the fourth book of the «Aeneid», give the setting in which they would have appeared and identify all persons concerned.

13 Evaluation

Questions involving evalution are best suited for the later years of Latin study, especially when they are studying the works of the masters such as Vergil. Here is an example of this type of question.

In the second«Aeneid» the Laocoon episode could have been omitted without destroying the story. Discuss the truth or falsity of the statement and give detailed reasons for your position.

Questions that are of an evaluative nature might include a discussion of the moral implications of a story or a certain character's action, the validity of the reasons alleged by a certain character for his action, the soundness or foolishness of a certain strategy, how the very expression of the thoughts fits the mood of the character and many others that alert and interested teachers may conceive.

14 Completing the story

Students are sometimes dissatisfield with the fact that authors seldom begin their story at the beginning and almost never end at the end. Teachers can occasionally in an examination give the imagination of their students full play and ask questions such as these, the answer to which will reveal much of the student's appreciation for the story.

Vergil ends the fourth book with the release of Dido's soul by Iris. Give your own version of her entry into the nether world and the judgment to which she was subjected.

Supposing Dido did not actually die but finally recovered under the skillful care of her physician. What would be a sequel to the fourth book?

This type of question can be given even in first year. The teacher gives the main elements of a story, and then allows the students to complete it in any way they wish. The completion that the student writes will clearly reveal his active knowledge of vocabulary and grammar.

A multiple-choice test

Very many of the foregoing types of questions can be used rather effectively in multiple-choice questions about a text. I submit the following as examples. The passage is taken from Caesar's description of the revolt along the seacoast as it appears in «Second Year Latin», p. 88, by Robert J. Henle, Loyola University Press, 1958.

Itaque, dējectīs antemnīs, mīlitēs summā vī trānscendere in hostium nāvēs contendēbant. Quod postquam barbarī fierī animadvertērunt, expugnātīs complūribus nāvibus, fugā salūtem petere contendērunt. Ac jam conversīs nāvibus in eam partem quō ventus ferēbat, tanta subito tranquillitās facta est ut sē ex locō movēre nōn possent. Quae rēs maxima fuit opportūna. Nam singulās nāvēs nostrī expugnāvērunt ut paucae ex omnī numerō noctis interventū ad terram pervenīrent. Ab hōrā ferē quārtā usque ad sōlis occāsum pugnābātur.

1 Function of the ablative absolute

«Dējectīs antemnīs» has the same meaning as

    1 quamquam antemnae dējectae sunt
    2 quia antemnae dējectae sunt
    3 ut antemnae dējectae essent
    4 postquam antemnae dējectae sunt

2 Function of a descriptive tense

«Contendēbant» implies

> 1 that the soldiers boarded all the ships
> 2 that the soldiers were boarding the ships while something else was going on
> 3 that it took quite some time for the soldiers to board the enemy ships
> 4 that the boarding of the ships occurred in a very short time

3 Comprehension

Once Caesar's plan was apparent, the enemy

> 1 counterattacked vigorously and with much success
> 2 fled at once
> 3 counterattacked vigorously but with no success
> 4 counterattacked half-heartedly and then tried to flee

4 Expectancy

The use of «tanta» indicates to the reader that the following subordinate clause will

> 1 tell the reason for the action of the main clause
> 2 give the result of the action of the main clause
> 3 seek further information about the main action
> 4 tell the purpose of the action in the main clause

5 Comprehension

«Conversīs... ferēbat» means that

> 1 the wind was helpful to Caesar's ships
> 2 the enemy turned their ships in order to sail away
> 3 the enemy headed their ships into the wind
> 4 Caesar's enemy accomplished flight by heading for shore

6 Knowledge of the Veneti and their ships which was explained in the notes of the text, hence a reference question.

After the wind died down the enemy could not escape

> 1 because the sails were fouled up
> 2 because the Veneti had no rowers
> 3 because Caesar's men used grappling hooks
> 4 for none of the reasons given here

7 Comprehension

Caesar's victory here was largely due to

1 superb strategy
2 overpowering manpower
3 a chance turn in natural events
4 poor strategy on the part of the enemy

8 Comprehension of the passage as a unit

In the Old Testament we read that in answer to Joshua's prayer God made the sun stand still so his victory could be complete. In the case

1 darkness made no difference for Caesar's men, so he did not need help
2 the enemy did not make use of the darkness to escape anyway
3 Caesar did not need extra time as all the enemy ships were captured
4 Caesar could have used such extra time as was Joshua's for a more complete victory

9 Comprehension of small units

Directions: In the following questions, words or phrases from the passage are given. These are followed by four Latin words or phrases. Select the word or phrase which is the best definition of the words taken from the paragraph.

summā vī

1 magnopere
2 fortiter
3 fortissimē
4 sine ūlla difficultāte

salūtem petere

1 servārī sē
2 servāre eōs
3 salūtem dare
4 servāre sē

10 Comprehension in Latin and change of forms in text

Directions: The following questions have incomplete Latin statements that deal with the contents of the passage. From the choices select the one that best completes the incomplete Latin statement in the question.

Paucae nāvēs effūgērunt...

1 quia tempestas orta est
2 propter tranquillitātem
3 quod nox intervēnit
4 quoniam ad terram nāvēs pervēnērunt

11 Variation on comprehension of the passage

Directions: In each of the following questions determine which set of words has the most contrast in view of their meaning in this paragraph.

189

    1 dējectīs antemnīs... conversīs nāvibus
    2 fugā salūtem petere contendērunt... subito tranquillitās facta est
    3 rēs fuit opportūna... ad sōlis occāsum pugnābātur
    4 contendēbant... pervenīrent

12 Variation in comprehension — applying «opportūna» to the Veneti rather than to the Romans.

Caesar's use of «opportūna» implies
    1 bad fortune for the Veneti
    2 a stroke of good fortune for the Romans and the Veneti
    3 good fortune for the Veneti
    4 nothing about fortune for either side

13 Summary-type question

A good title for this paragraph would be
    1 Tranquillitās parit victōriam.
    2 Nox ēripuit victōriam.
    3 Multās hōrās pugnātur.
    4 Nāvēs expugnātae sunt.

Testing of vocabulary

We might preface this treatment of vocabulary testing by stating that English should be used as little as possible in order to make certain that we do not force the students to act contrary to the proper procedures in the learning of vocabulary. It is our ideal that students will directly associate the Latin word with the object or thought. This direct association will impose some limitations on testing but they are not significant.

Vocabulary should be tested in context and not in isolation, since it is the context that gives the real meaning to the word. For example, «rōbur» can have many meanings: oak tree, oak, hard wood, lance, planks of oak, strength, vigor, power, and usually only one meaning will fit a definite context.

Neither should a long list of disparate words be given as this is entirely contrary to the normal use of words and puts an undue burden on the memory. Were we to ask a student to sit down and write out as many words as possible that he knows, he would find it difficult even in his native language. He would soon come to the point where he could not add more words. Then if we were to ask him to define each one he would probably have much more difficulty; however, if we would put these same words in context, the student would probably not have much difficulty in defining them.

Here are some suggested ways of testing vocabulary.

1 Pictures

In the very early stages of language learning pictures offer a convenient way of testing vocabulary and they can be used in a variety of ways. The teacher can make the drawings on a ditto page and then duplicate them for distribution to the students during the test. Students are asked to identify the objects in the pictures. Needless to say, the pictures must be rather simple with only a few objects represented.

If the teacher has a set of pictures, he might distribute one to each student and follow the procedure outlined above. Should he wish each to have the same picture, he will have to resort to duplication, or he might use an opaque projector.

At other times he distributes the pictures and asks the students to write a sentence or two about each one; or he might ask them to write a series of sentences about the picture.

Should the teacher wish to test verbs, he must use a picture that concretizes the action or one that symbolizes it. The sentences then can be expanded by the use of suitable adverbs in the sentences they write, just as the sentences naming the objects can be expanded by means of adjectives or adjective equivalents.

2 Synonyms and antonyms

If the teacher has given the students some paragraphs of Latin, he underlines certain words and asks the students to give synonyms or antonyms for these words.

3 Related words

At other times the teacher underlines certain words in a paragraph or two of Latin and asks the students to give the related words. For example, if the verb «regō» appeared and were underlined, the student could then supply such words as «rēx» and «rēctor».

4 Proportion

Proportion is a handy way of testing vocabulary and at the same time it gives the teacher a definite knowledge of the student's capacity to see the relationship between words. For example, if this is the question

   mīles : exercitus :: nauta : _____

the student would fill in the word «classis» in the blank space.

5 Attribution

This type is question is helpful in testing adjectives. It will also definitely indicate whether the student knows the meaning of the word or not. These are difficult to compose but are worth the effort since they are so searching. For example, suppose we instruct the students to pick the adjective that can best be used with the noun in this question,

> canis — honestus justus
> crūdēlis palūster

the student should choose «crūdēlis».

6 Fill in

This type of question is particulary handy for testing the student's knowledge of conjunctions: coordinating and subordinating. In the following paragraph students are asked to supply the conjunctions or connecting words.

> Potestne tibi haec lūx, Catilīna,
> _____ hūjus caelī spīritus esse jūcundus, [aut]
> _____ sciās esse hōrum nēminem [cum]
> _____ nesciat tē prīdiē Kalendās Jānuāriās [quī]
> stetisse in comitiō cum tēlō?

As can be gathered from the example, this type of testing is searching. The difficulty can be increased if a sight passage is used. This type can also be used for testing the student's knowledge of prepositions.

> _____ timōrem in montēs ex proeliō sē recēpit. [propter or ob]

Adjectives and adverbs can also be tested, provided that the teacher leaves the student free to insert any adjective or adverb that makes sense in the context.

7 New words

Testing for the meaning of new words is very much like giving the student a sight comprehension passage in a text test. In drawing up the question the teacher should be careful to use at least nine familiar words out of every ten in order to permit the student to arrive at the meaning of the new word from the context. This type of testing should be used sparingly since it is difficult, as can be judged from the following paragraph. The student should be able to conclude to the meaning of «auceps».

Formīca sitiēns cum ad fontem dēscendisset ut biberet, in aquam cecidit nec multum abfuit quīn misera perīret. Columba quaedam in arbore sedēns, misericordiā tācta, rāmulum in aquam injēcit. Hunc assecūta est formīca eīque innatāns mortem effūgit. Paulō post adfuit auceps, quī columbae īnsidiābātur. Formīca, ut piae columbae opem ferret, ad aucupem arrēpsit et tam vehementer eum momordit ut arundinēs prae dolōre ābjiceret. Columba, strepitū arundinum territa, āvolāvit ac perīculum incolumis ēvāsit.

When composing questions that involve the arriving at the meaning of new words, the teacher will do well to restrict his questions to physical objects and action words. Abstract words create too much of a problem.

8 Composition

Give a list of words and ask the students to compose meaningful sentences using the words.

It may be objected that such testing of vocabulary involves too many other skills that might distract the student. However, if the list of words is not too lengthy, students usually manage to use most of the words in a sentence or two.

9 Translation

Translation can form a minor part of a vocabulary test, provided that the words in the test were used in sentences. The teacher will know from experience what words in a series of readings cause difficulties for students. Or it may be that when they were reading he marked the words that caused problems for the students. These words the teacher uses in the composing of Latin sentences. He then asks for a translation, or he suggests several translations from which the students are to choose the best. Here is an example.

From the context established in the question determine which of the choices gives the correct meaning of the underlined Latin words.

<u>Somniat</u> <u>hic</u> quī dīvitiās habet, nam mors omnia subtrahet.

   1 he is full of joy
   2 his is a tranquil life
   3 a dreamer is he
   4 he is full of hopes

This type of question is good for testing the unusual perfects of verbs. Here is an example.

The best meaning for the underlined word in the Latin sentence, «Animālia <u>pāvēre</u> parvulōs suōs», is

1 to spare
2 [they] were astonished
3 to pave
4 [they] have fed, [they] have nourished

If translation is used to test vocabulary, the Latin sentences should be very simple, consisting for the most part of subject, predicate, and object, together with their modifiers.

10 Matching

It is presupposed that all the matching questions will be drawn from a reading that appears at the top of examination page. If the text is not given, the vocabulary is being tested in isolated forms. Such testing puts an undue burden on the student's memory and will not disclose his real knowledge of vocabulary.

Matching questions are rather easy to draw up, and if they are not too long they readily show the student's knowledge of vocabulary. This type can be used in a variety of ways.

In the first list are found the Latin words. Synonyms and antonyms are in the second list. Students are asked to match them.

Draw up a list of Latin words, and in the second column give a number of English derivatives. Ask students to indicate the source of the derivatives.

In the first list give a number of nouns or proper names and in the second give adjectives that will describe one or other of the nouns. Now and then synonyms for the adjectives that appear in the text should be used.

In the first list give nouns or proper names and a verb to form sentences. In the second list give adverbs that might have appeared in the text. Ask the students to match them.

Occasionally a teacher will give a list of Latin nouns, and in the adjoining column he will put the English meanings. Students are then to match them. Since these are taken from the text which the student supposedly knows, they are not being tested in isolation.

11 Relationships

List several conjunctions that appear in a paragraph of Latin. Ask the students to describe the connection between the two clauses. For example, «ut» in a purpose clause would be answered something like this: he did the

194

thing but it is not just merely the doing of it for he had a definite purpose in mind, namely, to circumvent the enemy's plan. Such a question tries to find out how much the student knows about the conjunction and what it does in a sentence.

A much more difficult question would be one like this.

Determine what relationship (disregarding meanings) exists between the words in the question. Then find that same relationship between the sets of words that are given in the choices.

vel......inde

    1 quotiēns .... simul   3 sīve................... tandem
    2 recēns .... tumulus 4 fors................... ops

Since «vel...inde» are a conjunction and an adverb, that is the relationship the student must look for in the choices and this he will find in the words «sīve...tandem».

It may justly be objected that this type of question is too scientific, but despite this objection it could at times be used to stress the differences between words.

Other relationships that might be tested in this way are: noun and adjective, adjective and adverb, transitive and intransitive verbs, regular and deponent verbs.

12 Misplaced item

Give a list of four words and ask which one of them is out of place or does not fit with the other three. Here is an example.

    nāvis   nauta   mare   arbor

«Arbor» is the one that is clearly out of place. Such questions can be made very difficult as in this example.

    nūmen   penātēs   dea   sōl

If «sōl» were capitalized then it would fit with the others.

13 Substitution

In questions involving substitution the teacher gives a Latin sentence and underlines certain words. He asks the student to substitute other words for the underlined ones with this proviso, that the resulting sentence be a meaningful one. This type is particularly useful for the multiple-choice questions in an examination. Here are some examples.

Spērō senem prōditūrum esse cōgitātiōnem suam.

 1 aetās...somnus
 2 Archias...lūmen
 3 Ennius...carmen
 4 doctrīna...sēdēs

«Spērō Ennium prōditūrum esse carmen suum» makes a meaningful sentence, whereas the other combinations do not.

Mīror Catōnem eum honōre dōnāsse.

 1 Hēraclīensis.... somnus 3 scrīptor............. lūmina
 2 Mūsa.......... ars   4 regiō............... spatium

«Mīror Mūsam eum arte dōnāsse» makes a meaningful sentence. Note that in this type the student would be expected to put the substituted words into their proper cases.

14 Drived meaning

Give an English word that you are rather certain the students have not seen before, but make certain that is connected with or is derived from a familiar Latin word. Give several meanings for the English word and ask the students for the correct one. They make their choice from the knowledge they have of the Latin word.

Here are a few examples. Note that this type can be used best in situations that call for multiple-choice type questions.

pendant
 1 thoughtful
 2 pentagon   [pendant is derived from the Latin
 3 ornament   word «pendeō», hence the meaning
 4 pool   "ornament."]

allocution
 1 perception
 2 address   [allocution is derived from the Latin
 3 protection   word «alloquor», hence the mean-
 4 allowance   ing "address."]

There are many possibilities for testing dervied meanings such as this.

From the choices given, select the Latin word that does NOT have a connection with some English word in the sentence.

Military regulations prohibit our transporting civilians.

1 mīlliēs
2 trānsportō
3 cīvitās
4 rēgnum

15 Context questions

In each question a definite situation is established. The students are expected to pick the word that will complete the incomplete Latin sentence. We presuppose mankind's normal reaction to the situation that is established.

Mīles occīsus est. Ergō māter ējus...
1 gaudet
2 canit
3 dolet
4 audit

Mīles trāns pontem īvit. Igitur nunc est in rīpā...
1 proximā
2 angustā
3 ulteriōre
4 inferiōre

16 Definitions

Directions: From the choices given, choose the one that best defines the Latin word in the question.

īnsula est...
1 terra quae habet fluviōs
2 terra quae undique habet aquās circum sē
3 magna terra prope mare
4 maxima terra quae nōn habet aquās

Conclusion

It may be objected that many of the foregoing types of questions for testing vocabulary are nothing else than intelligence questions. That may be true, but do not the intelligence tests search out the student's knowledge of English vocabulary? Students who have read widely in English and whose vocabulary therefore is usually quite broad do seem to do well on intelligence tests. It would seem then that there is a definite connection between

197

an abundant experience in reading and a knowledge of vocabulary. Our testing is not for assigning students to an intelligence category, but rather to find out what vocabulary they know in Latin.

Testing of morphology

Morphology should be tested in context and this can be done either by the strict essay-type questions or by the multiple-choice type questions. The strict essay question is more difficult for the student since no answer is suggested. Here are some possible ways of testing morphology.

Completion

The completion-type question is perhaps the easiest to use when testing morphology. And here are some suggestions.

Gender In colle _____ castra posita sunt.
     [summus, -a, -um]

Case Carnem _____ dedit.
     [canis, -is]

Number Castra _____ ā Caesare in colle summō.
     [pōnō]
    Inveniunt in hāc silvā _____.
        [multus, -a, -um] [leō, leōnis]

Person _____ in hunc mundum vēnī.
    _____ dēbētis hunc dīligere.

Comparison of adjectives
    Alter mōns est altus, alter est _____.
    Inter hōs mīles glōriōsus est _____.
        [fortis, -e]
    Dux est omnium _____.
      [sapiēns, -ntis]

Comparison of adverbs
    Alter dīligenter ēgit, alter _____ ēgit.
    Inter hōs omnēs _____ pugnāvit.
       [fortis, -e]
    Hōrum omnium dux _____ locūtus est.
      [sapiēns, -ntis]

Verbs

   Tense   Herī in castra _____ Caesar.
                        [veniō, 4]
           Crās in castra _____ mīlitēs.
                        [veniō, 4]

   Voice   Marīa ā Deō _____.
                        [amō, 1]
           Urbs mūrō _____.
                        [dēfendō, 3]

Substitution

Questions that involve substitution are handy for testing the student's knowledge of numbers. This type can also be used for testing other sections of morphology.

Numbers

   Students can be asked to write out the cardinal number for the Roman numeral that is used in the sentences.

   In silvā sunt XI mīlitēs.

   Diē XXX vēnit hospēs.

   II et II sunt IV.

Adverbs

   Students are asked to substitute an adverb for the underlined adverbial expression.

   Maximā cum cūrā copiās parāvit ut urbs caperētur.

      [Dīligentissimē]

   Magnā cum cūrā copiās parāvit.

      [Dīligenter]

   Majōre cum cūrā copiās parāvit.

      [Dīligentius]

   The question can be made easier by using expressions such as «maximā cum dīligentiā» wherein the adverb is suggested.

Transformation

The various ways of drilling the verb that were suggested in the chapter that treated the teaching of morphology can be used for testing, if proper directions are given, the students for making the transformations.

Teach the Latin, I pray you

1 Directions: In each of the following questions you will find an incomplete Latin sentence. From the adjectives that are suggested choose the one that will correctly complete the sentence. Note the number in front of the choice you made and mark your answer sheet accordingly.

Collis est
1 magna	3 magnum	[gender]
2 magnus	4 magnīs	

2 Directions: One word in the Latin sentence is omitted. Select the correct form of the noun that will complete the Latin sentence.

Carnem _____ dedit.
1 canō   3 cane
2 canī   4 canem

[case]

Mīles _____ pepercit.
1 hominī   3 homine
2 hominem   4 hominis

3 Directions: In each of the following questions one word in the Latin sentence is omitted. From the choices select the correct form of the verb that will complete the Latin sentence.

Castra _____ in Ītaliā.   [number]
1 est   3 es
2 sunt   4 estis

4 Directions: In each of the following questions there is a Roman numeral indicating the number of people. From the choices given select the correct cardinal number for the Roman numeral and mark your answer sheet accordingly.

In silvā sunt XI mīlitēs.
1 octō   3 ūndecim   [numbers]
2 decem   4 novem

5 Directions: In each question the Latin sentence gives a statement that is uttered today. From the choices pick the sentence that is correct IF the speaker wishes to indicate that the entire sentence was spoken yesterday.

Mīles labōrat.
1 Mīles labōrāverat. 3 Mīles labōrāret. [tense usage]
2 Mīles labōrāverit. 4 Mīles labōrābat.

Directions: Each question contains a statement. Immediately following the statement there is an adverb. From the choices that are given select the one that must be used with the suggested adverb.

200

Mīles pugnat. Herī...
1 mīles pugnābit. 3 mīles pugnābat. [tense usage]
2 mīles pugnāverat. 4 mīles pugnat.

Directions: From the choices that are given select the one that correctly completes the Latin sentence which appears in the question.

Pugnat ut...
1 vinceret 3 vincet   [tense usage]
2 vincat   4 vincerit

6 Directions: In each of the following questions you will find a Latin sentence with one word omitted. From the choices select the correct form that completes the Latin sentence.

Haec fossa est lāta, sed illa est _____.
1 lātius   3 lātiōris   [comparison]
2 lātior   4 lātē

Directions: In each of the following questions the Latin sentence makes a statement about one person or thing. From the choices select the one that must be used if a comparison is involved between two persons or things.

Crīnēs meī sunt rubrī.
1 rubriōrēs   3 rubrī   [comparison]
2 rubriōribus 4 rubriōrum

Directions: In each of the following questions there is a Latin sentence which contains an adjective or an adverb. From the choices select the form that must be used if the speaker wishes to indicate the greatest possible quality.

Via erat difficilis.
1 difficillima 3 difficile   [comparison]
2 difficilior   4 maximē difficilis

Rārē hoc fēcit.
1 rārius   3 rārior
2 rārissimē 4 rārissimum

Directions: From the choices given select the word or words that most nearly expresses the same idea that is found in the underlined portion of the sentence which appears in the question.

Maximā cum cūrā copiās parāvit ut urbs caperētur.
1 diligentius   3 dīligenter   [comparison]
2 dīligentissimē 4 dīligentiōre

7 Directions: In each incomplete Latin sentence the speaker wishes to say something about the ability of someone to do something. Select the correct

word or words that will complete the Latin statement.

Sī mīlitēs vēnerint, Caesar... gerere bellum.

    1 potest   3 potuit   [irregular verb forms]

    2 poterit   4 possit

8 Directions: Caesar is talking to his soldiers before the battle. Complete each of his statements by selecting the correct form or forms from the choices that are given.

Fortiter _____, mīlitēs.

    1 pugnāminī   3 pugnāre

    2 pugnā   4 pugnāte

_____ virtūtem nostram.

    1 exhibent   3 exhibeāmus   [grammar and forms]

    2 exhibeant   4 exhibēmus

_____ antequam hostēs oppugnant.

    1 nē pugnent   3 ne pugnātis

    2 nōlīte pugnāre   4 nōlī pugnāre

Testing of grammar

Little need be said about the testing of grammar because throughout the sections on the testing of text, vocabulary, and morphology we have been using grammar. For example, if a teacher wishes to test the student's knowledge of "wishes" he need but refer to the section where we spoke of drilling the forms of the subjunctive and he will have a ready way of testing the student's knowledge of "wishes." The same may be said about "temporal" clauses, and so forth.

In general, transformation-type questions will be most serviceable. For example, if the teacher wishes to test the students on conditions, he would draw up sentences that contain an ablative absolute instead of an if-clause. The students are then asked to turn the ablative absolute into a condtion. For example, «Custōdibus caesīs, urbs capta esset» becomes «Sī custōdēs caesī essent, urbs capta esset.» At other times the teacher might give a statement in the indicative and ask that the entire sentence be changed into a condition. For example, «Custōdibus caesīs, urbs capta est» becomes «Sī custōdēs caesī essent, urbs capta esset.» To indicate the type of condition, the teacher would not ordinarily use the tag "contrary to past fact" but would rather tell the student to express the thought in such a way as to indicate that the occurrence was impossible sometime in the past.

Situation-type questions are helpful, too. For example, the teacher gives the student two statements such as these: «Mīlitēs caesī sunt. Pugna cessāvit.» He tells the students to subordinate the first sentence to the second. This can be done by expressing causality («cum» with the subjunctive, «quod» with the indicative), or indicating a sequence in time («postquam» and the perfect indicative). The student may be allowed to choose the type of subordination, or the teacher can indicate which he wants.

Completion questions can be used for testing grammar. For example, the teacher asks the students to complete «Pugna cessāvit postquam...» with any thought that will not conflict with the main clause. If the student finished such a sentence with a tense in the perfect indicative, the teacher could rest assured that the student knows the proper grammatical usage.

It hardly needs be said that the testing of grammar should be a functional one, that is, the student should be asked to demonstrate his knowledge of the construction. He need not know how to "tag" it.

Grammar can also be tested by multiple-choice questions. Here are some by way of examples.

1 Directions: In each of the following questions there is an incomplete Latin sentence. From the choices select the word or words that correctly completes the sentence in the question.

Munīvērunt viam...
    1 cum lapidibus
    2 lapidibus   [ablative of means]
    3 lapidum
    4 lapidī

Caesar... vēnit in castra.
    1 cum suīs mīlitibus
    2 mīlitibus   [ablative of ac-
    3 suōrum militium   companiment]
    4 suīs

Recognōsco... mulierem.
    1 hoc   [agreement of
    2 haec   demonstrative
    3 hunc   pronoun]
    4 hanc

2 Directions: In each of following questions there are two Latin sentences. The second sentence involves some changes from the first, and one or more words are omitted in the second sentence. From the choices select the correct Latin word or words that will complete the second sentence.

Marīa amat Chrīstum.

Chrīstus ā Marīa _____.

   1 amāvit

   2 amātus est   [ablative of agent]

   3 amātur

   4 amētur

Mātre āmissā, canēs periērunt.

_____ canēs periērunt.

                              [function of an

   1 Cum māter āmissa esset   ablative abso-

   2 Postquam māter āmissa esset   lute]

   3 Quamvīs māter āmissa est

   4 none of these

3 Directions: In each question the Latin sentence gives an utterance that is spoken today. From the choices given select the sentence that is correct IF the speaker wishes to indicate that the entire sentence was spoken yesterday.

Dīcit mīlitem fugere.

   1 Dīxit mīlitem fūgisse.

   2 Dīxit mīlitem fugere.   [tense by relation]

   3 Dīxit mīlitem fugitūrum esse.

   4 Dīcit mīlitem fūgisse.

How will the sentence in the previous question be expressed if the speaker wishes to indicate that the soldier will act tomorrow?

   1 Dīcit mīlitem fugitūrum esse.

   2 Dīcit mīlitem fugere.

   3 Dīxit mīlitem fugitūrum esse.

   4 Dīcit mīlitem fūgisse.

4 Directions: In a debate one side or other often concedes a point to the opponent. Each of the following questions contains a statement that is to be modified by a concession. From the choices select the correct Latin clause that will complete the Latin sentence.

_____ repente cōnfessus est.

   1 Cum negāre posset

   2 Quamvīs negāre potuit   [concessive

   3 Ut negāre poterat   subjunctive]

   4 Quamquam negare posset

Conclusion

It is not to be supposed that the foregoing treatment of testing is by any means definitive or exhaustive. As more experience is garnered, the types of questions will undoubtedly be increased and their usefulness more fully appraised.

Experienced teachers should not hesitate to experiment with various types of questions. Teachers who are just beginning their career will do well to follow the more approved types that are presented in such courses as "Tests and Measurements". To this same type of course the teacher is referred for the correct format for examinations.

Chapter 9

The art of questioning

In the chapter entitled "Teaching the reading of Latin" much was said about questions that the student might keep in mind as he reads in order to learn how to interpret the various uses of the ablative case, namely, how, where, when, why, what kind. If such questions help the student interpret the use of ablative case, then the teacher should be able to make use of these when he wishes the student to give in reply one or other usage of the ablative. Generally, however, these five questions are too vague for indicating the student's precise knowledge of a particular usage. Therefore the teacher must have at his disposal a set of questions that will adequately reveal the student's knowledge.

The ideal in the reading of Latin is comprehension without translation. But how is the teacher to assure himself that the student is comprehending? This assurance can come only from the replies that the student gives to questions that are formulated by the teacher, whether such questions be oral as in the recitation period, or written as in the examination.

Theoretically questions can concern themselves with the structure of the language or with the content of what has been read. In the early phases of language training when the questions are simple, it is possible for the student to answer them without knowing the meaning. For example, suppose the student hears the sentence, «Nauta servum videt», followed by the question, «Quis servum videt?» He can in actual practice answer, «Nauta servum videt» without knowing the meaning since the answer is merely a matter of knowing which word is the subject of the sentence. In other words, the student needs know only that «nauta» is a noun in the nominative case.

Once, however, the student poceeds to the reading of connected discourse, the answer to the question «Quis servum videt» will not be so simple and for that reason it is most likely a reliable question indicating comprehension since the student will likely have to choose between several sentences and their subjects. The answer might also involve a proper name. Particularly would such a question reveal the student's comprehension if the text mentioned nothing about "seeing" and merely indicated the conversation between, for example, the master and the slave.

In practice, then, when questioning students about the content of a passage, the distinction between structural and content questions vanishes for the most part.

Earlier when giving some prohibitions in the matter of testing, we stated "Do not ask the student to 'tag' the grammatical usages." Teachers should not conclude that therefore no questions on grammar are given to the students. Grammar questions are still asked, but they are asked in such a way as to reveal the student's ability to use or understand the grammatical usage. For example, suppose the teacher wished to ask about the subordinate clause in this sentence, «Caesar imperāvit ut hostēs obsidēs trāderent.» He would more than likely ask a question such as this, «Quid Caesar imperāvit?» Such a question reveals to the student that the clause in question is a noun clause. And if the student gives the subordinate clause in his answer, the teacher can be satisfied that the student understands the thought and the fact that the clause acts as a noun. For reading purposes there is no further comprehension if the student call tell the teacher that «ut hostēs obsidēs trāderent» is a noun clause of purpose. If the teacher feels that such a question reveals too much to the student, he can easily rephrase the question somewhat after this fashion, «Quae jussa hostibus ā Caesare data sunt?» Now a correct reply undoubtedly reveals the student's comprehension of the thought, and the way he words the answer will also likely reveal his knowledge of the grammar.

The formulary that a teacher may use in questioning the student about the content of a text will vary in accord with the content of the text and what the teacher wishes to ask. Such formularies are as limitless as the capability of the language to express thought. However, there are some more or less standard formularies that the teachers find helpful when they wish to force the student to give definite answers about the text.

Rather than give a mere listing of question words such as one might find if he went through a dictionary, let us try to organize the question formularies around situations that might occur in the readings. The situations are arbitrary but it is hoped that they will be useful to teachers who are for the first time endeavoring to find out how much a student comprehends without resorting to the last means, namely, translation. Translation always relates the text to English and since we wish to teach the student to comprehend without the intermediary of English, teachers should use translation as a check on comprehension only as a last resort.

Persons and things

Subject

There are several ways of asking for the subject of the sentence. These include «quis, quid», «quīnam, quaenam, quodnam», «quisnam, quidnam», «quae rēs». If there is question of proper names, questions such as these may be used, «Quid est nōmen ējus quī pugnat? Quōmodo appellātur quī pugnat? Quōmodo nōminātur quī pugnat?»

Object

The interrogative forms that are used for eliciting the subject can, with proper changes for case, be used for requiring the object in the answer, «quem, quid», «quemnam, quamnam, quodnam», «quemnam, quidnam», «quam rem». The other questions, too, need change such as this, «Quid est nōmen ējus quem hominēs laudant? Quōmodo appellātur is quem hominēs laudant? Quōmodo nōminātur is quem hominēs laudant?»

Possession

To ask a question the answer to which will indicate the person who possesses something, a teacher can use one of several formulae.

Cūjus rosa est?	Marīae rosa est.
Quam rem Marīa habet?	Rosam Marīa habet.
Cui est rosa?	Marīae est rosa.

The plurals would, of course, use «quibus» or «quōrum, quārum». And «quam rem» will become «quās rēs». Note the use of the dative of possession.

There are other ways of asking for the possessor such as these:

Quis est possessor hūjus animālis?
Quis hoc animal possidet?
Quis est dominus hūjus servī?
Cūjus in potestāte est haec urbs?
Quis rēgnī potītus est?

Distinction

When the teacher wishes to find out which of two people did a certain thing, he will use «uter, utra, utrum».

Uter hoc fēcit?   Petrus hoc fēcit.

Receiver

In order to find out whether the student knows who is the indirect object, the teacher will use «cui» and in the plural «quibus» together with some verb like «dō, dare» or «offerō, offerre».

Dominus statuam puerō dat.
Cui dominus statuam dat?   Puerō.
Cui ā domino statua datur?   Puerō.

The teacher may wish to make use of circumlocutions such as these.

Quis statuam accēpit?   Puer.
Quis nunc statuam possidet?   Puer.

Accompaniment

If the teacher wishes to find out who it is that accompanied someone he needs but use «quōcum» and in the plural «quibuscum».

Quōcum servus venit?   Cum dominō.
Quibuscum dominus venit?   Cum servīs.

If the students are acquainted with deponent verbs, the teacher may wish to use a verb such as «comitor» or the noun «comes».

Quis mātrem comitātur?   Fīlia.
Quis est comes mātris?   Fīlia.

Agent

The ordinary way of asking for the agent is the use of an expression such as «ā quō» or «ā quibus». These are also used for the dative of agent that appears with the gerundive.

When the dative or ablative of agent appears in the text, the teacher may wish to change the questioning and word it as if the text itself were stated actively.

Urbs ā Caesare obsidēbātur.
Quis urbem obsidēbat?

Ā mīlitibus capta est urbs.

Quī urbem cēpērunt?

Instead of using «ā quō» or «ā quibus» for the dative of agent with the gerundive, the teacher can change the question to one that uses the verb «dēbet».

Hoc Paulō faciendum est.

Quis dēbet hoc facere?

Questions such as the above reveal very little of the structure to the student. Hence if they are answered correctly, the teacher can be assured that the student knows the use of the gerundive of necessity.

Means

When the teacher wishes the student to tell by what means something is done, he may use one of two expressions: «quō īnstrūmentō» or «quō auxiliō» making the proper changes when there is question of the plural.

Urbs fossā dēfenditur.

Quō īnstrūmentō urbs dēfenditur?

Quō auxiliō urbs dēfenditur?

Urbs mūrō et fossā dēfenditur.

Quibus īnstrūmentīs urbs dēfenditur?

Quibus auxiliīs urbs dēfenditur?

If the teacher does not wish the question to reveal so much of the structure, he might use questions such as these.

Quōmodo urbs dēfenditur?

Quā urbs dēfenditur?

Quibus rēbus urbs dēfenditur?

Description

When there is question of eliciting a description of a person or thing, the teacher will ordinarily use «quālis, quāle». The answer will ordinarily be an adjective or an adjective equivalent.

Quālis vir bene pugnat?

Fortis vir bene pugnat.

Homō quī multum ōrat laudābitur.

Quālis homō laudābitur?

Quī multum ōrat laudābitur.

Caesar propter lēgātōs occīsōs bellum gessit.
Propter quālēs lēgātōs Caesar bellum gessit?
Propter lēgātōs occīsōs.

Caesar erat vir summō ingeniō.
Quālis vir erat Caesar?
Vir summō ingeniō erat Caesar.

Est vir magnae virtūtis.
Quālis vir est?
Vir magnae virtūtis est.

If the teacher feels that the use of «quālis, quāle» reveals too much to the student, he may use circumlocutions. Here are some examples. These involve transformations and hence reveal clearly the student's knowledge.

Mīles fortis est.
Quā virtūte mīles ōrnātur?
Fortitūdine mīles ōrnātur.

Ille malus est.
Quō vitiō labōrat?
Malītiā ille labōrat.

Size

When there is question of adjectives such as «parvus, longus, brevis» the teacher will ordinarily use «quantus, -a, -um» in his question.

Ille mōns est parvus.
Quantus est ille mōns?   Parvus.

Reference

When a dative of reference occurs in a sentence, the teacher will use «cui» or «quibus» in his question.

Quotiēns tibi jam extorta est ista sīca dē manibus?
Cui jam extorta est ista sīca?
Tibi.

Comparison

Occasionally conditional clauses of comparison are met in reading. In such cases the teacher can word his question after the one in this example.

Sē gerit quasi rēx sit.

Cui assimilātur?

Rēgī assimilātur.

For the ablative of comparison the teacher will usually need to resort to circumlocution.

Patria tibi vītā cārior est.

Utra tibi est cārior, patria an vīta?

Quam rem plūris aestimās?

Multō tibi patria cārior est.

Quantō tibi patria cārior est? Multō.

Place

When there is question of some relation that has to do with space, the following questions will serve the teacher well.

Place where

Quō in locō est animal ferum?	In silvā.
Ubī est animal ferum?	In silvā.
Quō in locō est māter?	Domī est.
Quotā in pictūrā est senex?	Quīntā in pictūrā.

Place from which

Quō ex locō venit animal ferum?	Ē silvā.
Unde venit animal ferum?	Ē silvā.
Unde ortus est?	Ā Germānīs.

Place to which

Quem in locum abīvit?	In oppidum.
Quō īvit?	In oppidum.
Quōnam prōgressus est?	In oppidum.
Quem in locum īvit?	Rōmam.
Quem in locum cucurrit animal?	Sub lapidem.
Quō usque prōgrederis?	Ad caelum prōgredior.

Cause

When the teacher wishes to elicit an expression of cause, he can choose from a number of expressions. Each of the following can be used, no matter how the cause is expressed whether in a clause, a phrase, or an individual word (ablative of cause).

Quārē hoc fēcistis?

Cūr hoc fēcistis?

Quā dē causā hoc fēcistis?
Quam ob rem hoc fēcistis?
Quāpropter hoc fēcistis?

Purpose

When the teacher wishes the student to give a purpose clause in reply, he can use one or other of the following expressions.

Caesar vēnit ut urbem obsidēret.
    Quō cōnsiliō vēnit Caesar?
    Quō prōpositō vēnit Caesar?
    Cūr vēnit Caesar?

In order to elicit a dative of purpose in reply, the teacher can make use of the expression «cui bonō» or «cui ūtilitātī».

Decem cohortēs auxiliō mīsit.
    Cui bonō cohortēs mīsit?
    Cui ūtilitātī cohortēs mīsit?

One or other of the question signals for clauses could also be used to elicit the dative of purpose, but then the student will need to change the noun into a verb.

Quō consiliō decem cohortēs mīsit?
Ut auxiliārentur decem cohortēs mīsit.

Time

Students can be forced to use an expression of time in their reply if the teacher uses one or other of the following questions.

Time how long
    Quam diū pugnāvērunt?   Duās hōrās.
Time when
    Quandō advēnērunt?   Quartō diē.
    Quā in diē advēnērunt?   Quartō diē.
    Quota hōra est?   Sexta hōra est.
Time within which
    Quīnque diēbus veniet.
    Quandō veniet?   Quīnque diēbus.
Time how long
    Abhinc annōs decem mortuus est.
    Quandō mortuus est?   Abhinc annōs decem.

Time how long before or after
　Multīs post annīs mortuus est.
　Paulō ante proelium mortuus est.
　　Quandō mortuus est?　　　　Multīs post annīs.
　　　　　　　　　　　　　　　Paulō ante proelium.

When the teacher wishes to question students about clauses that express time, such as those introduced by «postquam, cum, dum» and «antequam», he can use no better signal than «quandō». If conjunctions such as «antequam» and «priusquam» are followed by the subjunctive, the teacher may wish to indicate the "purpose" idea by using a double signal such as «quandō et quō consiliō».

Space

When there is question of asking about extent of space, the expression «quam longē» is apt.

　Flūmen decem pedēs aberat.
　　Quam longē flūmen aberat?

Some clauses will permit the use of «quousque».

　Horātius impetum sustinuit quoad cēterī pontem interrumperent.
　　Quousque Horātius impetum sustinuit?

If it is thought advisable to bring out the idea of "purpose" in the subordinate clause, the teacher can use a double signal.

　Quousque et quō cōnsiliō (prōpositō) Horātius impetum hostium sustinuit?

The signal «quam longē» may also be used.

　Quam longē et quō prōpositō Horātius impetum sustinuit?

Number of occurrences

When there is a need to question the student about the number of times that an event transpired, the teacher will be able to use one or other of the question signals that appear in these examples.

　Quot cīvēs hāc clāde periērunt?
　　Sex cīvēs periērunt.
　Ter in terram cecidit.
　　Quotiēns (quotiēs) in terram cecidit?
　　Ter cecidit.

215

Clauses

There are many types of dependent clauses in Latin, but the teacher by judicious questioning can elicit from the student the exact clause that is wanted in the answer. Here is a listing of some of the more typical subordinate clauses and their eliciting question which have not appeared thus far in this chapter.

Conditions

Sī vīvis, sum fēlīx.
> Quā sub condiciōne sum fēlīx?
> Sī vīveret, gaudēret.
>> Quā sub condiciōne gaudēret?
>> Quā condiciōne gaudēret?

Concession

Quamquam dīves est, nōn est beātus.
> Quō concessō, nōn est beātus?
> Quamvīs dīves sīs, nōn es beātus.
>> Quō concessō, nōn es beātus?
>> Ut sīs dīves, nōn es beātus.
>>> Quō concessō, nōn es beātus?

If the teacher feels that the use of the term «concessō» reveals too much to the student, he might consider the use of this question-signal, «Quō argūmentō adlātō.»

Result

Sīc vītam agit ut omnēs eum laudāre possint.
> Quid sequitur sī vītam sīc agit?   Omnēs eum laudāre possunt.
> Nōn is sum quī fugiam.
>> Quālis vir nōn sum?

Noun clauses

In general noun clauses will answer to the signals that were given for the subject or object of a sentence. Here are some examples.

> Accidit ut nōs nōn vidēret.

216

Quid accidit?

Eīs persuāsit ut dē fīnibus exīrent.
  Quid eīs persuāsit?

Timeō nē veniat.
  Quid timeō?

Caesar rogat num mīlitēs pugnent.
  Quid Caesar rogat?

Dīxit sē pācem factūrum esse.
  Quid dīxit?

Bene accidit quod lūna plēna erat.
  Quid bene accidit?

Fierī nōn potest quīn veniat.
  Quid fierī nōn potest?

Nōn recūsāvit quōminus poenam subīret.
  Quid nōn recūsāvit?

Further case usages

Many case usages were discussed in the earlier part of this chapter. However, there remain other usages about which teachers may wish to question. We list examples of some of the more important usages and how to question to elicit them in an answer.

Vocative
  Pugnāte fortiter, mīlitēs!
    Quōs alloquitur?

Predicate genitive (elliptical)
  Mīlitis est pugnare.
    Cūjus mūnus est pugnāre?
  Gallia Populī Rōmānī nōn Ariovistī est.
    Cūjus in potestāte est Gallia?

Subjective genitive
  Adventus Caesaris erat opportūnus.
    Quis advēnit?

Objective genitive
  Timor Deī est initium sapientiae.
    Quem sapientēs timent?

Partitive genitive

Magna pars copiārum perīvit.
  Quārum pars magna perīvit?
Hōrum omnium fortissimī sunt Belgae.
  Quōrum fortissimī sunt Belgae?

Genitive of indefinite value
Permagnī eum aestimās.
  Quantī eum aestimās?

Genitive with verbs
Dēbēs oblīvīscī incendiōrum.
  Quōrum dēbēs oblīvīscī?
  Quae dēbēs oblīvīscī?
Taedet mē vītae.
  Cūjus mē taedet?

Genitive of the charge
Fūrtī mē accūsat.
  Cūjus mē accūsat?
  Cūjus reī mē accūsat?

Genitive with adjectives
Bellum est perīculōrum plēnum.
  Quōrum est bellum plēnum?
  Quārum rērum est bellum plēnum?

Dative limit of motion
It clāmor caelō.
  Quō it clāmor?
  Quousque prōgreditur clāmor?

Dative with verbs
Mūnītiōnī Labiēnum praefēcit.
  Cui Labiēnum praefēcit?
  Quae rēs est in potestāte Labiēnī?
Ventus nāvibus nocuit.
  Quibus ventus nocuit?
  Quibus rēbus ventus nocuit?

Double accusative
Tē imperātōrem appellō.
  Quem tē appellō?
Caesar exercitum flūmen trādūxit.
  Trāns quam rem Caesar exercitum trādūxit?
Chrīstus nōs viam salūtis docet.

Quam rem Chrīstus nōs docet?

Accusative of specification

Lacrimīs oculōs suffūsa est nitentēs.

Quibus rēbus lacrimīs suffūsa est?

Quās rēs lacrimīs suffūsa est?

Ablative of separation

Ā tyrannīs patriam līberāvī.

Quibus ā rēbus patriam līberāvī?

Ā quibus patriam līberāvī?

Ablative of manner

Mīlitēs magnā (cum) virtūte pugnāvērunt.

Quōmodo mīlitēs pugnāvērunt?

Ablative of respect

Lēgibus inter sē differunt.

Quōmodo inter sē differunt?

Quō respectū inter sē differunt?

Quōmodo inter sē nōn congruunt?

Ablative of degree of difference

Multō melior est.

Quantō melior est?

Ablative of price

Domum vīlī pretiō vēndidit.

Quantī domum vēndidit?

Various verb forms

Supine in «-um»

Lēgātī pācem petītum vēnērunt.

Quō prōpositō lēgātī vēnērunt?

Quō cōnsiliō lēgātī vēnērunt?

Cūr lēgātī vēnērunt?

Supine in «-u»

Mīrābile est dictū.

Quō respectū est mīrābile?

Quā rē est mīrābile?

Gerund

Pugnandī cupidī sunt.

Cūjus reī cupidī sunt?

219

Scrībendō sē dedit.
  Cui sē dedit?
Ad explōrandum missus est.
  Cūr missus est?
  Quō prōpositō (quō cōnsiliō) missus est?
Dē bene scrībendō locūtus est.
  Dē quā rē locūtus est?

Gerundive
  Ponte faciendō urbem servāvit.
    Quō auxiliō urbem servāvit?
    Quōmodo urbem servāvit?
  Urbs mīlitibus dīripienda trādita est.
    Quālis urbs mīlitibus trādita est?

Infinitive
  Ōrāre est bonum.
    Quid est bonum?
  Pugnāre possum.
    Quam rem possum facere?
  Pugnāre timent.
    Quid timent?
    Quam rem timent?

Conclusion

The foregoing examples of how to question should convince the teacher that it is possible to teach grammar more meaningfully if he is but hard enough to question in Latin. Questioning in Latin is not difficult and teachers who have not used it should adopt it. In the beginning they will need to prepare their questions in detail when preparing for class. As experience grows, the facility in formulating discriminating questions will increase and confidence will grow in proportion to facility.

The combination of confidence in the ability to question in Latin and the actual facility in questioning will give greater interest in the teaching of Latin. Both teacher and pupils will be aware of their power over the language for expressing their ideas. Since both teacher and pupils are using Latin constantly during the recitation, the Latin becomes a real medium of communication and that without the interference of English.

Teachers should be convinced that questioning in Latin and answering in Latin is one of the best means at their disposal to help students to read

Latin as Latin — facile responses in Latin cannot be given with direct comprehension, and rapid questioning in Latin cannot be done without thinking in Latin.

Chapter 10

Latin composition

The traditional approach

Most teachers of Latin rightfully feel that no student of Latin really knows the language unless he can write it creditably. It is the writing of Latin that reveals whether the student has an accurate knowledge of forms and syntax. Many students are able to read Latin with fair comprehension but they do not feel adequate when it comes to writing a paragraph or two. Students who can read and understand fairly well may be said to have a passive knowledge, while those who can also write the Latin well can be said to have an active knowledge of the language.

Certainly students who have studied the language for four years should be able to read and comprehend as they read. If they come to college with such a preparation, then the college teacher can teach them how to write the language. However, writing the language, at least in an elementary way, should be part of the student's experience while he is in high school.

In the past, most textbooks were satisfied to explain a usage and then ask the student to translate a large number of sentences from English to Latin. This exercise was supposed to fix the usage for the student. This it certainly did as is evidenced by the facility that many achieved in writing individual sentences without a mistake. Unfortunately though for most students, the training ended there. Little attempt was made to teach the student how to organize these sentences into paragraphs because all too often the sentences he had translated were disparate in thought. Some composition books, it is true, included exercises that involved paragraph work, but these always labored under the illusion that a student could become enthuiastic in expressing someone else's thought. Quite generally students diligently translated such paragraphs, but it was more out of a sense of duty and a conviction fostered by teachers that such procedures were necessary to learn the language adequately. Seldom, if ever, was the student given the opportunity of the interesting experience of expressing his own thoughts or feelings in the language he was studying. This may have been due to the somewhat artificial situations that authors attempted to create in their exercises as well as to the type of reading that the student did.

The new approach

The advent of modern devices for teaching has changed all of this considerably. Especially has the tape recorder forced teachers to re-evaluate the methods they have been using in the teaching of languages. Not only are such devices now used for drilling the student, but they are also helpful in teaching him how to comprehend in a living language situation.

In particular the use of the tape recorder has cast considerable doubt upon the efficacy of Latin composition as it was generally practiced until quite recently. Certainly the older teachers remember when ten or more disparate sentences were assigned for translation before the next class. This was intended as a drill for a particular usage. The difficulty was that students would write the theme, but it would be some twenty-four to thirty-six hours or more before it was returned. By the time it was returned, he probably forgot what he had written; particularly is this true if he had to make generous use of the dictionary and the grammar as he was composing the Latin that would faithfully mirror what the English sentence had said.

Drills need no longer labor under such difficulties because the tape recorder and the language laboratory can effectively take the place of theme writing. Oral drill is not only faster than written drill, but it has the advantage of being able to correct the student's error at once if he made such. Moreover, there is no distraction such as that offered by consulting a dictionary, fussing with a balky pen, or erasing a mistake.

Composition means communication

Because the tape recorder and the language laboratory have largely displaced the written drills in the teaching of language, it must not be concluded that all composition in the language is to be omitted. There is still need for composition to sharpen the student's knowledge to the point of real mastery, and composition is a necessary tool for arriving at this goal.

Note, though, the terms "composition in the target language". Composition is what the student needs, not translation from the English to Latin.

This presupposes that the student himself is active and has something that he wishes to communicate to others. Because the thought he wishes to communicate is his own, he is likely to be more interested in expressing it, and because he is more interested, he will be more alert to avoid errors, as these interfere with communication.

English technique in composition

In the teaching of Latin composition we might look to our teachers of English. Teachers of English do not for the most part have bilingual students. They cannot therefore ask the student to take something that is written in Polish and express it in English. The student who wishes to write English must practice by writing English. So, too, the student who wishes to learn Latin. He should write in Latin. The student who writes English is not hampered by the necessity of expressing someone else's thoughts; neither then should the student of Latin be so hampered.

Things presupposed for composition

Let's consider for a moment what the English teacher might do when he wishes to teach composition. There is, of course, the necessity of drilling students in correct usage and the rules of grammar, but such drilling is kept mostly to a minimum, or at least it should be. Grammar must be taught functionally and in context. But presupposing a knowledge of usage and fundamental grammar, what does an English teacher do concretely in his composition classes?

Preparation for composition

Before assigning a topic for composition, the teacher strives to set up a situation that will be meaningful for the student. This he does through assigned readings and discussion. The more he can stir the feelings of the students, the more likely he is to get a good composition. We are usually quite voluble about the things which affect us emotionally and can speak and write rather well under those circumstances. Witness the marshalling of arguments that even young students achieve when there is question of convincing the teacher that a test should not be given on the day following the biggest social event of the year.

Once the student has been given something to say, the teacher usually gives some help in the way of starting them off on an outline. He may even require that the outline be drawn up first and submitted for correction.

He may also indicate specific viewpoints that the students can adopt and expand or discuss. It is then the task of the student to write the composition. Adequate motivation and proper preparation enable the student to express himself without assuming any roles.

Correction and rewriting

After a composition is handed in, the teacher of English usually spends much time in correcting it. He usually does not have time to rewrite it and so indicates where the composition is faulty.

Quite generally English teachers require their students to rewrite a theme in order to correct the errors and to make it a more meaningful communication.

Composition in Latin

Such, in brief, might be the scheme that a teacher of English would follow if he wishes his students to advance in composition work. The same general scheme can quite profitably be followed by those who wish the student to write a composition in Latin. Each teacher, no doubt, will want to modify the scheme that we shall present, but it is hoped that the scheme for Latin composition will stimulate his approach to this important phase of the teaching of Latin.

Preparing for the composition in Latin

The first of the preparatory steps for a Latin composition consists, as in English, of reading. Since Latin is not a native language, the student will want to reread the Latin text many times in order that words, phrases, clauses, and even entire sentences, will remain in his memory — to be used later when he himself wishes to write Latin.

The second step will involve some simple translation from English to Latin. This translation should be based on what the student has read. If the text does not have a suitable passage, the teacher can easily compose one by retelling the story and possibly leaving out some of the less important elements. Usually the text for such a translation should be considerably less ornate and not nearly as difficult as the original, nor should the passage for translation be too lengthy.

This step leading to composition is likely to be of no help to the student unless the teacher gives a real impetus for the work of translating. This he can do in a number of ways, but this is perhaps one of the best. During the recitation period the teacher asks a student to go to the chalkboard in order that he may write down what the students suggest by way of translation. With the text of the original in front of them the class and the teacher cooperate in the translation of the English to Latin.

As soon as the translation is completed the teacher asks the student at the board to erase the Latin. Needless to say, no writing was permitted the students during the class composition. A well-trained memory is the student's most important asset in learning a language.

This translation from English to Latin is roughly parallel to the discussion that is usually carried on in an English class before the assignment of a composition. Discussion stimulates the interest and arouses the feelings of the students in English class. The class composition should arouse the interest of the students of Latin since they will readily realize that the more they remember of the translation the easier will their work be that night.

The next step, still a preparatory one for the final composition, will be taken the next day during the recitation period. During the time that the teacher is possibly working with the class on some new reading material, two students are at the chalkboard writing down their translation of the English to Latin passage. When their work is completed, the teacher calls for a correction of these versions. Correcting errors is necessary, but teachers should not omit this occasion of indicating the better expressions of the thought.

As the work of correcting the two themes at the board is in progress, the teacher can be going about the room glancing at the compositions that the other students have done. Since this phase of the work involves everyone in the same thoughts, most students can correct their themes by comparing them with the corrected versions that appear on the chalkboard.

The composition topic

With this preliminary work completed, the teacher is ready to assign the topic for composition. If the students have been reading a narrative piece, the teacher should indicate topics that more or less parallel the situation in the original text. If the subject matter for the composition is more or less parallel to the original, the student will be familiar with the vocabulary that he will need to tell the story. Students should, of course, be free to substitute their own parallel because composition should be an occasion for expressing themselves.

Helping the students

At this point the teacher may see fit to give some help, but usually it should be deferred. Such help can best be given after the students have done some preliminary work on their own. For that reason he gives the students several days in which to complete the work. Suppose the topic were assigned on Monday night; the teacher would ordinarily not ask for the composition until at least Wednesday and preferably Thursday or Friday of that week or even the following Monday.

During the recitation period that follows the one in which the assignment was made, the teacher might elicit questions on the work by asking if there are difficulties in the work. If this is the teacher's usual procedure, it will give the students a very concrete motive for starting their composition the very day that it is assigned. As all know, students are all too prone to leave assignments go until the last minute.

It is advisable that the teacher remind the students about the composition daily. It is during the days that intervene between the assignment and the collection that the teacher may wish to give reminders of what to do and what not to do in the writing of the composition.

Certainly students should be told not to consult an unabridged dictionary in order to find expression that they might use in the composition; they should restrict themselves to the vocabulary that they find in the text — the necessity of assigning topics that parallel the original now becomes more evident.

Students should be encouraged not to consult anyone while writing their paper — the teacher wants to know how they will express it, not how someone else will express it.

Ordinarily the teacher will assign some kind of limit to the paper, for example, it is not to exceed fifty words, or it is not to be less than fifty words. Beginning students in particular appreciate such a limitation; older students possibly do not need such a restricition.

The teacher might wish to give other suggestions that occur to him, such as the writing of a rough copy on the first day, then putting it aside, reading it over the next day in order to make corrections and emendations, and then writing the final copy a day or so later. The intervals are important because the student can come back to the paper after he has more or less forgotten what he wrote. Generally he will be able to see errors that would otherwise escape him. This is much the same advice that teachers of mathematics give their students. If you do not get the answer to the first problem, go on to the second and third, and only then come back to the first and you will generally see where you made the mistake.

Correcting the composition

After collecting the papers on the assigned day, the teacher has the task of correcting the composition. Really it should not be called a task in comparison with the older routine when teachers corrected papers, each of which contained the very same thing. Because each paper contained the same thing, he could correct rather rapidly. Since each composition now presents more of the student himself, they are much more interesting to correct although it must be admitted that more time must be spent on them.

During the correction of the themes it is not advisable that the teacher undertake extensive rewrites. Rather he will find that it will be more profitable for the student if he merely indicates the errors. In order to facilitate the correction, the teacher will use something of a code. Here is a partial one that he might use.

a – agreement; something is wrong in the agreement of noun and adjective, subject and verb, and so forth.

t – tense; in some way the tense is wrong, possibly in sequence.

c – case; possibly the student forgot that «parcō» takes its object in the dative case.

s – spelling; in some way the student has misspelled the word.

w – word order; possibly the student has forgotten that «causā» follows the genitive that it governs.

m – meaning; the expression of the thought is so poor that the teacher really does not understand what the student wishes to say.

The sooner the teacher can return the composition to the students the better, and ideally he will return them at the next recitation period. This is important because the longer the period between the writing and the rereading, the less effective will be the corrections that the teacher so laboriously indicates. During the period in which the papers have been returned, the teacher should discuss those errors that are common in this set of papers. Ordinarily he should not spend class time on those errors that are more or less peculiar to one individual. Discussion of these should be relegated to some other time that is convenient to the teacher and the student.

Rewriting the composition

Students should be expected to rewrite the paper and hand it in at the recitation period that follows. Sometimes the errors are few and the teacher may be satisfied with corrections clearly indicated on the original paper. If students are to rewrite the paper, both should be handed in.

Ordinarily the correction on the rewrites does not take too much of the teacher's time as he usually looks to the corrections only. If the papers were entirely rewritten he can scan them rapidly, particularly if they have been typed.

Before returning the rewrites to the student the teacher will find that it is good practice to call upon several of the students to read their rewritten composition to the class. Usually the better papers are chosen. Not only is this reading a recognition of work that has been well done, but it is at the same time an exercise in comprehension for the rest of the class. It might be remarked, too, that the reading of the composition by the author is a good exercise in public speaking. Younger students in particular appreciate this public recognition of their work.

Some cautions and observations

As experienced teachers read about such directions for composition work, they may be inclined to shrug their shoulders and say that it takes too much time. It does take time, but the results achieved are more than ample repayment and the interest that students show in such composition work should enkindle the interest of the teacher in each student's progress.

Other teachers who have tried a similar scheme for a short time might object that the papers are so poor that the effort is not worthwhile. Perhaps it may be that such teachers were expecting too much of the students in the beginning. It must be remembered that the students are but new at the language, even though they may have studied it for two years because, after all, they are working with the language but a limited amount of time each day. Even English teachers at times indicate that they are all too often disappointed with the compositions their charges write, and in that case there is question of the native language.

Teachers must expect that in the beginning the compositions of the students will be full of errors. As the students do more reading and studying there should be a lessening of errors, though it must be admitted that such a diminution frequently is almost imperceptible. If the teacher has kept the papers that students write, he can see considerable improvement in the papers written in March as compared with those written in October. It is likely that there will always be some errors in the student's compositions since even seniors in high school seldom write faultless papers in their native language.

Composition an index of the reading level

Composition work as outlined in this chapter will keep the student working in and with the Latin and since he is not restricted to the expression of someone else's thought such compositions will reveal much to the teacher. If the student follows the directions, he will clearly show how much vocabulary he has mastered in an active way. His knowledge of grammar, too, will be revealed since ordinarily he will not take the time to look up a construction with which he is not too familiar. Hence, composition work is an indirect index of the level at which the student is reading in Latin.

Just as English teachers occasionally give an examination in composition, so too should the Latin teacher. It is always possible for students to consult with others when writing their paper, but during a class period the teacher has control over the helps that are at the disposal of the student. At times he will wish them to write the composition with no helps; occasionally he allows the use of text since it is quite possible that a student may vaguely remember a construction and would like to use it but feels that he must check his knowledge first. Such open-book compositions will therefore be much better and will likely be a clearer indication of the student's reading level.

A broader view of composition

Composition work is also entailed when teachers give assignments such as these:

retelling the story by changing the time from the present to the past or the future

changing all indirect discourse to direct or vice versa

changing grammatical constructions such as indirect questions to direct, temporal clauses in the indicative to those that use the subjective, and so forth

changing the story from the third to the first person

It is true that such composition work does not allow the student to express his own ideas, yet he does put into the rewrite something of himself and his own knowledge of the language.

The writing of digests of what they have read is also an exercise in composition for students. Even though the story supplies the vocabulary and much of the grammar, yet the student must choose from these and organize them in such a way that they make a meaningful communication. Teachers will do well to handle the correction of digests in much the same way as the more formal compositions in which the student tells his own story.

It should be remembered, too, that when a student answers a comprehension question he is doing work in composition. And then there are situations in class when oral answers must be given to questions. This, too, may be considered a type of composition.

When teachers conduct their classes for the most part in Latin and when the students do a fair amount of reading of Latin and give most of their replies in Latin, there is a constant training in composition. That is why there need not be as much written work in the Latin class as formerly when English was the chief medium of communication in a Latin class.

Major composition topics

Many teachers like to have a major project for the class at the close of a semester or when they have completed the reading of a sizeable portion of one of the masters. A fairly lengthy composition in Latin is excellent as a project. If students know in advance that some such work will be assigned, they will have an added motive for mastering the materials they read.

Here are some suggestions that will undoubtedly evoke other possibilities in the minds of the experienced teacher.

Writing an autobiography in Latin is interesting for sophomore students and it provides abundant opportunities for them to show their knowledge of such items as dates and proper names for places. If they are reading Caesar, then they might wish to give a newspaper reporter's account of some episode, as for instance Caesar's landing in Britain. Telling the story as it appeared to one of the captives, composing a speech that the leader of the enemy might have made in the council meeting before joining battle with Caesar, or telling the story of the battle as seen by some of the elders, these and topics like them give the student abundant opportunities to display his skill in writing Latin.

If the students in third year are reading Cicero's speeches against Catiline, they could be told that they have three or four minutes in which to make a reply to what Cicero said. If they are reading the third Catilinarian, they may wish to give the report that the captain of the guard might have given about the capture of the conspirators, or the affair at the Mulvian bridge. A newspaper account of the crucifixion of a Roman citizen might be suggested during the course of the reading of the Verrines. Such topics permit the student to use the vocabulary of the author as well as many of his expressions.

It might be remarked in passing that such composition work helps to fix the words and phrases of an author in the student's mind, since using a word or phrase in one's own composition is an excellent means toward making it one's permanent possession.

Composition in Latin need not be neglected in fourth year. Vergil offers abundant opportunities for composition topics. The «Aeneid» offers many situations in which the imagination can be brought into play. For example, an account of Dido's judgment when she reaches the underworld, the record of Priam's judgment when he arrives there, what would have happened had the Trojans opened the wooden horse. Such compositions can in fact make the students keenly aware of the differences between prose and poetry, for example, the grammatical usages as well as the expression of the thoughts.

Conclusion

Listening in order to comprehend what is said, speaking in order to actively master the Latin usages, these are but means to the one goal — that of reading Latin and comprehending as we read. Hearing with the imagination the cadence of a Ciceronian period or the smooth flow of a Vergilian hexameter will only add to the enjoyment of reading. And if students can be brought to the point where they enjoy the reading of Latin, we can hope that reading Latin will not be confined to their school days, but that it will be something to which they will later return in their leisure moments just because they enjoy being in contact with the masters of that language from which our own native tongue has borrowed so many words — the masters who represent a culture of which ours is but a continuance.

Chapter 11

Review and spiral teaching

Whenever review is mentioned, both students and teachers react rather strongly. The latter are much exercised to find ways and means of making this necessary part of learning at least somewhat interesting while their real interest centers around the time when they can proceed to new matter with its inherent interest. This last reaction of the teacher is also part of the student's attitudes, since new material has a thrill of exploring unknown lands without the dangers involved in an exploration. Experience teaches that students find nothing so dull as review even though they, too, will attest to its importance. Therefore in any consideration of the techniques associated with the teaching and learning process it is important to explore ways and means of making review effective without at the same time exposing the process to elements that can lessen if not entirely destroy the interest of both teacher and student.

Sustained interest

In this search for enlivening the review that all agree is so neccesary, teachers occasionally fasten upon methods that are quite superficial and lack the capability of establishing and sustaining genuine interest. Among these dubiously effective methods are to be found such items as declension and conjugation games, word-games, and grammatical identification spelldowns. This is not to say that these cannot with proper use upon occasion make for a well-conducted and high spirited class, but the inherent weakness of such artificial method must be recognized. They are but a brief interlude and spirit they engender cannot ordinarily be sustained over a period of several classes. We must consequently look beyond such methods to something that gives a more stable and prolonged interest and involves teacher and student in the effective conduct of reviews.

In order to sustain the interest and effective work on the part of the teacher and student alike, it seems that review must be conducted against a varied background of fundamental learning activities. It is practically an axiom that things cannot be taught to mastery the first time that the teacher and student engage in an exploration of a new portion of the field of knowledge. This is particularly true when that new part is complicated or presents aspects that are quite foreign to the culture and background of the students. Repeated teaching is therefore quite in order and this involves review. The methods used in this review can help students to success and advancement in learning or they can leave him where he was before the review started.

Spiral teaching

Repeated teaching of the same material done in the same way will never enliven but only dull the interest of students and make of the teacher a mere automaton. To avoid these problems, we look to what has been identified as "spiral teaching". In general, this means presenting new material but not necessarily in its entirety. The teacher, of course, does not give a distorted picture; rather he presents the highlights and insists that these be learned. At the next presentation more details are added that will widen the student's horizon of knowledge. It is a presentation of the familiar against a background whose details are brought into clearer focus. If this process is followed, the student will be aware of the familiar and conscious of the new. It is this newness which has the thrill of exploration and which sustains his interest. Such an interest is intrinsic to the learning process and can therefore keep the student actively involved and learning. As a review technique, however, spiral teaching means presenting some few new elements — not, indeed, in their entirety but rather summarily — in close connection with material that students already know. Thus the old is not dissociated from the new; rather, the new grows out of and builds upon the old.

Morphology and spiral teaching

All modern texts of whatever approach agree that students must learn the morphology of a language if they wish to understand the various communications. Such knowledge is generally acquired during the first year of study. Yet there is consensus among teachers that the lasting mastery of morphology is not completely achieved in the first year. This failure is due to a variety of causes, such as lack of study, failure to retain what has been learned, and prolonged periods, such as vacations, in which the knowledge is not used actively. In order to keep the acquired knowledge active, teachers generally review morphology at the beginning of second year and again at the start of the third year. This constant repetition should give the mastery that will enable students during their fourth year to read with a certain amount of ease and appreciation. New elements must be injected into such review if the students are to retain their interest, and again we have the elements of spiral teaching.

Conducting the review in second year

Let us suppose that students by the end of first year know the five declensions, the four conjugations and «-iō» verbs, as well as some irregulars such as «sum». While this is quite a lot to learn, experience has shown that students can more or less master this body of knowledge in one year. What then is the teacher to do if he wishes to review this matter at the beginning of second year?

First of all, it is assumed that the second-year teacher will be using connected discourse in the readings that the students will study. This then is part of the new which is presented against the background of the familiar. It is essential that this reading material be graded so that adequate review can be conducted from the reading material itself. The graded reading will guard against introducing elements that are extraneous to the review and interfere with the energy and concentration of the student at any one given point. In the beginning the upgrading of the reading material can be quite rapid, but it should be slowed down as the review matter involves more complicated grammar.

More than likely the teacher will want to start with a review of the declensions. He can prudently assume that students know the five regular declensions both horizontally and vertically. The forms of these are readily recalled as progress is made in the graded reading. This is the familiar, but what of the new? Here are some suggestions.

* Present the declesion in the order in which the students first learned them. Then use different orders as presented in the various texts and ask students what advantages can be seen in the various orders.

* Review the locative case and indicate endings such as «-aī» and «-ābus» and the reason for this last form.

237

* Consider some gender exceptions in the second declesion such as «vulgus» and «pelagus»; the ending «-os» for the nominative singular; the occurrence of only one "i" in the genitive singular; and the syncopated form of the genitive plural.

* Give some of the unusual endings in the third declension, e.g., «-im» for the accusative as in «Thymbrim»; give the declensions of «vīs, bōs, sūs»; consider various general rules for gender; present nouns such as «fors» and «spontis» which do not have complete declensions; list some indeclinables such as «fās, māne, nefās»; give a brief consideration of heteroclites, heterogeneous nouns, and plurals with a change in meaning.

These and other items taken from standard grammars will lend interest to a review of the declensions while at the same time expanding the student's knowledge — true spiral teaching. The teacher need not present all the material himself. He can ask students to consult grammars. Each can be given a restricted area for investigation. Such students present the material they have gathered and become experts for that area. Care must be exercised that the welter of new details does not obscure the fundamentals of the declension and so lose the value of the review. In general the teacher should strive to present items that are not found in the student's text.

In the review of adjectives and adverbs the teacher can stress the irregular comparisons, the nine irregulars as a group («ūnus, sōlus», and so forth), the use of adjectives as substantives («bona» as possessions), and when reviewing numbers, the more common adverbial and distributive forms can be learned. In the case of pronouns more care can be devoted to the indefinites and some older forms such as «ollī» for «illī». These suggestions do not by any means exhaust the possibilities for the extension of knowledge amid review. Each teacher will choose those items from standard grammars that are helpful for achieving his purposes here and now while he keeps in mind what the students will meet in later readings.

When there is question of reviewing the conjugations, the teacher will be certain that alternate forms are presented («-ēre» for «ērunt»), as well as shortened forms («repudiāssem» for «repudiāvissem»). The future imperative forms can be presented along with one or two mottoes that illustrate the usage. There is possibly time to study more in detail the supines, the irregulars and defective verbs, the periphrastic conjugations and some impersonal verbs. Some of these may have been presented in first year, but it can be assumed that they were not learned to mastery. In most first-year texts the items mentioned are not taken in formal study.

The formal drilling of morphology is quite in place in the review that is conducted at the beginning of second year. The teacher will do well to use devices or language laboratory drills that were not used in first year in order to secure some change in the method itself. There should be new drills for use in the language laboratory and these should be based on the readings in the text in order to fix both morphology and text in the student's mind.

Using the reading matter as a basis of review

Basing the review on the text itself is a very effective approach and is to be preferred to conducting a review of forms and then beginning the reading. If the review is based on a definite reading, then the teacher should feel free to disregard the order of presentation of morphology that is to be found in standard grammars. Teachers can draw up a list of what they wish to review. They then read the text the students will see and determine the elements they wish to review in any specific paragraph. This scheme is handy when there is no possibility of using a graded reader.

As the reading and review proceed, the teacher checks on his master list the grammar that has been reviewed. The process continues until such time as the essential review is completed. Here is a typical paragraph and some suggestions for conducting a review. The Latin is simple so that students can read with comprehension. If they comprehend almost at once, then there is time for conducting the review of forms without unduly lingering on a single paragraph of a story.

> Trōia, magnum oppidum et pulchrum, est in Asiā. Post Trōiam sunt montēs altī et magnae silvae. In silvīs sunt multae ferae bēstiae. Ante Trōiam est campus lātus. Campus est inter Trōiam et ōceanum. Trōiae vīvunt Trōiānī et multī aliēnī populī. Multās dīvitiās Trōiānī habent. Trāns montēs vīvunt aliī populī et sunt amīcī et sociī Trōiānōrum. Clārum est rēgnum Trōiānōrum per terrās Asiae.

1 Draw up in declension form the nouns of the first declension.

	Singular	Plural
Nom	Trōia	silvae
Acc	Trōiam	dīvitiās
Abl	Asiā	silvīs
Dat	------	------
Gen	Asiae	------

239

As soon as this is completed, the teacher can ask for a complete declension of one or two of the words that appeared in the text. The work can be done orally or in writing.

2 Draw up in declension form the nouns of the second declension but ask the students to supply the forms that do not appear in the text. It is profitable to take an expression such as «multās dīvitiās» and by questions such as «Quae rēs sunt bonae?» force the students to give other cases.

3 Review the prepositions which appear: «post, ante, inter, trāns, per, in».

4 Ask about the gender of the first and second declensions, with students giving illustrations from the text.

5 Consider the locative case and ask for an example from the text.

As the teacher conducts the review of the items as illustrated above, he will keep in mind what was said earlier about new material. Thus, he will possibly include words such as «vulgus» and «pelagus» which are neuter gender and so exceptions to the general gender rule of nouns in the second declension ending in «-us».

The above suggestions would satisfy most teachers so far as review is concerned. Not too many items are included and for that reason the reading is not delayed too long. When there is question of reviewing more complicated material, more time will of course be taken for the actual review of forms.

Reviewing morphology in third year

What then is to be done in third year in the review of morphology, especially if we keep in mind the idea of spiral teaching? Again, it is essential that the students start with relatively simple reading material that is rather strictly graded. The pace at which the reading is taken will be considerably faster than it was in second year, since students should have a better grasp of morphology due to the review in second year. All review of morphology should be based on the reading which itself provides the new material against which the familiar is activated.

During this review of morphology in third year, the teacher will pay special attention to the quantities of all the endings. This is the new element and it is taken here to make the work of scanning in fourth year easier. And because of this attention to quantity, the teacher can insist more on a careful pronunciation — another help in the reading of poetry. Pairs of words that are contrasted in pronunciation and meaning can be presented, for example, «vēneris» and «vēnerīs». Such pairs can be used for oral recognition.

This is the year, too, in which the knowledge of groups of words is to be consolidated. For example, the words whose genitive and dative singular are irregular («ūnus, tōtus», etc.); the five verbs whose object is in the ablative together with an explanation of why these objects are considered an ablative of means; the verbs whose object is in the genitive case. Teaching the Roman method of setting dates can be helpful in reviewing the cases as well as the numbers, particularly if both their method and our way of reckoning is taught. The study of indefinite pronouns, an area in which students are generally weak, will add new knowledge amid the review of familiar forms.

Grammar review

Methodologies differ in the amount of grammar that is presented, and teachers themselves use different terminology. Some teachers, too, are intent upon formal grammar while others are content with a functional knowledge. No matter which position a teacher may take, and no matter what terminology is used, students should have a review of grammar at the beginning of second year and again when they start third year.

Review of grammar in second year

It is quite likely that many fundamentals of grammar will be remembered by second-year students even though a lengthy vacation may have blotted out some of the details. Teachers will therefore be wise if they check the syllabus of first year and even inquire of first-year teachers how much grammar was taught. Not all sections perhaps were able to complete the text that was used in first year. Once the teacher has this information he can readily determine the new elements that must be added to make for genuine spiral teaching.

As in the review of morphology, so in the review of grammar there is need for graded reading material in order to limit the amount to which the student is exposed at any one given point. This enables him to concentrate on the grammar that the teacher wishes reviewed. Unless the text already contains a set of review lessons, the teacher will do well to draw up a master list of what he wishes to review. As he proceeds, he checks the master list

241

to make certain that no significant elements are omitted. There is no reason why morphology and grammar cannot be reviewed simultaneously provided that the amount of material taken at any one time does not confuse the students or spread their area of concentration too much. The general ability of the class will largely determine how much review can be taken in a given assignment.

Now to proceed to some specific areas, by way of illustration, in which new items can be injected into the review. Let us start with the sequence of tenses. First, the familiar items are reviewed briefly, then the teacher writes on the chalkboard or distributes sheets that contain various sentences in which strict sequence is not observed. The first sentence might contain a perfect infinitive which is the reason for the secondary sequence in the remainder of the statement. Other sentences would indicate the historical present, or a use of the present perfect with its primary sequence. Result clauses, too, might be included. Class discussion will usually bring out the reason for the unusual sequence or it will at least help in the formulation of a rule covering the case. If for some reason the study of the subjunctive was deferred until second year, then the procedures indicated here can be used in the review during third year. If visual aid equipment is available, the teacher would flash only one sentence at a time on the screen and thus be certain that all students are working on the same sentence at the same time.

If the teacher is reviewing the ablative absolute construction, time can be taken to show how it substitutes for almost any type of clause. Another fruitful scheme will involve the comparison and contrasting of conditions and wishes. Direct and indirect commands will also give a new view to some grammar with which students in second year are somewhat familiar.

Review of grammar in third year

Those students who continue with their study of Latin into third year can definitely profit by a formal knowledge of grammar since this will help them organize and classify what they have learned to use functionally during the first two years. It is suggested that the review of grammar be centered around key ideas in order to bring the diversified elements within easy comprehension and retention. Such topics will include time, place, and space; all the uses of individual conjunctions such as «ut» and «cum» together with an indication of which meaning occurs most often; causality and the various ways of expressing it will organize a number of grammatical usages. The various expressions for purpose, concession, and result will organize many usages.

All too often teachers of Latin fail to make use of the available "live situations" in the teaching of Latin where communication in a meaningful context can be exploited for learning. Why not present the grammar in Latin? Students readily enough learn the technical terms and with a little practice are able to read the rules with ease. This ease of comprehension stimulates the students' interest and gives a sense of confidence in their reading. If teachers do not have the time for conducting the entire review in Latin, then they should from time to time bring in some such material just to increase the student's interest.

Students in the third year of high school who are studying Latin are mature enough to follow a unification of grammar according to the five linguistic functions. What these are has already been given on pages 15 and 116 ff. in this book. It is however advisable here to indicate how the various parts of grammar are organized under such headings. Here is a general statement of what each function embraces.

The «nominal function» embraces all items that act as subject or object in a sentence. Included here are all the uses of the nominative, several usages of the accusative, and many dependent clauses.

The «adnominal function» embraces those items which function like an adjective. Included are several usages of the genitive, one of the ablative, and many dependent clauses.

The «verbal function» treats of the various aspects of the verb in the sentence such as person, number, tense, and mood.

The «adverbial function» includes all items that act like adverbs. This includes most of the uses of the ablative, all uses of the dative, some uses of the genitive, and many dependent clauses.

The «directional function» concerns itself with the words that indicate how the clauses of statements are united and how subordinate clauses are linked to main statements. Hence we are dealing with coordinating and subordinating conjunctions.

The nominal function

The nominal function will include all the uses of the nominatives as well as infinitives and clauses that function as subjects or objects of verbs. Appearing here will be all the uses of the accusative except those few noted in the adverbial function. The nominal function includes accusative with the infinitive, indirect questions, noun clauses of purpose, noun clauses of result, dependent clauses that act as subjects of impersonal expressions such as «fierī potest», clauses and verbs of fearing, hindering and impeding, and explanatory clauses introduced by «quod».

The adnominal function

The adnominal function will include the ablative of description, the genitive of possession, subjective and objective genitives, the partitive genitive, and the explanatory genitive. Also included are relative clauses both with the indicative and with the subjunctive. Some prepositional phrases, especially if they express time or place, are classified under this function. In general, however, prepositional phrases act as adverbs and so appear in the adverbial function.

The adverbial function

This function is by far the most extensive and includes the accusative in exclamations, accusative of respect, and those accusatives that express extent of time and space. Here are found the ablative of agent, ablatives of separation, manner, accompaniment, instrument or means, respect, comparison, cause, price, and measure. All the usages of the dative case are to be found in this category as well as some usages of the genitive such as the genitive indicating indefinite degree («Tantī eum aestimō»), the genitive after verbs like «oblīvīscor» and «egeō», and the genitives found with verbs like «interest, piget, condemnō» and those genitives that occur with adjectives such as «cupidus».

Most prepositional phrases are adverbial in function, and expressions of time and place are also included in this category.

In this category, too, we find the ablative absolute, purpose and result clauses that do not function as nouns, temporal clauses, and comparative clauses.

The verbal function

Under this heading the various aspects of the verb are gathered so that the student can remember the elements more easily. Included are the general meaning of the various moods, the different meanings of the tenses, for example, the inchoative, inceptive, and repetitive imperfect. Various usages of the infinitive which indicate the stage of an action with reference to the main verb, the sequence of tenses, syncopated verb forms, and the use of tenses in connected discourse where sentences are used paratactically.

It should be noted that the above listings are not exhaustive. They do, however, provide a sufficiently wide range of knowledge for the average student to enable him to read Latin and correctly interpret it.

Reading and spiral teaching

Review and spiral teaching should also be evident in the reading materials that the students are to use. By the end of first year it can be supposed that the students have achieved a certain level of proficiency in reading. This no doubt will be lost to some extent during a prolonged vacation. It is advisable therefore to begin the second year with rather simple reading in order that the student may recall and review the skills he achieved earlier. The new element in such reading will probably be mostly the content of the story itself. The same process «dēbitīs mūtandīs» should be repeated at the beginning of the third year.

If it was not done in second year, then certainly in third year the teacher should present the helps for comprehension that were given in Chapter 6, pages 116–155, of this book. Thus the teacher, when he reviews the grammar, will at the same time indicate what students should do in order to interpret correctly the conjunctions they meet in their reading. Here is a typical example of what might be given the students for the interpretation of «ut» when they meet it in their reading:

> When reading Latin, your first reaction to an «ut» should be that it expresses purpose unless a clear signal such as «sīc» or «ita» have preceded it to indicate result. Vaguely in the back of your mind keep the possibility that «ut» may take the indicative and express time. Rarely will it express the idea of concession. And in a few instances it may mean "how" or "as".

This presentation of how to interpret a particular conjunction can be the new material that will give some life to what otherwise might be difficult review.

In order to review and strengthen the reading ability of the student, the teacher should write questions and directions in examinations in Latin using constructions that have already been reviewed. This is one of the so-called "live situations" that can be used in the teaching of Latin. The first time such examinations are given, the teacher can rapidly go over the questions and check for comprehension by asking for an English equivalent. In subsequent examinations the teacher should readily answer students' questions about the Latin. If new words or constructions are used in these latter examinations, time should be taken to insure that all understand the meaning.

If the teacher uses Latin in the questions of his examinations, and if the students are in better sections, they may be asked to answer in Latin. If this is done, more time than usual should be allowed for the examination. For classes of lesser ability it is probably better to allow students to answer in English since the barrier of expression in Latin might mislead the teacher in the matter of their knowledge of Latin.

Teachers have found that this device for reviewing reading is very much worth the effort expended. They take a paragraph of rather simple Latin that the students read earlier and rewrite it using new vocabulary and those constructions that have been reviewed. Both versions appear on the page that is given the students. Still later a third version is presented which embodies the grammar that was reviewed meantime. A fourth or even a fifth rewriting can be used.

Vocabulary and spiral teaching

At the beginning of second year and thereafter some teachers prefer to give their students lists of words. These are systematically reviewed during the first few weeks of the school year. This is good, but it is likely to be somewhat difficult to engender enthusiasm and interest. If, however, such lists are organized in categories, there can be more interest and certainly there will be more help for the memory. For example, categories such as these can be used: adverbs relating to time, adverbs relating to place, words expressing arrival or departure, asking and seeking, words relating to the body, the family, and so forth.

Some teachers prefer to dispense with such lists and secure the review by means of the reading itself. If the reading is graded, the review can be easily controlled and can even be associated with new words — a true spiral teaching situation. For example, if the word «frāter» occurs in the reading, the teacher will ask for the Latin for other members of the family. Students will recall those they have seen and the teacher can implement the list with new words such as «avus». This type of review can become quite efficient since it brings into use the words that are important here and now for comprehension and does not run the risk of recalling words that are seldom used or used only in a very specific type of writing. Moreover, it is easier to recall words in context.

It would be a great help for students if texts indicated by some special marking the words that have occurred in the earlier years. This device would alert the student and indicate to him what he should remember. If the new words were further marked with some device to indicate how often they will be used in a given text, the student would know what emphasis must be given to learning them independently of a given context.

The words in a text are an immediate occasion for conducting review that goes beyond the words themselves. Thus, if the student meets the expression «quaestūrā fūnctus», the teacher can review or teach the other words whose object is in the ablative case, or if they meet «dīgressus», the students can be asked to give the simple form of the verb and then proceed to the formation of the compounds.

Undoubtedly during the course of the first and second years the teachers have taught students how to interpret the various prefixes and suffixes that they have met. During this third year it is profitable to give students a rather extensive list of prefixes and suffixes and their meanings. If the text does not have them, then the teacher can easily draw up one or two pages that list them.

Another element that will give some new aspects to the review of vocabulary is a consideration of assimilation and vowel changes that occur in compounds. Standard grammars will provide the teacher with more than ample material for bringing in new aspects of these matters which were more than likely treated to some extent in the previous study of Latin.

In the third and fourth years the review of vocabulary can be made more meaningful by asking the students to give Latin synonyms and antonyms. If they do not remember such, then they can be asked to define the word in Latin. Such work could be part of the homework for specified words in the text.

Translation and question signals

If the first two years of the study of Latin were chiefly concerned with comprehension, the students are quite familiar with the question signals such as «quid agit, quid patitur», and so forth. They will also have been trained to respond to more complicated Latin questions. At the beginning of the work in third year these same questions will be useful for leading the students on to further work. Instead of answering in Latin, the students can now be trained to respond in correct English. The new is thus taught against a background of review of what they have already learned. The reverse procedure may also be used. The teacher gives a fine English translation of some part of a lengthy sentence and then asks the students to identify the Latin that warrants the English translation, or the student can be asked what Latin question he would formulate to force such a reply.

Appendix 1

All teachers and prospective teachers of Latin will do well to become acquainted with the field of linguistics. Those who have experience in the teaching of Latin will find that the reading in this field of science will stimulate their thinking since it will offer a new organization to many of the ideas and techniques about the teaching of Latin which experience has helped them formulate. Prospective teachers will find that a study of linguistics will considerably broaden their knowledge of language and prepare them to be better teachers.

Every science has its technical language, but this should not deter the teacher from starting to read in this field. The authors of books on linguistics adequately define the terms they use and so it is just a matter of some reading before the new terms become familiar.

Teachers who wish to know more about linguistics should, if possible, attend some university where courses in this field are taught. But since such study is not possible for all, those who are interested can get a good acquaintance with linguistics through private reading and study. The following list of books is not extensive but reading them will give a good introduction to the field of linguistics. In fact, even those who plan to pursue a formal course or two in that field will find it profitable to have read these books before starting attendance at the lectures.

Francis, W. Nelson, «The Structure of American English», New York: The Ronald Press Company, 1958, vii–614.

Gleason, H. A., «An Introduction to Descriptive Linguistics», New York: Holt, Rinehart and Winston, Inc., 1955, 1961.
The author gives an excellent bibliography to which the reader is referred for titles for further reading.

Hall, Robert A., Jr., «Leave Your Language Alone», Ithaca: Linguistica, 1950.

Lado, Robert, «Language Teaching — A Scientific Approach», New York: McGraw Hill Book Company, 1964, xiv–239.
An extensive bibliography is given on pages 223–229.

Palmer, L. A., «The Latin Language», London: Faber & Faber, Ltd., 24 Russel Square, 1954.

Sturtevant, Edgar H., «An Introduction to Linguistic Science», New Haven: Yale University Press, 1947.
The author frequently uses Latin by way of illustration.

Appendix 2

"Is the teacher a teaching machine or is the teaching machine a teacher?" Most teachers will unhesitatingly answer in the negative to the first part of the question, but what will they say by way of answer to the second part of the question? Teaching machines are so-called teachers, not so much because of the machine but because of the presentation of the material inserted into the machines. This method of presentation has received the technical name of "programed instruction".

Basically programed instruction is a small-step sequence of presentation, demanding an active response on the part of the student, reinforcing his response by the correct answer after each step, and thereby leading the student from the known to the unknown. Such a definition needs further explanation and exemplification.

Programing is a technique of constructing carefully a sequence of items leading the student to mastery of the subject with minimal error. Information is given to the student in small units to which he responds in some way — by completing a sentence, by working a problem, or by answering a question. Items are designed so that the student can make correct responses while progressing toward more and more complex material. Commonly associated with programming is the teaching machine, which is just one mechanical device for presenting programs. The programed textbook is far more common and practical at present since the machines still have many "bugs" and are not readily adapted to handle the new programing techniques that are so rapidly developing.

Programing is not a startling new technique. In essence it includes methods practiced for ages by good teachers — very clearly determining the goals in teaching this particular area of subject matter, developing the matter by logical steps so as not to lose the student by too big a jump, and always forcing the student to think actively along with the teacher.

Programing does have a place as a teacher-training tool, a sort of discipline to make a teacher determine the goal of his course or of a particular section of his course and to be able to break down into small steps his method of arriving at the goal. Programing also affects textbooks, especially those in the self-instructional field. Programing too is a help in determining the curriculum chiefly because it forces a rethinking of the goals.

The actual use of programs in the curriculum of our schools is enmeshed in many "if's, but's", and "perhaps". If teachers keep an open mind or, better still, a favorable attitude toward programs, they are likely to find that they will increase their teaching effectiveness. To try programing only demands that degree of humility necessary for all good teachers who are always looking for ways to improve their presentation of class matter and who are always striving for better results on the part of the student. But a call for programing must not be a total reversal of what teachers have been doing. To make use of a short unit of programing in a particular area is a much more sensible approach and one which can quite effectively prove the merit of a particular program without causing the teacher a great adaptation in approach. Quite frequently the use of a particular program is an effective way of reviewing familiar material.

If a teacher can take the time and will make the effort to try writing a few short units of programing for his course, he will quickly find how difficult it is to write a good program. He will also be able to determine in what areas a program is useful and effective, whether the program is to be used as a workbook exercise or a home study assignment. Besides offering a method for reviewing, programing is effective both in remedial work and in the enrichment of a curriculum.

By way of example here is a partial program that deals with scanning the dactylic hexameter for a Vergil class. A few frames (i.e. steps) from this scansion instruction are intended to teach both the recognition of the dactyl and the spondee as well as the correct spelling of both words. The answers at the right can be covered by a sliding tab or they can be put on the next page. Responses can be made orally or in writing. By immediately seeing the correct answer there is a reinforcement of learning if the response was correct, and if the response was incorrect there is immediate correction before proceeding with a wrong idea lodged in the mind.

If the program is a good one, the basic knowledge of scansion could be learned by the student in one or two home-study assignments. During class the teacher can drill and explain exceptions.

The use of programing must avoid two dangers. There is an inclination on the part of the teacher to look upon a program as a test; students, too, may at first have this attitude. This aspect of programing stems from the

252

26.
    (1)   (2)
ārmă vǐr|ūmquĕ că|nō
The pattern of one long mark followed by two short
marks is called a «dactyl». In the line above there are
(how many) dactyl(s).   2 dactyls

27.
    (1)   (2)
ārmă vǐr|ūmquĕ că|nō
A dactyl is a pattern of a _____ mark followed by two
_____ marks.   long–short

28.
    (1)   (2)
ārmă vǐr|ūmquĕ că|nō
A (   ) pattern is called a d--tyl.   dactyl

29.
    (1)   (2)   (3)   (4)   (5)   (6)
ārmă vǐr|ūmquĕ că|nō Trō|jāē quī|prīmŭs ăb|ōrīs
How many dactyls are in this line?   3 dactyls

30.
    (1)   (2)   (3)   (4)   (5)   (6)
ārmă vǐr|ūmquĕ că|nō Trō|jāē quī|prīmŭs ăb|ōrīs
(5) is an example of a dac--l.   dactyl

31.
    (1)   (2)   (3)   (4)   (5)   (6)
ārmă vǐr|ūmquĕ că|nō Trō|jāē quī|prīmŭs ăb|ōrīs
(3) is not an example of a d----l.   dactyl

32.
    (1)   (2)   (3)   (4)   (5)   (6)
ārmă vǐr|ūmquĕ că|nō Trō|jāē quī|prīmŭs ăb|ōrīs
How many patterns are <u>not</u> dactyls?   three

33.
    (1)   (2)   (3)   (4)   (5)   (6)
ārmă vǐr|ūmquĕ că|nō Trō|jāē quī|prīmŭs ăb|ōrīs
(3) is a pattern of a _____ mark followed by a
_____ mark.   long–long

34.
    (1)   (2)   (3)   (4)   (5)   (6)
ārmă vǐr|ūmquĕ că|nō Trō|jāē quī|prīmŭs ăb|ōrīs
The long-long (– –) pattern is called «spondee». Besides (3), ____ and ____ are each an example of a
spondee.   (4) and (6)

35.
    (1)   (2)   (3)   (4)   (5)   (6)
ārmă vǐr|ūmquĕ că|nō Trō|jāē quī|prīmŭs ăb|ōrīs
(3) and (4) and (6) are each an example of a s---dee.   spondee

36.
    (1)   (2)   (3)   (4)   (5)   (6)
ārmă vǐr|ūmquĕ că|nō Trō|jāē quī|prīmŭs ăb|ōrīs
(2) is not an example of a spon---.   spondee

37. A sp------ is a pattern of a _____ mark followed by a   spondee
_____ mark.   long–long

construction of the individual items and the demand for an active response on the part of the student. But the avowed purpose of a program is to <u>teach</u> and not to test. The second danger also stems from the construction of the program. When a teacher first looks into a program he will feel that the programer has made the acquisition of knowledge far too easy. The small-step sequence of items in a program, worded in such a way as to force the student to answer correctly, would seem to violate the theory that knowledge makes a bloody entrance. But two factors should be considered. First, we know from our own experience that learning is the more pursued the more conscious we are of our success and accomplishment. We like to be right and be told that we are right. Programs do just this. Modern psychology indicates that this is one of the most efficient and effective ways by which we acquire knowledge. Programed instruction, then, is only a method of taking advantage of our pride and drive for knowledge. Anyone who has actually tried to learn from programed textbooks will find the high degree of concentration demanded over a continuous period of time is still a part of the "bloody" entrance.

Teachers and prospective teachers who are interested in programing should contact: The Center for Programed Instruction, Inc., 365 West End Avenue, New York, New York 10024, or they may write to Encyclopaedia Britannica Educational Corporation, 425 North Michigan Avenue, Chicago, Illinois 60611, for information about Professor Waldo E. Sweet's programed texts for Latin.

Index

255